Accountability for School Psychologists:

Selected Readings

Edited by Thomas N. Fairchild

University Press of America™

DEDICATION

To my mother, Bea Kalblinger,
whose hardwork, kindness, and unselfishness
will always be appreciated and remembered.

ACKNOWLEDGMENTS

This book of selected readings reflects my philosophy that school psychologists need to be accountable for the services they provide. Considerable time and energy has been spent in the process of editing this book of readings. This task has taken over three years and its conception and completion reflects the influence, support, and assistance of many persons. I would like to express my sincere appreciation to my family who has encouraged and supported me through the difficult times; Dr. Theodore N. Clair, who stimulated my interest in accountability for school psychologists; Mary Jane Kindschy and Dr. Jean Fitzgerald who helped me to grow so much professionally; my wife Carolyn, Marcy Taylor for typing the first draft of the manuscript; Sherri Newell for typing the final draft; and Gannett Pitkin, Margo Davis, Marti McDowell, and Carolyn Fairchild for proofreading.

CONTENTS

"Can School Psychology Survive in the 70's?" was the title of an article published by the Journal of Professional Psychology (Fall 1971) and written by Theodore N. Clair and John Kiraly, Jr. at the University of Iowa. The article addressed some of the current problems confronting school psychologists, and offered suggestions for school psychologists who wanted to remain within the mainstream of education. The importance of accountability was highlighted by the following statement:

> "School people are beginning to make specific demands upon their school psychologist, and his effectiveness is seriously being evaluated. In many situations the psychologist is in trouble because he cannot furnish substantive proof as to the positive outcomes of his performance." (p. 385)

Although accountability has received widespread acceptability, it has been perceived as the responsibility of classroom teachers and administrators. Ancillary personnel have often considered themselves exempt from accounting for their services. Consequently, very little progress has been made in the area of accountability for school psychological services. Recently, however, school psychologists are becoming more and more aware of the need for accounting for their services and documenting their effectiveness. Numerous articles relating to accountability for school psychological services are appearing in the professional journals.

In a recent article the writer noted:[1]

> "If school psychologists are being called upon to provide evidence with regard to their effectiveness, school psychology training programs have an obligation to prepare school psychologists with self-evaluation skills. ... A formal course in self-evaluation and accountability techniques that outlines specific techniques should be provided. These techniques could be applied during the practicum or internship experiences, which would allow the students to try them out first-hand and select the techniques that they can manage effectively,

[1] Fairchild, Thomas N. An analysis of the services performed by a school psychologist in an urban area: Implications for training programs. Psychology in the Schools, 1974, XI, 3, 275-281.

yet still would provide them with pertinent data as to the efficacy of their services." (p. 281)

This text was a by-product of that recommendation. Since there was no organized information in the area of accountability for school psychological services the author decided to synthesize the available accountability research into a text of selected readings for use by practitioners and students in training programs.

The literature has been thoroughly review in an effort to include all of the available reserach on accountability. New material that has not been printed in the professional journals has also been included.

The text should be of primary value to school psychologist practitioners. The writer hopes the selected readings will provide school psychologists with practical information which will help them as they develop means of accounting for the services they provide their schools.

The text should also be of particular value to directors or coordinators of school psychology training programs. The writer ,believes that course work in accountability methods and self-evaluation is of utmost importance during pre-service training, so that future practitioners appreciate the need for accounting for their services and have some knowledge of the available techniques for gathering information regarding their effectiveness.

Tom Fairchild

SPECIFYING GOALS AND OBJECTIVES

The importance of specifying goals and objectives has received considerable support within the educational community - goals for ourselves as educators and more importantly goals and objectives that we would like our students to achieve as learners and persons. In an age of accountability, specifying goals and objectives is of critical importance because they provide us with the means of evaluating our effectiveness as school psychologists. The specification of goals and objectives can be conceptualized within three separate frameworks or levels as they relate to the successful functioning of the school psychologist. These three levels can be identified as the (1) systems level, (2) individual school psychologist level, and (3) the student level.

First, we can specify goals for the school psychological services delivery system. Humes discusses the Planning, Programming, Budgeting Systems (PPBS) approach. In the model outlined by Humes, goal statements serve as a frame of reference for decision-making, planning, and evaluation. In the PPBS model consumers of services were afforded the opportunity to participate in the formulation of goals. This is an excellent approach. A lay-professional committee recorded the major goals, sub-goals, and objectives for the school psychological services in their community.

The second level for conceptualizing goals involves specifying goals and objectives at the individual school psychologist level, rather than at a systems level. In an effort to promote the use of behavioral objectives Leviton offers a list of objectives which can be perceived as a description of a school psychologist's responsibilities. School psychologists should recognize the necessity for describing their role in behavioral objective terms which provides them with the opportunity to evaluate and demonstrate their effectiveness. The list presented by Leviton is a tentative one, and allows individual psychologists the chance to modify it to suit individual needs.

The third level for conceptualizing goals and objectives is much more specific than the preceding two levels. At this level, the school psychologist is concerned with specifying goals and objectives for students that relate directly to intervention strategies. These Supportive Instructional Objectives (SIO's), as described by Grimes, Dublinske, and Easter, provide school psychologists with the means of obtaining feedback on the effectiveness of their recommendations. They emphasize the importance of teacher involvement in formulating the SIO's. Morrow's article provides further support for the need to outline specific behavioral objectives for students. Morrow's approach emphasizes a team approach in preparing the objectives. Input on objectives is then requested from parents and students, and a recording system is used which provides immediate and continuous feedback regarding the effectiveness of the recommended plan.

SCHOOL PSYCHOLOGIST ACCOUNTABILITY VIA PPBS

Charles W. Humes, II

Summary: Accountability for school psychology is presented through the Planning, Programming, Budgeting Systems (PPBS) approach. The nature of goals and objectives in this model are explored in detail. The actual goals and objectives as developed in the Greenwich (Conn.) Public Schools are used as an illustration.

As has been pointed out frequently, this is the decade of accountability for public education. The demand for outcome-oriented results has continued to climb and it is anticipated that the peak will occur during the mid-decade. Every part of the educational enterprise is undergoing this kind of scrutiny (Lieberman, 1970). One of the last bastions to be attacked is school psychology. The slowness of the public to press for outcomes in this area is perhaps related to two factors: (1) the seemingly esoteric nature of the discipline, and (2) the difficulties seemingly associated with measurement in the affective domain. However, the press is on and alternative programs or actual survival may be the issues in question (Silberberg & Silberberg, 1971).

In many ways school psychology is more accessible to measurement than school guidance or school social work for it tends to deal with result-oriented data (Clair & Kiraly, 1971). The school psychologist's principal delivery tool has traditionally been the psychodiagnostic evaluation, and the various factors connected with this service are susceptible to outcome measurements. As school psychology approaches the task at hand, albeit somewhat reluctantly, there are implications for other kinds of psychological services, namely college, clinic,

SOURCE. Reprinted from Journal of School Psychology, 1974, 12, 1, 40-45. By permission of the author and the publisher. Copyright 1974 by the Journal of School Psychology, Inc. Published by Behavioral Publications, New York.

etc., where practicing psychologists are employed.

There are a variety of ways in which to approach accountability for school psychological services (Tomlinson, 1973) but a useful omnibus approach is through Planning, Programming, Budgeting Systems (PPBS). The Greenwich, Connecticut, Public Schools have been involved with PPBS on a district-wide basis since 1970. In the intervening years some 50 separate school programs have been identified with goal statements and evaluative criteria (Humes, 1972). One of the extant programs studied is that of School Psychological Services.

GOALS

In the PPBS model there are goal statements which are general and timeless. A goal is a frame of reference for management decision-making and for program planning and evaluation. Goal statements should always relate directly to specific problem situations requiring psychological services. A goal reflects the desired end result and not the quantity of activities and services applied to achieve the result. The existence of goals helps redirect program emphasis away from process orientation to effect. The development of goals becomes an important device toward the delivery of maximum psychological services. However, they should be realistic and developed within the constraints of the organization.

In order that the development of goal statements play a significant role, there must always be broad participation of staff personnel. Broad participation assists in the process of acceptance and a concurrent commitment to the activity. In most situations broad participation means involvement of personnel other than psychologists. It is essential that consumers of psychological services have an opportunity to participate in the formulation of goals.

OBJECTIVES

Objectives are specific achievement targets to be accomplished within a given time span which will represent measurable steps toward the goal. Objectives should be comprehensive in nature and cover all activities leading to the achievement of a goal. In this manner there may often be several objectives related to a given goal.

Although both quantifiable and nonquantifiable objectives may be utilized, it is always more appropriate to use objectives that permit quantitative measurement of achievement. Nonquantifiable objectives should always be used sparingly when trying to develop an objectively based evaluation system. It frequently happens that when problems have not been clearly defined, objectives are often described in terms that do not lend themselves to quantification.

4

In psychological services it may be difficult to establish quantitative measures of effectiveness. It will be observed in the illustrative objectives to be presented that efficiency measures are sometimes used as alternatives. While efficiency measures are process-oriented, they serve a useful purpose in beginning stages by defining the manpower required to perform a given activity, the frequency of a specified service, or the required number of contacts. Thus, efficiency measures are directed to output, and effectiveness measures are related to outcomes. Efficiency measures, or activity counting, is usually the first step in trying to organize a discipline into manageable parts. The typical school psychologist knows generally what his role should be, but he is often hard-pressed to define it in specifics. While efficiency measurement will be an inevitable part of the initial development of objectives, it is highly desirable that some effectiveness measures be interspersed among them. The long range plan would be to have all objectives stated as outcomes, i.e., client impact indices.

As objectives are developed, and even approach the outcome measures, it is essential to point out that (a) effectiveness standards are not necessarily maximum objectives, and (b) all standards must be reviewed periodically so as to insure relevance and appropriateness. The development of goals and objectives is an iterative process and must always be related to current needs and situations.

APPLICATION

In the Greenwich experience, the development of goals and objectives for school psychology occurred in three phases. They were as follows:

1. Development of tentative goals and objectives by professional staff in a primitive format.

2. Refinement of the tentative goals and objectives through the medium of a management consultant.

3. Finalization of the goals and objectives through the device of a lay-professional committee composed of psychologists, representation from other disciplines, and citizens.

As the goals and objectives went through the above three-phase process, it became increasingly clear that each subsequent review produced evaluative criteria that were more outcome-oriented. However, the prime movers in the insistence on such outcome indices were often those committee members other than school psychological services staff. It was obvious that psychologists tended to stay with input or process-oriented statements along traditional lines. Apparently, consumers were far more interested in results than those who practice the discipline.

5

MAJOR GOAL

To increase the intellectual and emotional development of all students, through general and specific services to students, parents, and all professional staff, in order to foster a positive learning environement.

SUB GOALS

1. To serve as a resource to students and school personnel for discussion of common developmental problems encountered by students.

2. To provide direct intervention for those students who present specific learning or behavior problems.

3. To provide consultative services to staff and administration regarding atypical children.

4. To serve as a resource to parents concerning the understanding of their child.

5. To provide for professional growth by improving psychological services, making contributions to the field, and engaging in, and keeping informed of, ongoing research activities.

OBJECTIVES

1.0 Students or staff desiring these services will meet on an individual or group basis. Initial acknowledgment of all requests will be within two school weeks. A record of the nature, extent and effectiveness of such contacts will be maintained and available for review by the Director of Pupil Personnel Services.

2.0 Psychologist will respond to the referring source indicating the status of all cases referred for service, and all cases referred will be reviewed for future action by the end of the school year.

2.1 Fifty percent of students referred for evaluation within any given school year will be assessed through appropriate techniques. Written reports of findings with recommendations will be provided to appropriate school personnel.

2.2 The referring source will learn through consultation with the psychologist and other involved staff appropriate academic prescriptions, plans for classroom management, and student-teacher interactions that accomodate individual needs. This will be done in 90% of the cases of evaluated students. The progress of 100% of the evaluated students will be determined through a

6

follow-up study reflecting whether specific recommendations have been implemented and the effect of their implementation upon overall adjustment. The format will be developed by the psychologists by February, 1974.

2.3 Selected students will be exposed to individual or group counseling in order to facilitate growth in learning and/or behavior. Such contacts will be recorded by the preparation of a confidential summary concerning each student and observations of improvement, if any, noted by the psychologist in conjunction with the counselee.

3.0 Pupil Personnel Services and administrative staff will be assisted in the development of special programs for all exceptional children by the participation of the psychologist in meetings regarding such programs. A record of the nature and extent of such participation will be maintained and available for review.

3.1 School personnel will be assisted in most appropriate placement of students in special programs by psychologists' involvement in devising screening procedures for such placement and by their participation in Pupil Planning and Placement Team meetings. Screening procedures will be reported in written format annually to the Director of Pupil Personnel Services.

3.2 Staff and administration will be aided in the advancement of these programs through psychologists' participation in regular team meetings which deal with the progress of individual students and revisions in the program. A record of the nature and extent of such participation will be maintained and available for review.

3.3 Mentally retarded students will be re-evaluated to ascertain continuing appropriateness of placement, as required by state law. A written report will be prepared following such re-evaluations.

4.0 Parents of evaluated students will be prepared to understand their children better through interpretations of the findings and recommendations of psychological evaluations in 70% of the cases. Such interpretations will be conducted within six weeks following the completion of the evaluation, and the effectiveness of such contacts will be determined by the observations of the psychologist.

4.1 Parents' understanding of the functioning of psychological services will be enhanced by the preparation of a brochure outlining psychological services in the schools. This will be completed by June, 1974, and submitted to the Director of Pupil Personnel Services for dissemination to the public.

7

4.2 Parents' understanding of students' problems of growth and development will be enahnced by psychologists' participation at least once annually in a parent meeting, panel, or workshop. A report of the effectiveness of such contacts will be determined by the observations of the psychologist.

5.0 Student growth and adjustment will be enhanced by increased awareness on the part of the psychologist of current research and the need for additional research in the school system. Psychologists will establish a sub-committee by October, 1973, to review current research activities and to consider relevant issues in education as possibilities for a future research design. Their findings will be reported to the psychologists who will select (by May, 1974) a topic for research.

5.1 Students will benefit from psychologists' participation in at least two in-service training workshops per year to enhance diagnostic and counseling skills and to increase understanding of the relationship between psychology and education. Opinion data on the value of the workshops, will be reported to the Director of Pupil Personnel Services.

5.2 Students will benefit from the psychologists' attendance at least one workshop or conference annually to keep abreast of new developments in the field and of how they related to his responsibilities within an educational milieu. Opinion data will be reported to the Director of Pupil Personnel Services with comments on how the conference relates to the psychologist's professional responsibilities within the school setting.

DISCUSSION

The presentation of these goals and objectives will be criticized for a variety of reasons. Perhaps the principal one will be that they do not adequately tap the qualitative nature of the services. This is a valid criticism and one that applies equally well to all programs of whatever type. The only rationale that can be used in countering such criticism is to answer that quantifiable measures can never do justice to all aspects of a given program. All that such quantifiable measures should purport to do is assess those segments of the services that are measurable. Obviously, other parts of evaluation will continue, particularly those which are concerned with supervisory responsibilities. The point to be made is to beware of a general, rather than a selective, rejection of quantifiability. It is much to easy to deny categorically the feasibility of outcomes quantification on the bases of difficulty, inappropriateness, or lack of validity. Although these roadblocks may be present in varying degrees in some area of the job description, they do not necessarily apply to all parts of the school psychology job. In fact, the task of the school psychologist is probably no more difficult to assess than many other parts of the educational enterprise. Unfortunately, the general rejection of quantifiable measures is often related to a general disapproval and distaste for accountability. It should be reaffirmed that no part of public education will be exempt from the accountability thrust. If one assimilates this fact it is possible to develop a mind set that permits the exploration of such possibilities. Any approach to outcome measurement must be a positive one or it is doomed to premature failure. In this respect it has been stated (Hartley, 1968) that all human systems can be systematized.

It is crucial for key school psychological services staff members to initiate and promote an approach to accountability lest someone outside the discipline attempt to do it. The hidden, and often overlooked strength, in this new performance model is grass-roots involvement in what a program should offer. It represents an opportunity for staff members to be heard as never before. This involvement can produce an outcome-oriented functional job description that will be more viable and less subject to tampering than anything yet seen. If school psychologists, in different school settings, will apply themselves to this reality, we may be able to formulate some models that the total profession may want to endorse on a regional or national level.

References

Clair, T.N., & Kiraly, J. Accountability for the school psychologist. Psychology in the Schools, 1971, 8, 318-321.

Hartley, H.J. Educational planning-programming-budgeting. A systems approach. Englewood Cliffs, N.J.: Prentice-Hall 1968.

Humes, C.W. Accountability: A boon to guidance. Personnel and Guidance Journal, 1972, 51, 21-26.

Lieberman, M. An overview of accountability. Phi Delta Kappan, 1970, 4, 194-195.

Silberberg, N., & Silberberg, M. Should schools have psychologists? Journal of School Psychology, 1971, 3, 321-328.

Tomlinson, J.R. Accountability procedures for psychological services. Psychology in the Schools, 1973, 10, 42-47.

PROMOTING PROFESSIONAL GROWTH FOR THE SCHOOL PSYCHOLOGIST

Harvey Leviton

One of the key current concerns in contemporary education is professional accountability. That is, educators are being required to specify their goals and to substantiate how these goals have been attained. This specification of goals, or objectives as they are called more frequently, is being required of classroom teachers and administrative personnel as well as those who provide supportive services, such as nurses and school psychologists. For example, the Management by Objectives approach has been designed for use by administrators to help them to specify objectives and evaluate the degree of satisfactory attainment of these objectives. In a similar manner, the Instructional Objectives Exchange provides instructional objectives for the various curriculum fields in order to assist teachers to specify what they are trying to teach so that they can measure how effectively they have been taught.

The development of objectives varies in difficulty according to the specificity of the goal desired. For example, it easy for the kindergarten teacher to state an objective such as, "By December 1, 85% of my class will be able to identify correctly all the letters of the alphabet." It is more difficult for the administrator to state his objectives, but this can be done specifically in such areas as in-service training of teachers, relationships with the PTA, discipline of students, etc. It is even more difficult to state specific objectives for supportive service personnel who work on referred problems, and this is especially true of the school psychologist. He works with referred cases that usually involve exceptional children, and his concern is with academic and behavioral improvement as well as attitudinal change. Yet it is imperative that the school psychologist be able to specify and evaluate his objectives if he is to survive in this age of educational accountability. Be specifying objectives, not only is the school psychologist able to evaluate his efficacy, he is also able to grow. One year he may concentrate on some objectives more than

SOURCE. Reprinted from Psychology in the Schools, 1974, XI, 3, 260-262. By permission of the author and Clinical Psychology Publishing Co., Inc.

others so that he can improve areas in which he feels a weakness. Through the structure provided by behavioral objectives, the school psychologist is able to promote his own professional growth as well as demonstrate his efficacy.

In order to promote the use of behavioral objectives for school psychologists, the following list of objectives is presented as a preliminary job description of what a school psychologist can do. While he would be held responsible for most of the objectives, in any one year he could emphasize certain ones. The objectives have been divided arbitrarily into four basic areas for ease of conceptualization: instruction, assessment, community relations, and professional growth. The objectives are not a comprehensive list, but a preliminary conceptual framework for a job description of the role of the school psychologist in behavioral objective terms.

BEHAVIORAL OBJECTIVES RELATED TO INSTRUCTION

1. To counsel with individual students with regard to personal problems and needs.
2. To convene case study conferences to determine appropriate alternatives to meet an individual student's needs.
3. To consult with individual tutors with regard to students' needs and regularly review progress.
4. To prescribe appropriate activities to remediate learning problems in such areas as behavioral management, perceptual and motor training, language development and classroom climate.
5. To recommend to the principal special services to meet an individual student's academic or emotional needs.
6. To interpret the results of a student's evaluation to teachers so that they may individualize instruction.
7. To provide communications to principals, teachers and counselors with regard to results of individual psychological evaluations.
8. To interpret to the student the results of his individual psychological evaluation in order to increase his personal awareness.
9. To assist principals, counselors, teachers and parents to determine the feasibility of academic retention or promotion.
10. To assist principals to assign students to particular teachers who best can meet the pupil's individual needs.
11. To assimilate all available information on a student's current functioning and present it in a comprehensive manner.
12. To serve as a psychological resource person to teachers when classroom discussion is centered on such topics as mental health, learning theory, abnormal behavior, psychometrics, etc.
13. To assist elementary principals to determine grade placement of a student.

11

BEHAVIORAL OBJECTIVES RELATED TO ASSESSMENT

1. To evaluate achievement at it relates to potential.
2. To evaluate personality as it affects achievement and behavior in school primarily, but also in the community.
3. To evaluate intellectual ability in order to determine the level of academic potential.
4. To interpret the results of individual psychological evaluation to a student's parents so that they may understand his individuality and help to develop appropriate expectations.
5. To develop and implement programs for early identification of children with learning problems.
6. To identify and diagnose the optimal learning modality of an individual student and recommend specific activities to increase his educational effectiveness.
7. To evaluate perceptual and motor development to assess developmental readiness and recommend accordingly.
8. To follow up students referred in order to determine the effectiveness of their individual programs.
9. To assist in the development of evaluative procedures of educational programs.
10. To assist administration to change organizational procedures in keeping with relevant psychological knowledge.

BEHAVIORAL OBJECTIVES RELATED TO COMMUNITY RELATIONS

1. To discuss school psychological services with interested community organizations.
2. To serve as a member of the interdisciplinary staffing team for students with behavioral problems.
3. To serve as a liaison between the school staff and medical and mental health services in the community.
4. To conduct short-term counseling with students and their families in order to facilitate communication and mutual respect.

BEHAVIORAL OBJECTIVES RELATED TO PROFESSIONAL GROWTH

1. To develop and construct programs to assist teachers to create a positive, constructive, respectful emotional climate in their classrooms.
2. To interpret to faculty the proper use of school psychological services, special education services, proper interpretation of psychological reports and psychological principles.
3. Provide in-service education to faculty to help them to meet the needs of particular exceptional children whom they may have in their classrooms.
4. To assist in the planning, monitoring and evaluation of innovative educational procedures.
5. To keep current with literature and relevant journals in areas of specialization.
6. To contribute to the body of knowledge by engaging in research, publishing and making presentations at national or local conventions.

CONCLUSION

This paper has presented behavioral objectives as a means to further professional growth for all educational personnel. The direct implications of this approach for the school psychologist have been presented in the form of specific behavioral objectives. This is not a definitive and exhaustive list of objectives; it is a tentative one that should be modified to suit differing needs. By emphasizing different objectives each year, the school psychologist can promote his own professional development.

INCREASING INTERVENTION EFFECTIVENESS THROUGH IMPROVED COMMUNICATION

Jeff Grimes, Stan Dublinske, Jerry A. Caster

Educational intervention is a dynamic process because neither the problem nor the educational environment remain static. To cope with this condition, the approach frequently taken by Special Service Personnel (SSP)* is to attack the problem in general and often an ambiguous manner. What is suggested is that the problem be addressed specifically from a treatment orientation that focuses maximum attention on child behavior that is desired and activities necessary to attain that behavior. This is accomplished through use of Supportive Instructional Objectives (SIO) and specific educational recommendations.

The major benefit of this approach to intervention is that the probability of instructional action on behalf of the child is increased. Another benefit is that by using Supportive Instructional Objectives, the SSP is in a position to obtain feedback on the effectiveness of recommendations. It is contradictory that performance feedback is recognized as essential for pupil achievement, but concrete feedback on child change resulting from SSP intervention is so woefully neglected. Because of their specificity, the use of SIO's provides a method by which feedback can be obtained with a minimum of difficulty.

** SSP (Special Service Personnel) are personnel employed to provide professional skills which enhance pupil learning by working with personnel who are responsible for the instruction of the child. This includes psychologists, educational consultants, and also personnel such as speech clinicians and resource or itinerant teachers who may provide some direct instruction but who must rely on the classroom teacher for assistance in making change.

SOURCE. Paper presented at a Special Study Institute on Improving Intervention Effectiveness and Communication, Department of Public Instruction, State of Iowa, February, 1972. By permission of the authors.

Basic assumptions permeate any article that describes a method useful in improving services to children. In such cases, acceptance of methodology is dependent in large part on agreement with those assumptions. Underlying the methods offered in this paper are the following assumptions:

1. Special Service Personnel (SSP) are employed to enhance the learning of children. Regardless of information collected and recommendations offered, unless child change occurs, the basic purpose and expectation of intervention has not been fulfilled.

2. SSP must affect child change through working with others, primarily the classroom teacher. Because SSP do not have direct control over implementation of recommendations, responsibility for child change is necessarily a shared one and success in getting recommendations implemented is dependent to a large extent on effective communication.

3. In communicating, as the specificity of recommendations or desired outcomes increases, so does the probability of child change. This results from the application of more deliberate and controlled pedagogy to the defined problem.

INTERVENTION PROCESS

The process of intervention tends to be consistent for all SSP. (Figure 1) It begins after the teacher has identified that a problem exists. The problem may be that the child is not achieving, presents management difficulties, or does not seem to be adjusting adequately. The significant factor in every situation is that the teacher has dealt with the child, has tried the educational strategies she is familiar with, but is still looking for a different response pattern from the child. The involvement of the SSP starts when the teacher decides that assistance is needed in achieving the desired child change and contacts the professional who is most able to assist her.

Following the request for assistance, the SSP applies the skills appropriate to the problem. At this point a crucial event occurs. The SSP begins to formulate the report that will be delivered to the individual, usually the teacher, who will be working with the child. After the report for child change has been delivered, the SSP becomes at least temporarily inactive in the intervention process. The report serves as the ammunition needed by the teacher to start anew in the attempt to affect child change. Once the report has been implemented, the last step in the intervention process can be completed, i.e., evaluation. It is this final step in which the achieved and anticipated outcomes are compared and alternatives for future action are explored.

15

FIGURE 1

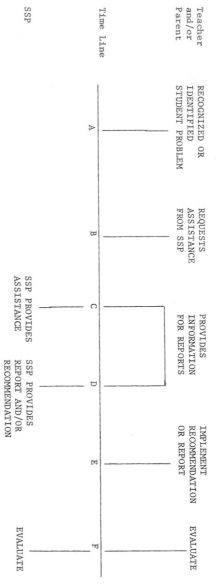

Teacher
and/or
Parent

RECOGNIZED OR
IDENTIFIED
STUDENT PROBLEM

REQUESTS
ASSISTANCE
FROM SSP

PROVIDES
INFORMATION
FOR REPORTS

IMPLEMENT
RECOMMENDATION
OR REPORT

EVALUATE

Time Line

A   B   C   D   E   F

SSP

SSP PROVIDES
ASSISTANCE

SSP PROVIDES
REPORT AND/OR
RECOMMENDATION

EVALUATE

INTERVENTION REPORTS

The written report is the primary vehicle used to communicate recommendations to those who request SSP intervention. Certainly, this written report does not negate the importance of conferences as an important and necessary part of communication. Rather, the report, as one type of communication, offers a record of the recommendations that can be referred to by the teacher when the SSP is not available and also serves as documentation for use in the more distant future by others who work with the child. Unfortunately, reports are often laden with jargon, professional terminology and test names which have no meaning and are frequently confusing to the user. While technical information may have relevancy to the SSP, the teacher is generally looking for other types of information. Because the teacher is looking for directions in social or academic programming for a child, recommendations desired are those that offer specific suggestions for classroom application. Since the teacher has posed the question, "What should I do in the classroom ....?", an attempt must be made to communicate with brevity what is needed to accomplish the desired child outcomes in that environment. Appendices A, B, and C are considered examples of reports that meet this requirement.

To give direction to the evaluation and the report, the teacher's question should be formulated into a statement of critical decisions. A critical decision is one that makes a significant difference in programming for the student. For example: "To help Bret verbally participate in class discussion." or "To help Sue improve spelling proficiency and decrease the hitting on the playground."

While the recommendations permit the teacher to act, they must be founded on something else that is also specific. That is, the Supportive Instructional Objective (SIO), a statement of performance or behavior that is desired of the child if the intervention is successful. Example:

By March 10, 1972, Bret will ask at least one question during three consecutive class discussions led by Mrs. Brown. Questions will be recorded by Mrs. Brown.

SIO's provide a method of communicating expectations of the intervention process in terms of child behavior. It is developed by the SSP in conjunction with the teacher, parent or others involved in implementing the recommendations and it projects desired pupil behavior at a future point in time.

17

Formulating the Supportive Instructional Objective is a necessary prelude to finalizing recommendations for two major reasons. First, unless agreement is reached on an acceptable level of performance it may be questionable whether the recommendations will be implemented because of diversity of perceived outcomes set by the teacher, parent or SSP. Also, if recommendations are implemented and child change occurs, child performance may be viewed as unacceptable regardless of progress because of unclear expectations for success. Unfortunately, in such cases it is the child who is penalized. The second major reason for the development of a SIO is that it will provide a purpose for the recommendations. Without the statement of desired performance, the individuals working with the child will have no clear method of monitoring progress. This monitoring is imperative if apprioriate judgements and corresponding modifications are to be made regarding the recommendations.

A Supportive Instructional Objective is a statement of a specific behavior and desired accomplishments that can be measured within a given time frames. To be measurable, a SIO must meet the following criteria:

1. WHEN is it going to be done.
2. Who is going to do it.
3. WHAT is going to be done.
4. TO WHOM is it going to be done.
5. CRITERIA that will indicate accomplishment of the objective.
6. EVALUATION method that will be utilized to determine if the objective has been completed.

The following are examples of Supportive Instructional Objectives:

After completing the language activities in book three of the Michigan Language Program, presented by Mrs. Peterson, Nancy will be able to read with less than 10% error, high first grade level children's literature books. Charts of error rate and list of books read will be kept by the teacher.

After completing the recommendations carried out by Mrs. Richards, Pete will have turned in at least 60% of all homework assignments due in a two month period ending April 1, 1972. Teacher will record data on homework assigned and returned.

Components of objectives may be put together in numerous ways as shown in Figure 2.

FIGURE 2
EXAMPLE COMPONENT ALTERNATIVES IN WRITING OBJECTIVES

Component	Examples of Components	Question Answered by Component
1. WHEN	By June 30, 1973 After completing Series A After 15 sessions	"When can I expect, or hope, to see change in the student?"
2. WHO	Teacher Clinician Parent Aide	"Who is going to make sure the objective is carried out and completed?"
3. WHAT	Read Hit Compute Stay in his chair	"What behavior will the student be able to have performed?"
4. TO WHOM	John Donahue The student	"Who does this obejctive pertain to?"
5. CRITERIA	60% correct at least 5 one or more complete all activities	"What constitutes success?"
6. EVALUATION	NW Syntax test counting classroom behavior work completed	"How will the evaluation be done to determine if the criteria was met?"

The purpose of the Supportive Instructional Objective is to improve communication. Dublinske (1971), Hernandez (1971), and Mager (1962) provide numerous examples and practice with planned feedback to help the reader develop proficiency in writing measurable objectives.

19

RECOMMENDATIONS

The educational recommendation is the vehicle required to transport the child from present behavior to desired behavior. Bringing about change through educational recommendations can be most effective when they are written as a physician prepares a prescription. This approach entails specifying (1) what is to be done, (2) how many are to be done, and (3) how often. It is demanded that the physician define the exact nature and scope of treatment rather than describing the condition and delegating treatment decisions to the pharmacist. In education, describing the behavior and expecting the teacher to independently define the treatment is ignoring the reason for the request for assistance. That is, the teacher has already drawn from her repertoire of skills without success and wishes specific guidance.

An example of an academic recommendation that includes the components of what, how much, and how often is as follows:

Example of Academic Recommendation
1. Use the <u>Hartly Reading Workbook #2</u>, beginning with exer-
                      WHAT
cises dealing with sight word reinforcement (pp. 47-74)

and follow instructions as indicated in the manual. The

student should do <u>one or two sight word activities per day</u>
                   HOW MANY
and work on this <u>at least four times per week</u>.
                  HOW OFTEN
Example of Social/Behavioral Recommendation
2. <u>Praise</u> Mary when she completes her work. Verbal praise,
   WHAT
<u>one comment</u> such as "good work," "fine," etc. should always
HOW MANY
follow immediately after she has completed her work. The

<u>first two or three days, praise all efforts, then verbally prais</u>
                       HOW OFTEN
<u>approximately half the time</u> and in three weeks, praise

approximately every third or fourth task completed.

EVALUATING SUPPORTIVE INSTRUCTIONAL OBJECTIVES

In the final step of the intervention process, the SSP, teacher and/or parent have to determine if the intervention was successful. This is done by interpretation of data collected with the evaluation component of the Supportive Instructional Objective. Evaluation is always done in terms of the criteria that has been set to indicate

success. Obviously, establishing criteria for objectives is not an
easy task. Difficulty arises in that some children presented with
a new learning strategy will quickly reach and may surpass the
criteria set up; others may now show as much change as originally
anticipated. Thus, SSP, teachers and parents must be comfortable
in approaching the complex problems presented in intervention situations in a manner that acknowledges that decisions regarding criteria for success reflect best judgement at a given time and are
always improved as new data is obtained. Just because the child
did not meet stated criteria does not mean that the recommendations
were ineffective. It may be that the criteria was set to high
initially. However, it is not intended that this be used as an
excuse for not making change in the child. Interpretation of information obtained from the objective is the crucial event in decision
making about future programming for the child.

EVALUATING THE TOTAL INTERVENTION PROCESS

To evaluate the total intervention process, we can use a model
designed to analyze intervention effectiveness.

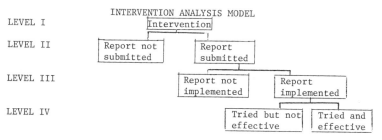

Input for the analysis model is obtained from the individual Supportive Instructional Objectives provided to teachers and parents.

EXAMPLE OF INTERVENTION ANALYSIS

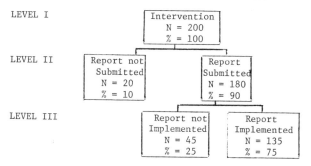

LEVEL IV	Tried but not Effective N = 35 % = 25	Tried and Effective N = 100 % = 75

Level I is the total number of SIO (Supportive Instructional Objective) developed by a SSP during a given period of time such as a year. For purposes of illustration let's consider this 200 SIO's. Level II separated those SIO's in which the teacher received written or verbal report of the consultation. In the example, 20 or 10% evaluation yielded no reports and 180 or 90% showed reports provided to teachers. Level III divides the 180 reports received into those implemented (total of 135 or 75% and those not implemented (total 45 or 25%). Level IV measures child change according to the SIO. Of the 135 reports implemented, those which were found effective (total of 100 or 75%) as measured by the students behavior indicated in the Supportive Instructional Objective are divided from those found not to be effective (total of 35 or 25%).

Based on this information the SSP can begin to look at methods for improving impact. For example, if only 10% of the reports submitted or objectives written are implemented, a change is necessary. To do so, information is needed on which to base these changes.

With the kinds of information available from using the SIO and the intervention analysis model, objective decisions can be made regarding why reports are not implemented, why they were ineffective, what parts of the report were ineffective, and what changes occurred in the behavior of children. If such decisions cannot be made, intervention cannot be improved. For improvement to occur, objective feedback regarding effectiveness is mandatory. Use of Supportive Instructional Objectives and the intervention analysis model will provide this kind of information.

The methodology indicated in this article will provide SSP with a method of promoting change in children as they work with parents and teachers; and, also allow the SSP to evaluate the effectiveness of intervention. To bring about change as SSP, effective communication is crucial. This is best done by making reports as specific as possible and by collecting information that will allow us to evaluate the child outcomes of intervention.

References

Dublinske, Stan. Instructional objectives in speed pathology. _Journal of the Iowa Speech and Hearing Association_, Polk County Board of Education, Spring, 1971, 15.

Mager, Robert F. _Preparing Instructional Objectives_. Fearon Publishers Palo Alto, California, 1962, 60.

Hernandez, David E. _Writing Behavioral Objectives_. Barnes and Noble, New York, 1971, 45.

Tom Student is a 6-year-old boy who is in first grade at Elm Elementary School, Main School District, and was evaluated February 1, 1972. Tom was referred for service by Miss Brees, classroom teacher. The boy is encountering difficulty in reading, especially immediate recall of sight words and when printing he is reversing letters such as b, d, p, and q. While intelligence measures indicate Tim is above average, he is presently below average in development of visual motor skills. The boy's general attitude towards school and home is positive.

The critical decisions are: how to decrease reversal in handwriting and increase sight word recognition.

OBJECTIVES AND RECOMMENDATIONS

The objectives and recommendations below were developed by the reporting psychologist and Miss Brees. As the recommendations are implemented, it may be found that changes are needed or other activities added to this program. Changes in recommendations should be made as warranted. If further assistance is needed, please contact this psychologist (281-3176). Follow up will be initiated by the psychologist after April 15.

Supportive Instructional Objective: By April 15, 1972, after completing the recommendations submitted to Miss Brees, Tom should be able to recognize and orally read, unaided by the teacher, at least 40 sight words from the Dolch Word List. A list of words given and those read will be maintained.

1. Use Games for Reinforcing Sight Words (see enclosure) at least one per week in school. Request the parents also provide this activity at home twice a week or more. Use the Dolch words and words from the basal text.

Supportive Instructional Objective: By April 15, 1972, after implementing the recommendations provided to Miss Brees, Tom should be able to copy sentences (total 30 words or more) from the blackboard, using primer paper and beginner pencil, with 3% or fewer reversals. The teacher will evaluate and record responses.

1. Use Frostig Workbook #1 beginning at page 47 and workbook #2 using the directions indicated in the manual. The pupil should spend approximately 10 to 15 minutes per day with the Frostig materials

23

and work this task at least four times per week.

2. Use DLM Parquetry blocks and patterns,
Visual-Memory Alphabet Recall cards and sandpaper
tracing letters (instructions enclosed) two or three
times per week. Work with these materials should
not be more than 30 minutes per day. The parents
could assist and provide these activities at home.

APPENDIX B
SUMMARY

Dale Syntax is an 8-year-old student enrolled in the third
grade at Kinsey Elementary School and was evaluated February 1,
1972. This student was referred by Mr. Fischer, school principal.
He has many speech difficulties and has problems in expressing what
he wants to say. He has poor body coordination. His attention span
is short and he gets very confused when trying to follow even the
simplest directions. His retention is very poor and at times he
appears to be in a "daze" in the classroom. On testing his nonver-
bal tasks were within the normal range and it appears that he has
average intelligence.

The critical decisions are: how to help Dale follow classroom
directions and increase language output.

OBJECTIVES AND RECOMMENDATIONS

Below are objectives and recommendations developed by the
reporting psychologist and Mrs. Harmon, Dale's teacher. As the
recommendations are implemented it may be found that changes are
needed or other activities added to this program. Changes in recommendations should be made as warranted. If further assistance is
needed, please contact this psychologist (281-8176). Follow up will
be initiated by the psychologist after May 1.

Supportive   By May 1, 1972, after completing the recommendation
Instructional   provided to Mrs. Harmon, Dale should be able to
Objective: receive and correctly follow directions with three
                parts, as judged and recorded by the teacher.

1. Use Valett's Remediation of Learning Disabilities. The section on providing skills for
Auditory Reception should be completed. Do one
activity each day, 3 times or more per week.

2. The section on auditory perception in Aids
to Psycholinguistic Teaching should be completed.

24

Begin with the activities suggested for first grade
students and continue until all activities for third
grade have been completed. Do two activities per
week.

3. Place articles relating to the same general
topic on the table. Instruct Dale to do three things
with the articles, e.g., policeman's hat, whistle,
gun -- Instruct him to "put on the hat, blow the
whistle, and shoot the gun." Session 10 to 15 minutes, two or three times per week.

Supportive   By May 1, 1972, after completing the recommendation
Instructional   provided to Mrs. Harmon, Dale should be able to
Objective: name and indicate two or more objectives per picture
                  for 10 pictures. Teacher will evaluate and record
                  correct and incorrect responses.

1. Use the Peabody Language Development Kit -
Level Two picture stimulas cards for clothing and
other tangible objects. Use the picture and a similar object to show Dale the relationship between
items. Have him say and describe the articles of
clothing. A 10-18 minute session twice a week would
be desirable.

APPENDIX C
SUMMARY

Mary Cavett is a 10-year-old girl in the fourth grade at
Dooley Elementary School, Main School District, and was evaluated
February 1, 1972. Mary was referred by Mr. Jenkins, School Guidance
Counselor. For the past two years she has shown an increasing tendency to socially withdraw in the classroom when confronted with
frustrations of an academic or social nature. Her achievement in
all basic skill areas is within one year of her grade placement.
Measures of mental ability indicate Mary is within the average
range of intelligence. The teacher's record book indicates she has
turned in only 20% of the assigned homework over the past 9 weeks.
She has begun to lay her head on the desk and cover her eyes when
encountering a problem she cannot immediately solve. During a 10
day period the teacher observed Mary's "Head on desk behavior"
occuring, on the average, of 2 times per hour while in the classroom.

The critical decisions are: how to increase the amount of
homework turned in, decrease withdrawal behavior and help Mary
establish social relations with peers.

25

OBJECTIVES AND RECOMMENDATIONS

The objectives and recommendations were developed by Mr. Jenkins and the reporting psychologist. As the recommendations are implemented it may be found that changes are needed or other activities added to this program. Changes in recommendations should be made as warranted. If further assistance is needed, please contact this psychologist (281-3176). Follow up will be initiated by the psychologist after May 1.

Supportive Instructional Objective:

By May 1, 1972, after the recommendations offered to Mr. Jenkins have been implemented by school personnel, Mary should have voluntarily completed and turned in at least 60% of her current homework assignments for the period of time from April 19 to April 30. A list of homework given and returned completed will be kept by the counselor.

1. Counselor, teacher, and psychologist should hold a conference initiated by the school with both parents. The purpose of this conference is to share the school's view of Mary's problem with the parents and enlist their support in designing and implementing a home program aimed at improving Mary's accomplishment with homework and improving relationships with peers.

2. Praise Mary when she brings in homework. Mark only correct responses (whenever possible). Check and see if she understands the printed instructions on all the homework. Make a chart which you both plot indicating if homework is completed.

Supportive Instructional Objective:

By May 1, 1972, when the recommendations offered to Mr. Jenkins have been implemented by school personnel, Mary should have established a friendship with a classmate "s" and should have sought out one peer of her own volition, 2 or more times for 3 out of 4 consecutive days. Mr. Jenkins will keep a report of Mary's in school relationships as reported by school personnel.

1. The counselor should discuss the importance of praise with all special subject teachers who have Mary, such as Art, PE, and Music. They should not praise her excessively (such as 100% of the time) and should avoid all criticism. They too should encourage "good" peer relations whenever possible.

26

2. The teacher or counselor should take a sociogram. Arrange Mary's seat at least 50% of class time so she is seated next to or with a student who chooses her in the sociogram. Encourage team efforts in working on classroom assignments whenever possible.

Supportive Instructional Objective: By May 1, 1972, when the recommendations offered to Mr. Jenkins have been implemented by school personsel, Mary should demonstrate "head on desk" behavior no more than once every 3 hours for five consecutive days. Teachers will record incidents of "head on desk" behavior and time of occurance.

1. All of the above recommendations should indirectly effect this objective.

AN ALTERNATIVE APPROACH TO THE DELIVERY OF SCHOOL PSYCHOLOGICAL SERVICES

Lonny W. Morrow

School psychologists are frequently criticized for not effect-ing change in students referred to them. This article describes one model-process which the author, while functioning as a school psychologist, successfully implemented to elimintate this criticism. Adoption of this approach should result in the school psychologist's being perceived as a viable force in the diagnostic-prescriptive process, rather than merely a tester of gatekeeper for special educa-tion.

An all too frequent criticism leveled at school psychologists is that teachers do not receive any additional information after the psychologists' evaluation is completed that will help them effect change in their student's behavior. Although I believe this criti-cism is often valid, it need not occur. I am going to outline one approach which I have used (1971-1973) as a school psychologist to successfully effect change (measured by criterion-referenced objec-tives) and alleviate this criticism (Grimes and Dublinske, 1972). Although the program was instituted in a classroom of trainable lev-el students, I believe it would work as successfully with any self-contained or resource room of "exceptional" as well as "normal" students.

This approach is truly student-oriented in that it focuses attention on the individual student's needs. Initially, implemen-tation of this program requires a great deal of time and effort on the teacher's and ancillary personnel's part. However, once every-one concerned becomes proficient in the process, it does not require any more time than other approaches.

SOURCE. Reprinted from Psychology in the Schools, 1975, XII, 3, 274-278. By permission of the author and Clinical Psychology Pub-lishing Co., Inc.

The formulation and use of behavioral objectives has been aptly described elsewhere (Esbensen, 1967; Mager, 1962, 1968). Basically, behavioral objectives are operationally defined student-centered objectives, meeting the following criteria:

1. They are stated in terms of expected pupil behavior.
2. They clearly describe what behavior the pupil should emit following each step in a lesson or unit plan.
3. They clearly outline the conditions under which the behavior can be observed.
4. They state a minimal level of performance criteria which is acceptable as an indication that the objective has been met (they may prescribe a time limit or percentage correct, etc.).

The first step in the process is a team evaluation of the student. This team optimally will consist of a school psychologist, classroom and/or special teacher, learning disabilities or special education consultant from the education field, as well as such other professional as pediatricians, optometrists, psychiatrists, etc. All professionals working with the student should be on the team whether that be many or few. After each of the team members has had the opportunity to assess the student's strengths and weaknesses informally, a conference is held. The basic purpose of the team conference is to share information and draw up specific behavioral objectives for the student, capitalizing upon his strengths to remediate his weaknesses--not just to label him. Whenever it is deemed appropriate by the team, the student could, and should, be involved in the setting of objectives.

The team members thus function as a support system for the classroom teachers and the parents. Specific help is given the classroom teacher and parents as they strive to help the student achieve his behavioral objectives agreed upon at the team conference. Once the behavioral objectives are formulated and recorded, a parent conference is held. The parents must be helped to understand that they are a viable component of the total team. They should be encouraged to ask questions and make recommendations, both pro and con, about the objectives. Their ideas and desires must receive respect and consideration; if they reject any objective, the team must revise the unsatisfactory element to the parents' satisfaction. Once this is accomplished, the objectives are implemented by all teachers involved.

An essential component of this approach is the recording system which accompanies it. It has been devised so that any team member (or the student) can look at it and immediately see how much progress the student is making toward the successful completion of each of the behavioral objectives. A standardized form is used to record the student's weekly assessment results. There is one form

per objective with the objective typed across the top. The weekly
dates are typed on the horizontal axis and the rate, frequency,
etc., of output on the vertical axis. The histogram's simplicity
and consistency facilitates both the recording process and parents'
understanding of their child's performance.

If continuous progress evaluation conducted on a weekly basis
indicates the student is making satisfactory progress toward
achieving the objective, the teacher continues the original plan
until the objective is successfully completed. In the event that
the weekly progress evaluation reveals that the student is making in-
adequate progress, a team conference is called. Questions such as,
"Was the original objective unreasonable?" or "Have we prescribed
the wrong materials?" or "Have we not prescribed the right teaching
techniques?" must be asked and answered. Once the team has come
up with a revised plan of action for accomplishing the objective,
this is implemented. As before, the support team continuously
monitors the student's progress.

For example, the team might decide that the reason a student
is having difficulty in multiplication is that he does not understand carrying. They could formulate a behavioral objective such
as "By March 8, Stan will compute a worksheet within five minutes
and with 100% accuracy of 20 two-digit multiplication problems
requiring carrying." Curriculum materials and various teaching
techniques would be suggested. Stan's progress in correctly com-
puting multiplication problems would be monitored on a weekly basis.

Another example might be after assessing a student emitting
aggressive acting out behavior such as hitting or kicking to get
what he wants instead of politely asking for it, the team might
formulate the following behavioral objective: "By April 10, Herb
will politely ask for any object he wants 100% of the time on five
consecutive days." Strategies suggested to the teacher might include using a timeout procedure in conjunction with positive reinforcement in the form of social reinforcers and free time. The
school psychologist would gather baseline data, set up the schedule
of reinforcement and make changes as necessary, frequently observe
the classroom interaction to make sure the program is working, and
help the teacher chart the number of hitting and kicking incidents
and the number of times Herb politely asks for an object. If these
undesirable behaviors do not decrease at an acceptable rate, as
reflected on the charting form, a new strategy such as modeling
might be implemented.

Once the student has successfully completed the behavioral
objective, whether that be before, on, or after the originally set
completion date, the next sequential obejctive is formulated and
the process begins again.

Obviously, if we are to truly individualize the curriculum for the student, the number of objectives, the areas covered by objectives, and materials and strategies used to accomplish them would be dependent upon the student's individual needs.

What are the potential advantages of utilizing this approach? It seems to me that the following are of particular relevance to educators:

1. The system builds in accountability. The teacher and support personnel receive continuous and immediate feedback as to the efficiency of their efforts to bring about desired academic, social, or emotional behavior from the student. This prevents wasting valuable learning time for the student-- time which can be spent on more appropriate learning tasks with the student. The recent advent of "cook-book" remedial approaches to students who are not learning in the usual manner, rate, or sequence makes it all the more imperative that school psychologists, remediation specialists, and teachers receive frequent, regular feedback as to the efficacy of their recommended and implemented remedial strategies and curriculum materials.

2. It fosters positive school-parent relationships. Parents can now feel a viable part of the team which is concerned about their child's educational progress. Seventy-five percent of the parents whose children were in the original program felt that they now had an important role in determining their child's curriculum. In addition, parents have the opportunity to work on some of the same skills at home that the teacher is working on at school. This helps foster over-learning and provides opportunities for generalization of learned academic, social and emotional behaviors outside the classroom.

3. It fosters communication between team members. This prevents needless duplication of effort and conflicting recommendations from the support personnel to the teachers involved and to the parents.

4. This approach assures the student that he is receiving his share of the teacher's time and attention. Too many times, due to different reasons, the exceptional student is neglected in the classroom (Bryan, 1974). Not only does the student fail to learn at the rate of which he is capable, but neglect often results in various behavioral problems.

5. Once the process is functioning smoothly, the teacher can write behavioral objectives that she would like the child to achieve. The school psychologist can then function as a consultant to the teacher for those problems unamenable to change.

31

The teacher is now more viable and involved in the diagnostic process. Instead of the frequently heard comment that "the received diagnosis only confirms what the teacher originally knew," diagnosis is now oriented to the student by developing strategies to meet the behaviorally stated objective.

6. This approach facilitates making the learning process sequential in nature instead of the usual hit-and/or-miss (shotgun) approach. This prevents wasting the student's time in needless duplication of effort.

7. Since many exceptional students see special resource teachers (remedial reading, learning disabilities, speech, etc.), everyone concerned with the student can work on accomplishing the same behavioral objectives, but from their own area of expertise.

8. The entire team will be able to agree (thus high reliability) on when the student has successfully completed the behavioral objective and is ready to advance.

9. This approach should foster the concept that teachers are responsible for the learning of their students--not commercially prepared curriculum materials. Teachers should become more aware of the advantages and disadvantages of each commercially prepared series they use. Teachers should learn to pick and choose the best components of each series and integrate them to meet the student's needs instead of routinely following the teacher's manual. This approach might even force publishers to do more thorough research as to whether or not their materials do what they claim. Money currently spent on making the materials attractive and attention-catching could instead be spent on field-based research.

10. Administrators should become more aware of the need for a number of different curriculum series, as opposed to buying several sets of the same series. Curriculum materials salesmen might have to start becoming knowledgeable about learning and the products they sell.

11. Utilization of this approach could have drastic effects upon the current grading system used by most schools. Instead of receiving a mark for reading or arithmetic, parents can now see records of the specific skills which their child has mastered or is currently working on. One hundred percent of the twelve parents whose children participated in the program preferred this method which showed their child's charted progress over the previously traditional method which had been in operation.

12. This could also facilitate schools implementing criterion-referenced testing which some educators (Proger and Mann, 1973) have recommended as opposed to the currently used norm-referenced testing.

By virtue of his position and training, the school psychologist has the opportunity and obligation to assume a leadership role in helping to effect change in those students referred to him. Utilization of this approach is one field-tested method of permitting the school psychologist to be perceived as a viable force rather than a tester or gate-keeper for special education.

References

Bryan, T.S. An observational analysis of classroom behaviors of children with learning disabilities. Journal of Learning Disabilities, 1974, 7, 26-34.
Esbensen, T. Writing instructional objectives. Phi Delta Kappan, January, 1967, 48, 246-247.
Grimes, J., and Dublinske, S. Planning for and monitoring TMR progress. Child Change, March, 1972, 1, 1.
Mager, R.F. Preparing instructional objectives. Palo Alto: Fearon Publishers, 1962.
Mager, R.F. Deriving objectives for the high school curriculum. National Society for Programmed Instruction, March, 1968, 3 7-14.
Mager, R.F. Developing attitudes toward learning. Palo Alto: Fearon Publishers, 1968.
Proger, B.T. and Mann, L. Criterion referenced measurement: The world of gray versus black and white. Journal of Learning Disabilities, 1973, 6, 72-84.

Section II

DETERMINING AND IMPROVING PERSONAL EFFECTIVENESS

When a discussion centers around accountability for school psychological services, school psychologists offer numerous explanations for not accounting for their services. One of the more popular arguments is that it is extremely difficult to assess many areas of school psychological services. For instance, does one assess the effectiveness of counseling, of consultative services, or of referral services? Many school psychologists consider their discipline too esoteric to be realistically discussed in quantifiable terms and measurable outcomes.

At the time this writer was developing methods of accounting for his services and implementing them in his job, he had doubts regarding the feasibility and practicality of attempting to document his effectiveness. However, the writer was able to develop several methods which school psychologists could employ to account for their services. This further reinforced the idea that a school psychologist can evaluate their services. The fact that accountability for school psychological services is not only necessary but a reality was supported by a review of the current literature devoted to this topic. Numerous and creative means of accountability have been described by various writers. Clair and Kiraly differentiate results-oriented data, and person-oriented data and discuss how these two types of data might be gathered. They also introduce the concept of psychological auditing in which a school psychologist's services could be audited by an external review board.

Tomlinson discusses the use of behavioral criteria in developing an accountability system. The effectiveness of psychological services in a metropolitan school system was based on information obtained during follow-up interviews. The interviews were designed to determine what changes had occurred in the target behaviors which were identified during the assessment.

Grubb, Petty, and Flynn discuss how they were able to improve school psychological services after conducting formal and informal evaluations of their role in selected buildings. The feedback from teachers regarding the present services being offered, and further input regarding desired services helped the writers to establish a role that was compatible with the needs of the building staff.

Fairchild offers several suggestions for accounting for school psychological services which include (1) keeping a daily log, (2) collecting time elapsed information, (3) scheduling accountability interviews, (4) follow-up questionnaires, (5) telephone follow-ups, and (6) behavioral consultation. The techniques and their rationale are described.

Conti and Bardon's proposal for evaluating the effectiveness of school psychologists involves 3 scales to be completed by consumers of school psychological services. The scales include an evaluation of the school psychologist's written report, an evaluation of the school psychologist's verbal communication, and information regarding how the psychologist is perceived by pupils with whom he work

Although Conti's follow-up study of referral outcomes was a descriptive study regarding the school psychologist's referral function, the concept of referral follow-up is extremely relevant in a discussion of accountability procedures. School psychologists make no systematic efforts to evaluate the referral function. However, in order to evaluate the effectiveness of the referral process, psychologists need to collect data regarding referral outcomes. A school psychologist's effectiveness can be enhanced if he or she can identify what referral agencies are most effective, or what specific referral problems different agencies are most successful with.

In this writer's opinion, visibility has always been a critical variable in facilitating a school psychologist's effectiveness. The writer utilized his follow-up questionnaires, telephone follow-ups, and 100% parent conferences as one method of visibility. Other methods include speaking at PTA meetings, and community service organization meetings, or presenting in-service presentations to teachers and parents to explain the role and function of the school psychologist. Hatch and Lynch discuss the concept of a school psychologist newsletter which affords the school psychologist the opportunity of communicating to all the district personnel what services he or she is involved in. This has the advantage of eliminating some of the mystique which traditionally surrounds the role.

The Erwin and Cannon article relates to accountability because they are concerned with minimizing the significant delay that transpires between the assessment and teacher receipt of feedback.

One means of reducing the time that elapses before teachers receive feedback would be to use audio-tape recorded staffings, so that recommendations could be implemented immediately.

The yearly report outlined by Fairchild is essential since the school psychologist must share the data he has collected regarding his personal effectiveness. The accountability data collected can be organized readily into a communicable written report which can be disseminated to building staff, directors, and the superintendent.

There are numerous ways for school psychologists to determine and improve their personal effectiveness. The writer hopes that the reader will be stimulated to adopt some of the methods discussed within the following section or devise other techniques of accounting for his or her performance. In either case, the individual school psychologist, as well as the profession of school psychology, will be enhanced.

ACCOUNTABILITY FOR THE SCHOOL PSYCHOLOGIST

Theodore N. Clair and John Kiraly, Jr.

As the public demands that educational institutions -- like other agencies of the government -- account for the sum total of their activity, the school psychologist, as a member of the educational staff, will be expected to prove his worth as it relates to the social, emotional and academic growth of children. Because he is aware that parents are becoming quite vociferous about the rising cost of education and are dissatisfied with the school administrator's utilization of available resources to facilitate the educational growth of youngsters, the psychologist can expect that soon he will come under closer scrutiny by those concerned with his functional behavior.

A DEFINITION OF ACCOUNTABILITY

Educational scholars have provided various definitions for the term "accountability". Lessinger (1970a, 1970b) states that it implies an agreement by school staff members to contract on the basis of providing a service answerable to stipulated performance standards. Without it, he cautions, good educational practice lacks both identification, documentation, and verification. Barro (1970) supports this view of accountability, for he stresses that it places responsibility for educational outcomes on all professional educators. Accountability for the school psychologist requires a definition of his role according to specific behavioral objectives and further dictates how these objectives can be quantified.

SOURCE. Reprinted from Psychology in the Schools, 1971, VIII, 4, 318-321. By permission of the authors and Clinical Psychology Publishing Co., Inc.

NEED FOR ACCOUNTABILITY

In any school the psychologist is effective only if he has a clear understanding of the administration's defined objectives. These objectives, which may differ from one educational setting to another, should facilitate collectively the creation of an optimal learning experience for children (Gray, 1963; Lopez, 1970). With the superintendent and the principal, the psychologist will be responsible for the evaluation of the educational program and assessment of the educational product. The psychologist must serve the school district as both its consultant and facilitator. Instead of being concerned primarily with testing or completing a predetermined number of case studies, he helps management to specify goals and behavioral objectives for the instructional program as well as in other facets of school life.

ACCOUNTABILITY AND THE COMMUNICATION PROCESS

Within a school organization, accountability facilitates clearer communication and can provide the means whereby all staff members are better informed as to their defined role and the behavior that results from that role. To fulfill his mission as a communicator, the school psychologist must make certain that the superintendent and the principal understand what he is doing. If he is to communicate, he must speak to teachers about the diverse needs of their pupils. If he is to know whether he is effective as a disseminator of information, he must be informed as to the outcome of his recommendations with objective data -- a test score, an observable performance.

ACCOUNTABILITY AND THE SCHOOL PSYCHOLOGICAL PROCESS

Accountability for school psychological services is relevant not only in terms of evaluation, reporting, and consultation, but also for student accomplishment. It links the practitioner's performance to results achieved by the pupil and requires the psychologist to assist in educational planning for the student (Reger, 1967). When he is dealing with an educational problem the school psychologist can be accountable for three major performance functions: diagnosis, intervention, and evaluation. The diagnostic performance function includes formal and informal observation of the child, psychological testing and a report on the results. This information provides baseline data for the second function, which is to attempt to solve the educational problem by designing relevant instruction. This intervention performance function incorporates decision-making processes to develop educational strategies in order to change inappropriate behavior selected within the components of the educational problem. Finally, the evaluation function demands both a quantitative and qualitative analysis of the performance. By means of evaluative research procedures and techniques to obtain feedback, the psychologist can recast any strategy in the intervention procedure in order to produce relevant change in the total process. This intervention need not be pathology-oriented, but can be directed toward curriculum development and improvement for total school program.

The school psychologist shoulders responsibility to the child, the parents, the teacher, and the administrative hierarchy; however, he should be accountable only to his supervisor. His supervisor is in an ideal and unique position to assess the need for psychological services by each member of the educational team. Likert (1961) and McGregor (1960) state that administrators are obligated to seek the goals of the organizations they represent, and thus the performance of individuals within the organizations is based on the relevance of this performance to achievement of those goals.

By the nature of his position, the administrator is able to view most objectively an evaluation of psychological service. In a discussion of the school psychologist administrator relationship, Reger (1965) supports this view in his statement that, "Administrators are obligated to do their best to be fair to all members of the organization without concern for personal likes or dislikes... (p. 112)." The administrator should be able to evaluate the performance of school psychologists on the basis of result-oriented data and person-oriented data (Lopez, 1970).

RESULT-ORIENTED DATA

Result-oriented data are derived from objective evidence that measures the school psychologist's functional performance. These data, gathered from his records, are amenable to both quantification and verification. Variables such as frequency of pupil-personnel contact, time needed to complete psychological studies of individual students, and number of in-service meetings can be measured easily.

Other data that pertain to the psychologist's daily efforts can be obtained from personal logs. These documents can be prepared to include information of a non-confidential nature relative to his mode of performance. This information, when processed, should reveal the outcome of the psychologist's prescriptive plan for the child. When he is devising the educational prescription the school psychologist must consider the problem variables, the situational variables, and the school variables. The measures obtained should reflect the results of the child's learning in terms of actual change compared with desired change and identify the degree to which the psychologist's intervention strategy has been responsible for this change. Specfic examples are given by Peter (1965).

40

PERSON-ORIENTED DATA

The administrator will judge the school psychologist not only in terms of result-oriented data, but as Lopez (1970) suggests, on the basis of his initiative, technical competence, and interpersonal competence. In his evaluation of the school psychologist's performance, the supervisor also may wish to consider mutual ratings by the psychologist's peers and the people he serves. Ratings can be made by these personnel on the basis of traits that they have chosen as important and by means of a scale of values on which they have agreed. The mutual rating plan affords the psychologist an opportunity to see himself as others see him. Further, it provides him with feedback as to his effectiveness on a continuing basis.

PSYCHOLOGICAL AUDITING

The quality of the school psychologist's services to his district can be audited by an external review board. Veteran school psychologists or diplomates in the field can be impaneled by their state or regional professional organization to examine and compare periodically the work of the practitioner in selected individual school districts. These experts can discuss their own experiences with each other and review guidelines established by the National Association of School Psychologists as well as Division 16 of the American Psychological Association and thus arrive at some agreement as to minimal standards of acceptable school psychological services. This kind of audit is different from evaluation in that it is oriented toward a statement of accomplishment (Kaufman, 1971). Of course, it is a system which, as Barro (1970) suggests, imposes a centralized quality control or "inspectorate" function upon the existing structure of autonomous local school systems.

CONCLUSION

The psychologist who is accountable for his services to the school must expect new power to innovate, for without it, he cannot be held answerable for his results. In his attempts to fulfill his commitment to maximize the learning of children he must not limit himself to diagnostic services, but rather must broaden his range of skills. He must translate demands for educational improvement into a program for educational improvement. He must share the teacher's burden of aiding youngsters to obtain relevant experiences appropriate to their growth and development, and his ability to fulfill these functions constitutes the very essence of his claim to professional status.

References
_____

Barro, S.M. An approach to developing accountability measures for
     the public school. Phi Delta Kappa, 1970, 4, 196-205.
Gray, S.W. (Ed.) The internship in school psychology, proceedings
     of the Peabody conference. Nashville: George Peabody College
     for Teachers, 1963.
Kaufman, R. Accountability, a system approach and the quantitative
     improvement of education -- an attempted integration. Educa-
     tional Technology Accountability in Education, 1971, 1, 21-26.
Lessinger, L. Every kid a winner: accountability in education.
     New York: Simon & Schuster, 1970. (a)
Lessinger, L. Engineering accountability for results in public
     education. Phi Delta Kappan, 1970, 4, 217-223. (b)
Likert, R. New patterns of management. New York: McGraw-Hill,
     1961.
Lopez, F. Accountability in education. Phi Delta Kappan, 1970, 4,
     231-235.
McGregor, D. The human side of enterprise. New York: McGraw-Hill,
     1960.
Peter, L.J. Prescriptive teaching. New York: McGraw-Hill, 1965.
Reger, R. School Psychology. Springfield, Ill.: Charles C. Thomas,
     1965.
Reger, R. The technology of school psychology. Journal of School
     Psychology, 1967, 5, 148-155.

ACCOUNTABILITY PROCEDURES FOR PSYCHOLOGICAL SERVICES

Jerry R. Tomlinson

The current emphasis on accountability in the public schools again has raised the issue and problems encountered in demonstrating the effectiveness of psychological services. In contrast to establishing performance goals for academic subjects, the helping professions have the problem of attempting to demonstrate their effectiveness across an almost infinite variety of problems that include the entire range of academic, motivational, management and social behaviors that occur in the classroom. It has been argued that the effects of psychological intervention are more global and less tangible than measures of academic performance or are in some way not amenable to measurement against objective criteria. However, with the advent of behaviorally oriented approaches to classroom problems, the use of specific behavioral criteria offers one possible solution to this problem (Bergan, 1970; Greiger & Abidin, 1972).

Through the use of behavioral criteria, the following accountability system was developed to evaluate the effectiveness of psychological services in a metropolitan school system.

METHOD

Behavioral Criteria

In most school settings psychologists function not as direct agents of change themselves, but as professionals who make recommendations to others with regard to the course of action most likely to produce desired changes in children's behavior. Therefore the effectiveness of psychological intervention must be evaluated against two criteria: the behavior of the mediator (did school personnel implement the psychologist's recommendations)

SOURCE. Reprinted from Psychology in the Schools, 1973, X, 1, 42-47. By permission of the author and Clinical Psychology Publishing Co., Inc.

and the behavior of the child (when the recommendations were implemented, did the behavior of the child change in the direction
desired).

The range and diversity of problems for which psychological
services are sought were included in the evaluation process by
defining a set of specific target behaviors for each case. Each
target behavior was described in terms of the current rate of level
of observable behavior. For example, motivational problems frequently were translated into target behaviors that involved the
number of assignments completed; hyperactivity was defined as the
number of times the child was out of his seat during a specified
period, special learning disabilities as performances in specific
tasks, and defiance as the number of occasions upon which the child
did not comply with teacher requests.

Target behaviors were defined whenever the psychologist assumed
some professional responsibility for the case, i.e., whenever the
psychologist suggested the plan to be implemented or made significant alterations in another plan. These included recommendations
to refer the child to another school service or agency as well as
techniques suggested for use by the classroom teacher.

Effectiveness Ratings

Effectiveness was determined on the basis of information
obtained during a follow-up interview designed to obtain specific
information as to whether the recommendations had been implemented
and, if so, what changes had occurred in the target behaviors.
This information was obtained from the individual with the greatest
opportunity to observe the specific target behavior in question.
In most instances in which specific techniques had been recommended,
follow-up information was obtained from the classroom teacher; when
referral had been recommended, this information was obtained from
both classroom teacher and the resource teacher. The length of
time between the initial contact and subsequent follow-up varied
according to the type of problem and the length of time in which
change reasonably could be expected to occur. In all cases, an
attempt was made to allow sufficient time between these two contacts
to assure some degree of stability in the behavior change.

No further information was recorded when the psychologist's
recommendations had not been implemented or when the case fell
into one of the following two categories: Withdrawn - when the
child had moved at the time of follow-up or change in the child's
life made any evaluation of the effects of recommended treatment
impossible (e.g., a change in family status, treatment from another
source, change in teachers, addition or elimination of physiological factors); Alternate - when an alternate plan not recommended

by the psychologist was implemented. In the remaining cases, each target behavior was rated by the psychologist according to the following definitions and on the basis of information obtained during follow-up:

1. Behavior reached and maintained at the desired level.
2. Behavior changed significantly in the desired direction, but further change desired.
3. No significant change in the behavior.
4. Behavior changed in an undesired direction.

A significant change was defined as any stable rate of change in the target behavior greater than had occurred in a comparable period of time prior to consultation with the psychologist.

Setting

These procedures were utilized during a 2-year period by a psychological services staff responsible for providing service to a metropolitan school system with a student population of 67,000. During this period, the department employed one director, two coordinators, and eight full-time psychologists.

Sample I. During the first year, three psychologists were assigned to a group of 12 inner-city schools and provided an average of 8 hours of psychological services per week to each school. Each psychologist maintained a record on every case in which he made a recommendation. Any information deemed appropriate by the psychologist could be included on these records, and any theoretical approach could be utilized when recommendations were made. However, the following information was required on each record: the target behavior(s) described in observable terms and their present rate of occurance and the criterion or desired level of performance and data on the target behaviors at the time of the follow-up contact. When subsequent contacts led to a change in the original plan or to the addition of new target behaviors, the same basic procedures for behavioral description and follow-up were followed.

A typical academic problem was the child who was reading two grade levels below his current grade placement. In such cases, the psychologist frequently recommended referral for special tutoring; the target behavior was reading skills as measured by performance on a standardized achievement test or level of progress in a graded reading series. A frequently encountered classroom management problem was the child who, although capable, was completing only a small percentage of assignments and who often engaged in mildly disruptive behaviors. A common recommendation for such cases was a direct suggestion to the classroom teacher that she establish a direct contingency between completion of assignments and an

45

available reinforcer. The target behaviors were in the percent of assignments completed and the number of disruptions during a specified period of time.

At the end of the school year, results were tabulated on all cases in which records were available, with the exception of cases in which additional follow-up contacts were planned for the following year. Data were available on 406 cases with an average follow-up of 12 weeks.

Sample II. A random sample of 176 cases from 62 schools (divided equally among eight psychologists) was drawn from a total of 1822 cases seen in the remainder of the city during the second year. Due to restrictive time limitations a record was not maintained on each of these cases; a copy of the report sent to the school principal was utilized instead. Whenever one of these reports did not specify clearly the target behaviors, the consulting psychologist defined a set of target behaviors on the basis of recommendations made in the report. The average time between the initial and follow-up contacts in this sample was 19 weeks.

RESULTS

The largest percentage (67%) of target behaviors fell into an academic category that involved either ability or skill (low reading, mathematics or general abilities) or performance (failure to start or complete assignments, requiring constant teacher attention). Management problems constituted 22% of the target behaviors, including such behaviors as nonattending, hyperactivity, attention-getting behaviors or inappropriate verbal responses. The remaining 11% were primarily social problems and included rejection by peers, absence of common social responses, cooperative behaviors, or anxiety related to school or specific social situations.

Approximately 60% of the psychologists' recommendations in both samples were for referral of the child, primarily to in-school services such as Special Learning Disability tutoring or resource help. The remaining recommendations were specific suggestions to teachers with regard to the handling of a particular child, e.g., establishing a contingency between desired behavior and reinforcement, reducing social attention after undesired behaviors, reducing or alternating assignments to correspond with current ability level or reducing or increasing negative consequences.

Of the 406 cases in the first sample, no action was taken on the psychologist's recommendations in 63 cases, 6 were handled by an alternate plan and 26 were withdrawn. In the remaining 311 cases, ratings were made on 438 target behaviors. Of these behaviors, 22% were rated as having reached the level desired, 54% were rated as having changed significantly in the desired direction,

22% were rated as indicating no significant change, and 2% were rated as changed in the undesired direction.

Of the 176 cases in the second sample, no action was taken in 17 cases, 9 were handled by an alternate plan, and 13 were withdrawn. In the remaining 154 cases, ratings were made on 231 target behaviors. Twenty-nine percent were rated as having reached the level desired, 55% were rated as having changed significantly in the desired direction, 16% were rated as unchanged, and no behavior was rated as having changed in the undesired direction.

DISCUSSION

When the effectiveness of psychological services was measured against the first criterion, the behavior of the mediator, the percentage of cases in which no action was taken on the psychologist's recommendations were combined with those cases in which an alternate plan was employed. The results indicate that the psycholgist's recommendations were not implemented in approximately 15% of the cases in both samples. Such information can be examined subsequently to determine the degree to which this may be a function of the type of case, the type of treatment recommended, the psychologist's role in a particular school, the psychologist's ability to convince the school staff of the efficacy of a particular treatment plan, or the inability of school personnel to implement certain recommendations.

When the effectiveness of psychological services was measured against the second criterion, the behavior of the child, the results indicate that in those cases in which the psychologist's recommendations were implemented, a significant change in behavior occurred approximately 80% of the time. This, of course, does not purport to be a "cure" rate nor as significant a behavioral change as might have been desired or achieved. Only about one-fourth of the behaviors were judged as having reached the desired level at the time of the follow-up contact; the remainder simply were rated as having changed more in the direction desired than had occurred in a comparable period of time prior to psychological consultation.

Such data, however, can be useful to identify some of the variables involved when recommended procedures do not lead to a demonstrable change in target behaviors. Once identified, changes in recommendations for certain types of problems then can be made and evaluation techniques can be refined further. For example, from an examination of our data, it appears that recommending specific techniques to teachers is most successful with management problems, while referring such problems is least successful. This suggests that we can improve our effectiveness with management problems by recommending specific techniques more often and reducing the number of such problems referred.

47

The information generated from applying this approach is subject to several possible sources of error, the first of which involves its reliance on verbal reports of teachers with regard to initial and subsequent behavioral description. As yet, teachers have not been demonstrated to be necessarily accurate in their observations of classroom behavior. However, the extent of this error may be reduced by the use of the rate of occurrence of specific target behaviors. It was necessary for teachers to translate vague evaluations such as "better" or "the same" into specific behaviors and their approximate rates of occurrence. Further, since it is the teacher who typically labels the child as having "problems," it may be of considerable significance that a teacher no longer applies this label to the child at the time of follow-up, although this may be a function of many variables other than an actual change in the rate of the target behavior.

Another source of error is the possible bias of the counsulting psychologist, who may lead a teacher to report or agree to a more significant change in the target behavior than would be supported by objective observation. In an attempt to reduce such a possible source of error, we currently are working on a system that involves college students or para-professionals as objective observers. Such observers would conduct the follow-up interview on the basis of target behavior descriptions provided by the consulting psychologist. This procedure could be extended by making such observations prior to psychological consultation and again at a predetermined follow-up date. Although not feasible for all cases, a sample might be chosen for such observations as a means to estimate the amount of error involved in teachers' verbal reports of classroom behaviors.

A problem arose with regard to the rating of behaviors that involve academic skills. Of these behaviors, 67% received a rating of "significantly improved", while only 14% were rated as having reacher criterion. This is, in part, a function of the fact that the length of time between the initial and follow-up contacts was insufficient for many of the skills in question to reach criterion. One possible solution may be to rate academic skills on the basis of changes in performance or learning rates subsequent to psychological intervention. One would note as having reached criterion those behaviors in which the rate of learning at the time of follow-up is commensurate with other available information, such as the child's level of intellectual functioning.

Finally, the lack of a control group precludes the possibility of any statement with regard to the specific effects of implementing psychological recommendations on subsequent behavior change. To determine what changes might have occurred in the target behaviors without psychological consultation would require comparison with a control group of matched cases in which the psychologist is not involved.

However, these evaluation techniques were not employed to demonstrate experimentally the effects of psychological intervention. Rather, such a procedure was designed to provide information, on the basis of which psychologists may identify systematically those instances in which their recommendations are not implemented or when they do not result in a significant change in behavior, as the first critical step toward modifications in their procedures or techniques. Such data also can be employed to evaluate the effectiveness of psychological services in specific schools or areas of the city, to evaluate new or alternative techniques, to determine the effectiveness of various referral resources and to develop behavioral goals for psychological services.

These procedures require minimal expense and professional time and are not restricted to a particular method or technique; they require only that the intended outcome be stated in terms of observable changes in behavior. Initial resistance to the use of behavioral criteria was based on a concern that only the most easily defined behaviors would be employed to select target behaviors. However, with increasing familiarity with behavioral descriptions, psychologists were able to translate more complex concepts such as self-image, into a set of behaviors that were acceptable as a reflection of their definition of that concept.

Although they do not provide rigid scientific evidence of the effectiveness of psychological consultation, the data provided by the use of such a technique are a step in the direction of demonstrating, in observable terms, the effectiveness of psychological services in the public schools to boards of education or legislators.

References

Bergan, J.R. A systems approach to psychological services. Psychology in the Schools, 1970, 7, 315-319.
Grieger, R.M., and Abidin, R.R. Psychosocial assessment: a model for the school community psychologist. Psychology in the Schools, 1972, 9, 112-119.

FUNCTIONAL ANALYSIS AND ACCOUNTABILITY OF PSYCHOLOGICAL SERVICES

Jerry R. Tomlinson

As demands for accountability in the public schools expand to include services other than those that directly involve the instruction of children, it becomes increasingly more important to develop accountability systems that take into account the unique elements of psychological services.

In an earlier article (Tomlinson, 1973) an accountability system in which effectiveness was defined in terms of changes in specific target behaviors was outlined. The following is a description of subsequent modifications in that system to include functional information and results obtained when applied to the entire population of children who received psychological services during a school year.

METHOD

Data Cards

To facilitate the recording of specific target behaviors for each child, with additional information about services performed, a card format was employed. This data card was a standard (7 3/4 x 3 1/4) IBM card, designed so that certain types of identifying, functional and effectiveness information could be recorded for subsequent computer tabulation and analysis. Identifying information included school, grade, special education status and whether previously seen for psychological services. Functional information included school personnel contacted, type of child contact, whether information or recommendations were made and to whom and whether parent and agency contacts were made. Sufficient space was provided for the child's name, teacher and school, a description of the target behaviors, recommendations and follow-up information. Problems that involved academic skills were described on one side of the card, nonacademic problems on the reverse.

SOURCE. Reprinted from Psychology in the Schools, 1974, XI, 3, 291-294. By permission of the author and Clinical Psychology Publishing Co., Inc.

A second card described any services that did not involve a specifically referred child, e.g., assisting school personnel to develop alternative approaches to classroom management or educational resources, but was not designed for data processing.

Effectiveness Ratings

Follow-up information was obtained in each case in which the psychologist made a specific recommendation to determine whether the recommendation had been followed. If so, each specific behavior was rated as: having reached the desired level, having changed significantly in the desired direction (but not yet at the desired level), or not having changed in the desired direction.

To avoid an earlier problem, in which academic skills tended to fall in the second, "improved" category because they rarely reached desired levels in the 12- to 15-week follow-up period, a modification of this rating system was developed for problems that involved academic skills. Through the use of a simple 8 X 22 grid printed on one side of the card, any useful measure of the skill in question was plotted on the ordinate, and the number of months or years in school was plotted on the abscissa. The student's current level then was plotted and a line drawn to the zero point to represent approximate rate of progress to date. On the basis of factors considered important by the psychologist, (e.g., intellectual ability, specific disability) a predicted progress line was drawn based on expected change in the rate of progress if the recommended treatment is effective. On follow-up, academic behaviors were rated as follows: actual rate of progress approximates or exceeds predicted rate, rate increased but short of predicted rate, or rate approximates previous rate of progress.

Setting

These procedures were utilized during a 1-year period by a staff of 14 psychologists who were providing services to a metropolitan school system with a student population of 6700.

RESULTS

Functional Data

A total of 2479 children received some type of direct psychological service during the school year, 67% of whom had not received prior psychological services. Three-fourths of all cases were in elementary schools; the largest number (267) were in first grade with progressively fewer cases in each succeeding grade.

Of services that directly involved the child, 55% involved some type of evaluation or testing, 15% were observed in the classroom and 8% were interviewed. In the remaining 22% the child was

51

not seen by the psychologist; information and recommendations were made on the basis of teacher interviews, reports and records. Psychologists met with teachers and provided information and/or recommendations in 75% of the cases and with parents in 20% of all cases.

In 208 instances, services other than those related to a specifically referred child were provided. The largest single group of such services were informational presentations to school staff or parent groups. Assistance in the development of additional techniques for classroom control, social relations, etc. was provided in 51 instances. The remainder involved administrative changes that led to improvement in the delivery of psychological services, development of alternative educational programs, treatment groups conducted by the psychologist, assistance with staff problems and research projects.

In 31% of the cases, the psychologist provided information to school personnel or parents or agreed with a plan or recommendation already under consideration, but did not make additional recommendations. In the remaining 1700 cases in which a specific recommendation was made, 43% involved academic skills while 57% involved behavioral, motivational or social problems. Approximately one-third of these were referred to some type of school resource, while in the remaining two-thirds recommendations were made directly to school personnel, usually the classroom teacher.

Effectiveness

Psychologists' recommendations were followed in 74% of all cases. Of these, 43% of the specific target behaviors were rated on follow-up as no longer being a problem, 45% were rated as having significantly improved and 12% remained essentially unchanged. There was no difference in there percentages between academic and nonacademic problems.

DISCUSSION

The finding that 44% of all services was performed in grades K-3 reflects both school and departmental emphasis on early intervention and lends support to a recent study by Kraus (1973) that suggests that most children who display behavior problems are identified before the end of third grade.

Findings with regard to the amount of repetitive service answer a question of some concern, namely the extent to which psychologists may be involved with a small number of problem children throughout their education. The findings suggest that only about one-third of the referrals were for children previously seen for psychological services, the greatest percentage of whom were referred from secondary schools.

52

When the psychologist has direct contact with the child, individual evaluation is still the most frequently performed service. It is perhaps more significant, however, that in slightly less than one-half of the cases individual evaluation was not involved, i.e., sufficient information was available from classroom observations, teacher interviews, and existing records. This may represent both a decrease in the number of requests for test scores and an increase in requests for consultation and specific recommendations. This is supported further by the finding that psychologists met with teachers in 75% of all cases.

There were several differences in these findings from our previous sample data. While the sample data indicated a much higher percentage of academic problems, this is most likely due to our redefinition of academic problems to include only those in which there is a need to improve a specific academic skill; motivational problems, failure to complete assignments, etc., thereby are excluded.

By including an "informational" category to identify those instances in which the psychologist does not consider himself critical to the subsequent plan adopted in a particular case, the percentages of cases referred to school based services was reduced. In addition, the role of the psychologist in such referrals has undergone a change in the past year, with more responsibility for such decisions placed on the school based team. This also may account for the reduction in the percentage of recommendations subsequently implemented, a reduction of about 10%, since many previous routine referrals to school based services now are included in the informational category and hence are not included when determining effectiveness, i.e., the psychologist is making fewer routinely implemented recommendations.

The increase in percent of behaviors rated as being no problem at the time of follow-up is due in part to the change in rating academic behaviors. In the sample data only 14% of academic behaviors were rated as having reached criterion, while after the change to the use of changes in the rate of progress as the criterion, 44% were rated as being no further problem.

The data card provides a reasonably small number (47) of easily checked categories for the recording of functional data as well as sufficient space to record specific target behaviors, a summary of recommendations made, and follow-up information. An attempt was made to make the cards as functional as possible, and when data has been transferred for data processing, the basic card was included in the departmental records for each child.

Both functional and effectiveness data provide a base line against which subsequent changes in functioning, introduction of new techniques,or approaches and shifts in the demand for different types of service in the future can be compared. The system provides information to make analyses of any type of service in any school or combination of schools and also provides a means to measure any specific type of service against corresponding effectiveness data.

References

Kraus, P.E. Yesterday's children -- a longitudinal study of children from kindergarten into adult years. New York: Wiley, 1973.
Tomlinson, J.R. Accountability procedures for psychological services. Psychology in the Schools, 1973, 1, 42-47.

A STRATEGY FOR THE DELIVERY OF ACCOUNTABLE SCHOOL PSYCHOLOGICAL SERVICES

Richard D. Grubb, Sharon Z. Petty, and Dale L. Flynn

A survey of representative teachers in a school district of 8,000 students was used as a basis of evaluating psychological services. Reactions suggested that teachers were dissatisfied with: (a) the wait in receiving service, (b) the nature of the services provided (not enough placement in special programs), and (c) limited follow-up of cases. A new procedure for providing psychological services is described which handles many of the teachers' concerns. The advantages, possible limitations and initial reactions to this "accountability" model are further presented.

School psychologists traditionally have had the role of describing and interpreting the academic and social behavior of children for the use of other people, primarily teachers and educational administrators. Many of the evaluations by school psychologists have been completed for the purpose of making administrative, educational placement decisions, such as the placement of a child in a special classroom. In recent years, special class placement has come under attack. Dunn (1968) asserted that such placements were counterproductive and suggested that new roles be sought for special educators involved in this process. The attack on special educators, generally, and school psychologists, specifically, has come from a variety of sources. Barclay (1971) reports of a survey which indicated that more than 70% of New York City's teachers considered the work of school psychologists of "no help, detrimental, or not relevant to teaching." The courts have become involved in the attack, occasionally ruling that the traditional evaluative role of the school psychologist results in decisions which are discriminatory and which may do irreparable harm.

As a result, school psychology is in search of a new identity and school psychologists are playing roles in addition to or in

SOURCE. Reprinted from <u>Psychology in the Schools</u>, 1976, XIII, 1, 39-44. By permission of the authors and Clinical Psychology Publishing Co., Inc.

place of the traditional role. Some school psychologists have
become experts in subject matter programming for groups and individual programmed instructional materials. Other psychologists are
involved in in-service roles conducting workshops for school personnel; conducting research with a commitment to exploring local
issues (as well as issues of a more general nature); developing
programs as needs are delineated; and engaging in "action counseling" (Krumboltz, 1966). A consultative role with "on the spot"
consultation to parents, teachers, and administrators and a role as
an arranger of antecedents and consequents of behavior for individuals and groups of individuals are still other services being adopted by school psychologists. Some school psychologists see their
role as a learning theory expert who should be able to influence
educational policy and practice at all levels within the educational
structure.

Some role prescriptions for school psychologists have been
"dictated from the top," e.g., state departments of education,
institutions of higher learning, expert opinion via journal articles.
Of greater importance to the school psychologist is the role prescriptions which come from within -- from the consumers of such
services. For this reason, an evaluation (formal and informal) of
school psychological services was undertaken in the Ferndale School
District, the result of which was to propose and ultimately implement a new model for school psychological services, a model which
at the time of this report has been in operation for one year.

THE DISTRICT

The Ferndale School District, a K-12 district with approximately 8,000 students, is a suburban district which includes all
socio-economic levels from the upper managerial level to the social
welfare level. Ethnic minorities comprise approximately 11% of the
population. The district provides comprehensive special education
services aimed at essentially all areas of handicap for all age
groups. The district employs approximately 400 certified teachers,
37 of whom are in special education. Previous to the evaluation
of psychological services, the role prescribed for the district's
two school psychologists was essentially of the Refer-Test-Report-
Recommend model.

THE EVALUATION

The formal evaluation was completed by 18 teachers in a
district school (grades K-6). It consisted of: (a) teachers'
perceptions of currently available psychological services, and (b)
teachers' rank-ordered preferences for alternative types of services
which were not available at that time. The informal evaluation was
completed by interviewing teachers in other schools in the district.

Of the persons responding to the formal evaluation, 83% had used psychological services in the past; 78% indicated that the services had not provided what they wanted. The most frequent negative comment regarded the wait (three to four months) for service, which was seen as much too long. Another stated major concern was that psychological services benefited a child only when the child was "properly placed in a special education program" and such had been an infrequent result. The fact that children were seen on only one or two occasions by a school psychologist was also perceived negatively, with teachers indicating that much more follow-up was necessary. The school psychologist was generally seen as one who should be able to solve the problems for which the child was referred. Teachers believed that this role had not been fulfilled; e.g., "the same children are still problems in higher grades."

In spite of the generally negative reaction, 100% of the teachers indicated that they would refer a child needing help. Teachers generally indicated that they were "at least doing something" by referring a child when they made another professional person aware and partially responsible for the problem. Seventy-eight percent of the respondents agreed with an item stating "the real problem with psychological services is the time lag which could be solved with more psychologists." Previous psychological services were seen as benefiting referred children "somewhat", but as benefiting the classroom teacher to a lesser extent. Previous recommendations made by school psychologists were considered "not suitable for classroom use since they required too much of a teacher's individualized help to implement." Several teachers regarded written interpretations as superficial and recommendations as vague.

Although approximately a fourth of the respondents indicated that psychological interpretations added little to what they already knew, such interpretations were generally seen as "somewhat helpful." By contrast, psychologists' recommendations were seen as "largely irrelevant" of "totally irrelevant" by half of the respondents. Although 83% of the teachers saw reports as "necessary" or "helpful," qualitatively they consistently indicated that "psychologists should spend more time with the students and teachers and less time with paperwork." The referral form at the time of the evaluation was seen as too lengthy (two pages), confusing and in need of revision. Two-thirds of the respondents perceived its greatest use as helping teachers to clarify their thinking about individual children.

To ascertain the reasons for which a representative group of teachers should refer children for psychological services, reasons for referral (open-ended referral) from the previous three years were tabulated and categorized. The majority of the referrals had been submitted by a relatively small number of persons. The

57

resulting 42 categories were then presented to the 18 teachers. All teachers agreed that four of the 42 categories: (a) suspected mental retardation, (b) passive, withdrawn -- "child just sits," (c) "perceptual" problems, (d) identity crisis, were valid reasons for referral. At the other end of the continuum, "smoking" was considered a valid reason for referral by only one-third of the teachers. Responses to all categories suggested that teachers generally believed that most of the categories were valid reasons for referral. Teachers' model response indicated that approximately one-fourth of their students could use the services of the school psychologist, yet the 18 teachers collectively had referred only 18 children that year -- an average of 1.0 per teacher.

As part of the evaluation, teachers were asked to indicate preferences for a number of role models. Roles involving direct service to teachers (consulting) and children ("therapists"/counselor) constituted the top preferences. Roles including psycho-educational evaluation (the traditional role), researcher, classroom change agent, and subject matter specialist were ranked as moderate preferences of teachers. Finally, roles involving administration of group tests, providing in-service workshops, serving as a "sounding board," and assisting in in-class behavior modification were ranked as the least preferred. However, qualitative information from both the formal and informal evaluations indicated that teachers believed that psychologists should be able to fulfill all eleven of these roles as well as others! Spontaneous comments indicated a general belief that psychologists should change the child to fit his current environment (including his regular class and current teacher), so that "everyone else can live with him." In situations where the child could not easily be fitted to the situation, it was generally stated that he should be removed from that situation to a special classroom (7 of the 18 teachers made some comment to this effect). To a lesser extent, individuals (2 of the 18) requested that the psychologist give them suggestions regarding adjustments that they, the teachers, could make. Several teachers indicated that psychologists should analyze the sources of children's problems and work for the solution of these underlying causes. Roles were also seen for the psychologist in terms of dealing with difficult parents, one-to-one consultation with children ("chats with an outside friend"), and early identification and remediation of children's problems. The need for more psychologists was a general comment; e.g., "A psychologist is needed in each elementary building."

Teacher willingness to become involved was disappointing. In answer to the statement, "Would you be willing to serve on a Child Study Team?", 12 of the 18 people indicated either (a) "not at all or (b) "only if released time was made available." Only one person indicated he would be willing to serve on such a team "before school, during lunch hour, during a free period, or after school;" three individuals were willing to meet on one or two of these times.

THE NEW PROCEDURE

Results of the evaluation indicated a need for a number of changes in psychological services. A system was needed which would be more effective, efficient, direct, consistent and continuous; which would streamline referral procedures, reduce the number of individuals tested (in favor of alternate means of problem solving), minimize psychological report writing and maximize the use of auxiliary services and outside agencies. Increased involvement by parents, teacher, and others at the building level was seen as a procedure which would place more problem-solving responsibility with those persons. A more open system which would reduce the amount of confidential information, avoid the labeling process, provide feedback mechanisms for evaluating the effectiveness of strategies used with children, provide continuous monitoring of psychological services, and continuous "feed in" for new operating alternatives would be helpful. Finally, a need was felt for a mechanism which would bring the teacher and school psychologist into closer communication (as contrasted to a system where the psychologist prescribes and the teacher consumes), where each teacher-school psycholgist interaction was considered a teacher training seminar as well as a psychologist training seminar.

As a first step, the teacher filled out a special services conference request form. The school psychologist then met with the teacher, and together they worked out a common problem focus as determined by the needs of the child and the needs of the teacher. A step-by-step plan for dealing with these problems and a mutually agreed-upon strategy was formalized on the spot (in contrast to the old system where the psychologist wrote out a formal report at some later time). The Conference Request form which evolved from the formal and informal evaluations resulted in 11 categories for referral. After checking these categories the teacher was asked to indicate how the problem was perceived, a procedure which in some cases would result in specific problem definition, and would suggest "steps to be taken" by the psychologist.

In asking the teacher how she was currently dealing with the problem, the implication and expectation was that the problem was being dealt with in some way. Questions regarding the involvement of parents, administrators, or counselors provided some feedback in regard to what these persons had already accomplished and also carried an implication regarding their involvement -- "if you haven't, maybe you should."

To encourage teachers to look at the "positives" in referral, a question regarding strengths or abilities was asked. This question served a dual purpose, in that it also gave the psychologist a starting point, in terms of something to build on. The question regarding the Basal Reader was placed on the conference request as an unobtrusive measure of the level at which the teacher had made the educational placement of the child.

Most conferences were held within five to ten school days after receipt by the school psychologists. However, it was still true that if testing was one of the recommendations agreed upon by the teacher and psychologist, the wait for testing took greater periods of time. Teachers seemed to accept the wait, since they had some immediate contact regarding the child and some realistic expectation as to when the agreed-upon strategies were to be implemented.

CONFERENCE REPORTS

Reports were not written routinely but only as requested by an outside agency or when written justification was needed for a child's file. Teachers, instead of "being allowed the opportunity of reading a report written by a school psychologist," participated in the planning. The teacher and psychologist conferred to clarify and redefine the problems listed on the conference request and decided which problems were to be the common focus. After the determination had been made, step by step strategies were decided on with a resultant one-to-one correspondence between items in the common focus and items in the mutually agreed-upon strategy. Persons at the conference signed the conference report form which prevented much of the previous "who said what, when" phenomenon. In this way, everyone who had some responsibility for the referred child had, in effect, signed his name to a contract. Times, dates, and responsibility were assigned on this form and dates for follow-up were scheduled if such appeared to be necessary.

OPERATION AND OUTCOMES

The Positives

With this system school psychologists could become involved in the total range of comprehensive psychological services; e.g., consultation with parents, building administrators, and teachers; some direct one-to-one work with children in and out of classrooms; establishment of behavior modification programs; and psychoeducational evaluations (approximately one out of every seven children referred).

All interpretative information based upon test results, observations, etc, was discussed with the teacher during a conference rather than being put into a formal written report, since such reports have little meaning to a teacher one or more years hence. This short circuits the labeling process, insuring that labels will not "follow a child forever" and that reports which were time and place appropriate do not outlive their usefulness. In addition, the system is not burdened with a great deal of unnecessary confidential information.

The new procedures seem to have produced a change in referral patterns. For one thing, some teachers who tended to refer a large portion of their class have decreased their number of referrals. On the other hand, the type of teacher who likes to become involved in decision making, planning, and innovation has been significantly involved. This changed pattern seems to have opened the door to more operating alternatives, greater professional growth and development on the part of teacher and psychologists, and less role model repetition.

The Negatives

Problems also exist with the new procedure. To some extent, school psychologists probably have had less direct contact with children, since they are not spending as much time in the one-to-one testing procedure. Since the child's perception of his own needs is paramount and since the psychologist purports to be serving those needs, a degree of insulation from children in one-to-one situations is a negative result which requires further planning.

Another problem area is the use of the teacher's "planning" time (guaranteed by contract) for conference time. A few teachers requesting service have been reluctant to use their planning time for conferences; thus alternatives are being sought; e.g., classes taught by principals or substitutes during conferences.

The Feedback System

The final step in the new procedures for psychological services involves a feedback system administered through the director of special education, which is sent approximately two weeks after the time of the first conference between the teacher and the school psychologist. This form, in addition to providing feedback for evaluation and continuous modification of the system, provides information on the effectiveness of procedures used with individual children.

Feedback from teachers and administrators regarding the new delivery system has been extremely positive. Teachers verbalized appreciation for "the greatest personal contact," "the opportunity to discuss problems at length," and "the continued communication with the psychologist regarding a child throughout the year." On the negative side, a smaller number of teachers have indicated that "students still are not being placed in programs any quicker," "there is not enough time to implement the program developed with the psychologist," and "psychologists have failed to solve some of the more serious problems students are having." When such concerns are known through the formal feedback mechanism, an opportunity exists for further interaction with that teacher.

Ten elementary principals were requested to evaluate the new services. Six responded and indicated that the new procedures were "simpler," "more direct," "more effective," "more efficient," "more relevant," and "more personal." They further indicated that the procedures encouraged teachers to refer children needing help and resulted in quicker service with immediate suggestions for teachers.

References

Barclay, J.R.   Descriptive, theoretical, and behavioral character-
    istics of subdoctoral school psychologists. American Psycholo-
    gist, 1971, 26, 257-280.
Dunn, L.M. Special education for the mildly retarded--is much of it
    justifiable? Exceptional Children, 1968, 35, 5-22.
Krumboltz, J. (Ed.) Revolution in counseling. New York: Houghton
    Mifflin, 1966.

ACCOUNTABILITY: PRACTICAL SUGGESTIONS FOR SCHOOL PSYCHOLOGISTS

Thomas N. Fairchild

Increased emphasis on accountability in education has led to
an increased emphasis on accountability for ancillary personnel
such as the school psychologist. Traditionally school psychologists
have been associated with diagnostic testing and special education
programs. Criticisms of psychological tests and special class
placement is placing school psychologists in a precarious position.
Psychological services, heretofore taken for granted, are being
questioned. Psychologists will be called upon to justify their
presence in the schools. It is imperative that school psychologists
provide substantive proof regarding the efficacy of their performance.

ACCOUNTABILITY: SIX TOOLS

While working for the Cedar Rapids Community School District,
Iowa, the writer developed and field tested various techniques that
would enable a school psychologist to account for the services provided to the school system. These accountability techniques are
described herein, and their inherent accountability value discussed.

The Daily Log

Description. The daily log is a time analysis of the services
performed by the school psychologist during the school year. In
developing a log the school psychologist needs to identify the various services that he performs.

The investigator identified the various services that a psychologist might perform and organized them within the five general
services categories of Assessment, Intervention, Evaluation, Consultation, and Administration. A code was then attached to each subservice category to facilitate daily recordings. Table 1 lists the

SOURCE. Reprinted from Journal of School Psychology, 1975, 13, 2,
149-159. By permission of the author and the publisher. Copyright
1975 by the Journal of School Psychology, Inc. Published by Behavioral Publications, New York.

services and their corresponding codes.

Table 1
School Psychological Services and Corresponding Codes

Code	School Psychological Services
	Assessment
AT	Administration and scoring of formal and informal tests
ARW	Report writing
ACO	Consulting other professionals* regarding a student
AIS	Diagnostic interviews with students
AOI	Interviewing other professionals* to gather diagnostic information
ATI	Teacher interviews to gather diagnostic information
AOB	Observational techniques
API	Parent interviews to gather diagnostic information
ACR	Reviewing cumulative records
	Intervention
	Indirect Intervention
IPC	Parent consultation to recommend intervention strategies
ITC	Teacher consultation to recommend intervention strategies
IOC	Consulting with other professionals* regarding intervention strategies
INS	In-service presentations
IST	Staffings
	Direct Intervention
IC	Counseling
	Evaluation
	Follow-up conferences to determine efficiacy of intervention
EFP	Conferences with parents
EFT	Conferences with teachers
EFO	Conferences with other professionals*
	Research on efficacy of school psychological services
ERL	Daily log
ERQ	Follow-up questionnaires
ERTE	Time elapsed data
EINS	In-service evaluation
ERF	Role and function
EFR	Final Report

*Counselors, principals, social workers, etc.

Table 1 (continued)

Code	School Psychological Services
	Administration
T	Travel
RM	Review of mail and copyreading psychological reports
M	Miscellaneous (unable to categorize)
SUP	Supervision of practicum student
PREP	Preparation for testing and conferences
ME	Attendance at meetings
PD	Professional development
PR	Public relations
COR	Correspondence

*Counselors, principals, social workers, etc.

A record was then kept of the amount of time devoted to each service, as well as the percentage of the psychologist's time consumed by that service. This was accomplished in the following manner. First, the writer recorded daily the services performed. For example, the following might be recorded in the psychologist's notepad for a typical day:

ITC	8:00-8:30	Smith re. Bob R.
ATI	8:30-8:45	Jones re. Susan G.
ACR	8:45-9:00	Susan G.
AOB	9:00-10:00	Susan G.
AT	10:00-11:00	Susan G.
IPC	11:00-12:00	Bob R.
T →	12:00-12:15	Sch Office
	12:15-12:45	Lunch
ARW	12:45-2:00	Larry M.
T →	2:00-2:15	Office School
IST	2:15-3:00	John T.
ARW	3:00-3:30	John T.
IPC	3:30-4:45	Connie B.

Referring to the coded subservices in Table 1 would enable one to describe what the school psychologist had accomplished during that particular day. The morning began with a teacher conference designed to share assessment results and make recommendations for ameliorating a problem. Mrs. Jones was visited at 8:30 to solicit more information regarding the presenting problem of a student she had referred. The student's cumulative folder was reviewed, and she was observed in the classroom. At 10:00 the student was administered diagnostic tests. Mr. and Mrs. R were seen at 11:00, after which the examiner returned to his office. After lunch Larry M.'s psychological report was written, followed by traveling to another school to participate in John T.'s staffing. After the staffing the psychologist wrote up a staffing summary. At 3:30 a conference was held with Mr. and Mrs. B regarding Connie.

The second step involved in recording the amount of time devoted to various school psychological services involved summing the amounts of time devoted to each service. The writer accomplished this step by translating the codes from the notepad onto a weekly summary sheet. Below is an example of a weekly summary sheet with codes recorded for the daily log example discussed above.

The information from the weekly summary is then summed monthly by the following method. All of the service codes are listed and followed by spaces for tallying the number of times each service appeared on the weekly summary sheets. The information for our example has been transferred from the weekly summary sheets onto the monthly summary sheet.

Beginning at the top of the weekly summary sheet ITC was recorded twice. Consequently, it received two tallies on the monthly summary sheet. When four tallies have been recorded on a blank the next tally starts on a new blank as was done for codes ARW and IPC. Each blank corresponds to one hour of service time, so keeping track of the hours in this manner makes it easy to write in the number of hours devoted monthly in the right hand column of the monthly summary sheet.

At the end of the contract year the yearly summary is derived by collating all of the monthly summaries. The number of hours required for each service are listed and a percentage is calculated which indicates the percent of psychologist's time devoted to that service. An example of a yearly summary is documented in the literature (Fairchild, 1974).

Although the daily log may appear cumbersome and time-consuming, it is relatively simple to manage after one memorizes the code he had devised and consumes only a few minutes each day. Monthly summaries require approximately 1 1/2 hours. If the daily recording appears prohibitive, yet one recognizes the value of documenting his services, a school psychologist may want to record a random sample of the services he provides. This might be accomplished by recording one day a week for the entire year, one full week each month, or a month each semester, depending on personal preference.

WEEKLY SUMMARY SHEET
SAMPLE DAY

Beginning Date _____   Ending Date _____

School Psychologist _____

	Monday	Tuesday	Wednesday	Thursday	Friday
8:00	April 1				
	ITC				
	ITC				
	ATI				
9:00	ACR				
	AOB				
	AOB				
	AOB				
10:00	AOB				
	AT				
	AT				
	AT				
11:00	AT				
	IPC				
	IPC				
	IPC				
12:00	IPC				
	T				
	Lunch				
	Lunch				
1:00	T				
	ARW				
	ARW				
	ARW				
2:00	ARW				
	T				
	IST				
	IST				
3:00	IST				
	ARW				
	ARW				
	IPC				
4:00	IPC				
	IPC				
	IPC				
	IPC				
5:00					
After Hours					

67

			No. of Hours
AT	IIII		
ARW	IIII	III	
ACO			
AIS			
AOI			
ATI	I		
AOB	IIII		
API			
ACR	I		
IPC	IIII	IIII	
ITC	II		
IOC			
INS			
IST	III		
IC			
EFP			
EFT			
EFO			
ERL			
ERQ			
ERTE			
ERF			
EFR			
T	II		
RM			
M			
SUP			
PREP			
ME			
PD			
PR			
COR			

Rationale. The values in collecting a time analysis of school psychological services are threefold. First, it provides evidence of the types of services being made available to the school. Frequently school psychologists are perceived as psychometrists or testers within a narrowly defined diagnostician role. However, they are well aware that they provide many other valuable services. The daily log allows the psychologists to document these services and to help dispell the mistaken notion that he is just a tester. Secondly, monthly summaries allow the school psychologist to monitor his services on a regular basis. Inspecting the time analysis information makes the psychologist conscious of time devoted to various services, thus allowing him to determine if he is overlooking one important function at the expense of another function. For example, the time analysis may indicate that considerably more energy is being expended administering diagnostic tests than providing teacher in-service programs. If a psychologist's goals included providing more in-service than diagnostic testing, the time analysis would call his attention to the discrepancy. The time analysis might reveal that no time is being devoted to pupil staffings. This should make the psychologist conscious that he is not involving pertinent others in the decision-making process regarding intervention strategies. Finally, the daily log yields the frequency of contacts with students, teachers, parents, and other professionals. The $\overline{X}$ amount of time required to do an individual assessment can also be determined. This information is useful when evaluating one's performance.

Time Elapsed Information

Description. For each school served the writer kept a manila folder of referrals. Taped on the inside cover was a sheet upon which the following information was recorded for each student referred - grade, name, referral date, date of first contact, date that evaluation was complete, date report was written, parent conference date, teacher conference date, and the date of the agency conference if an outside agency was involved.

Time elapsed information is collected by keeping a record of the actual number of teaching days (only count days that school is in session) that transpire between (a) the referral date and initial contact date (1-2), (b) the initial contact date and date of the conference with the major referral source (2-*), and (c) the referral date and date of the conference date with the major referral source (total time elapsed).

In our example Kay B. was referred on 9-10-73. The teacher is requesting assistance. The psychologist does not see Kay until two days have passed and does not meet with the major referral source (Kay's teacher) until five more days have elapsed. Overall,

69

seven days have transpired since the teacher asked for help and received it. The major referral source (person initiating the referral) is denoted by an asterisk because a referral may be initiated by parents, teachers, or outside agencies. If parents initiate the referral and are requesting assistance, then the amount of time elapsing until they receive that assistance is recorded.

Collecting time elapsed data consumes little time and is a nice method of keeping oneself organized. One can see at a glance how many referrals one is behind, which students have not been completed, which reports need to be written and what conferenzes need to be scheduled.

Rationale. Collecting this information enables the school psychologist to take a close look at how much time, on the average, elapses from the time a teacher or parent requests service to the time meaningful feedback is received regarding the student referred. One criterion of an effective school psychologist should be the immediacy of feedback after a referral has been received. If the time elapsing between referral dates and conference dates is disconcerting, the school psychologist should seek means of rectifying the situation. Keeping a systematic record also forces the school psychologist to be more conscious of getting feedback to the teacher as soon as possible after the evaluation. It encourages the psychologist to take action instead of procrastinating with referrals or inconclusive completed assessments.

Time elapsed information would also be useful in justifying acquisition of new personnel. Rather than claiming ineffectiveness to administrators because of prohibitive caseloads, consider how much more meaningful it would be to present time elapsed information as justification for hiring more personnel. For example, if the $\overline{X}$ time elapsing between referral date and feedback date is 30 teaching days, the psychologist's effectiveness might be diminished. In order to improve psychological services to schools, it might be worthwhile to recruit another psychologist in order to reduce the psychologist-student ratios and to minimize the amount of time elapsing before teachers receive feedback.

Accountability Interview

Description. Building principals of the schools served are contacted and requested to meet with their staffs to elicit feedback regarding the school psychologist's mode of operation. Later, after rapport has been developed with the school staff, it might be more appropriate to meet directly with teachers. At midyear and again at the end of the year, the school psychologist meets with the building principals individually or in a group and discusses the staffs' concerns regarding his mode of operation. Before this

Time Elapsed Sheet

School _____

Gr	Name	1 Referral Date	2 First Contact	Eval. Complete	Report Written	Parent Conf.	Teacher Conf.	Agency Conf.	Time Elapsed 1→2	Time Elapsed 2→*	Total Time Elapsed
2	Kay B.	9-10-73	9-12-73	9-17-73	9-18-73	9-19-73	*9-19-73	--	2	5	7
6	John Q.	9-10-73	9-17-73	9-17-73	9-18-73	*9-24-73	9-19-73	--	5	5	10

71

interview is terminated, decisions should have been made concerning problem resolutions. Below are the notes recorded at one of the psychologist-principal meetings:

Conference with Elementary School Principals
June 14, 1972

Purpose: (1) To get feedback from the schools regarding
psychological services for the past year.
(2) To make recommendations for the coming school
year.

In general the feedback for the past year was positive. Some concern was expressed over the reluctance of students to come for counseling because of the stigma attached. It was recommended that I lead some class discussions in the upper grades. This would enable me to establish better rapport with the students and to acquaint them with the available services.

Teachers' responses to the combined schools in-service discussion on "Promotion vs. Retention" were favorable. The major criticism was that there was not more time available for interaction. In the future it was decided that presentations would be kept to a minimum, allowing for greater interaction between the teachers of the three schools.

Teachers had also expressed an interest in finding out more regarding psychological evaluations. What tests are used and how are they interpreted? An in-service was scheduled for August 23 in order to provide answers to these questions. At this time teachers will be asked for suggestions for further in-service.

The principals requested that I follow-up on parents who had been reluctant to become involved with outside agencies. I indicated that I had been contacting these parents regularly, but will contact them again.

It is important to record a summary of the conference and planning decisions for inclusion in the Final Yearly Report.

Rationale. The positive and negative feedback elicited during accountability interviews allows the school psychologist to monitor his services to individual schools and to head off potential problems with building staff through open communication. Teachers feel more actively involved because they are given the opportunity to voice their concerns about school psychological services and to provide input regarding the services they would like performed. Open communication with building staff has the additional advantage of improving rapport with teachers. The interview communicates to teachers that the school psychologist is interested in what they have to say and that he is concerned about how well he is meeting their needs.

Follow-Up Questionnaire

Description. Follow-up questionnaires and stamped, self-addressed envelopes are given to teachers and parents of students evaluated by the school psychologist. Anonymity is requested in order to eliminate the halo effect and to elicit sincere responses. The questionnaire consisted of the following three questions:

1. Did you have a better understanding of the child as a result of your discussion with the school psychologist?
2. Were recommendations realistic and/or practical?
3. Were the recommendations of the psychologist effective?

Respondents checked YES, NO, or NOT APPLICABLE. Room was available at the bottom of the questionnaire for comments and suggestions.

The questionnaire was purposefully kept brief in order to maximize the percentage of returns. During the two-year period the questionnaires have been in use the average rate of returns has been 75%. During the 1972-73 school year, when rates were recorded separately for parents and teachers, a higher rate was recorded for teachers (77%) than parents (61%). The results of the follow-up questionnaire for the school year 1973-74 are presented in Table 2.

Table 2
Results of Follow-up Questionnaire

Item	Teachers	Parents
No. of questionnaires distributed	66	81
No. of questionnaires returned	48	41
Percentage return	73%	51%
1. Did you have a better understanding of the child as a result of your discussion with the psychologists?		
Yes	94%	85%
No	4%	12%
Not applicable	2%	2%
2. Were recommendations realistic and/or practical?		
Yes	89%	87%
No	4%	13%
Not applicable	7%	0%
3. Were the recommendations of the psychologist effective?		
Yes	64%	73%
No	4%	7%
Not applicable	9%	0%
Cannot be ascertained	23%	20%

Rationale. The primary function of the school psychologist is
to help teachers design and implement appropriate intervention
strategies for ameliorating learning and/or behavioral problems.
If the school psychologist is to be accountable for this service,
he must discover how effective he is. To accomplish this it is
essential that he elicit feedback reagrding the efficacy of the
recommended intervention strategies. The follow-up questionnaires
yield such information. The follow-up questionnaire also communicates the psychologist's interest in helping the child and teacher
and shows teachers the psychologists, too, are accountable for
their services.

Telephone Follow-Up

Description. After the initial conference school psychologists
frequently contact the parents of students they have evaluated.
This typically occurs when a referral has been made to an agency
outside of the school and the psychologist calls the parents to
determine if they are following through with the referral for outside intervention. However, this telephone follow-up method of
accountability required that the parents of all students evaluated
be contacted at least once during the year by telephone. Parents
of students evaluated during the first semester were contacted at
midyear, while parents of students seen during the second semester
were called near the end of the school year. Telephone follow-ups
presuppose that all parents have met with the school psychologist
during an earlier parent conference.

Rationale. Two benefits are derived from the telephone follow-
up. First, follow-up allows the school psychologist to ascertain
the efficacy of recommendations made or to determine if recommended
contacts with outside agencies have been made. While the follow-
up questionnaire yielded a 61% rate of return for parents (1972-73),
the telephone contact allows a psychologist to elicit feedback from
100% of the parents. Second, a by-product of parent telephone
follow-up is improved public relations. The psychologist is perceived as a helping person who is genuinely concerned and interested
in children. This fosters a positive relationship with the public
which can carry over into the school. Psychologists are no longer
seen as threatening. Consequently, parents become less anxious
about having their children evaluated by school psychologists.
Data collected during the 1971-72 and 1972-73 school year appears to
support this contention. During the 1971-72 school year only 25%
of the referrals were initiated by parents. The following year
43% of the writer's referrals were initiated by parents.

Description. Upon receipt of a referral the school psychologist contacts the classroom teacher. Target behaviors (academic or behavioral) are specified, recording procedures are devised, and baseline data regarding rate of occurence are collected by the teacher and/or psychologist. Intervention strategies for modifying the student's behavior are then designed by the teacher and psychologist. A criterion of success is then specified. Data are later collected regarding the frequency of the target behavior.

Rationale. Accountability is inherent in behavioral consultation. The efficacy of the intervention strategy is automatically determined when baseline assessment and follow-up assessment data are compared. If the criterion for success has been met, the effectiveness of a school psychologist in designing appropriate intervention strategies is determined. Another value of behavioral consultation is teacher involvement. Teachers identify the target behaviors that need to be extinguished or increased and help collect baseline and follow-up data. Recognition that the student's progress is being monitored also makes the teacher more conscious of following through with the recommended intervention strategies.

The utility of the accountability techniques for the practitioner has been discussed above under each technique. The tools are useful in other ways. The writer has used the tools in research on school psychological services. The Daily Log provided a description of amounts of time devoted to various services and suggested areas where psychologists might profit from further training (Fairchild, 1974). The writer has also been involved in comparing two models of school psychological services -- the traditional diagnostician model and the consultant model. Comparisons regarding which model provides more immediate feedback to teachers (yielded by time elapsed information) and which model is the most effective (information yielded by follow-up questionnaires) were made.

Since the purpose of the six accountability tools is to help school psychologists documented their effectiveness and justify their presence in the public schools, a final yearly report is an integral part of using the tools. The purpose of the yearly report is to synthesize all of the information collected and present it in a meaningful manner for dissemination to building principals and superiors. At the end of the final report the school psychologist should outline personal goals for the next acedemic year. The goals should be a by-product of the accountability information collected.

CONCLUSION

School psychologists should quit paying lip service to accountability. The accountability techniques described offer a means of providing substantive proof regarding services offered and the efficacy of a school psychologist's performance should be integrated into a meaningful written evaluation of his services and disseminated to supervisors and building principals. The data within the written report should help to justify a psychologist's presence on the staff. The school psychologist's evaluation of his services communicates to administrators the psychologist's concern about his service to children.

The tools outlined in this article are not exempt from criticism, but they can easily be adapted to suit individual needs and preferences, or other methods of accountability can be developed. The writer's goals, however, is not to suggest that these techniques are the only means of accounting for school psychological services, rather, it is to emphasize that there are ways for school psychologists to account for their performances, and it is essential that they make a concerted effort to do so if they are to justify their membership on the pupil personnel team.

References

Fairchild, T.N. An analysis of the services performed by a school psychologist in an urban area: Implications for training programs. Psychology in the Schools, 1974, 11, 3, 275-281.

A PROPOSAL FOR EVALUATING THE EFFECTIVENESS OF PSYCHOLOGISTS IN THE SCHOOLS

Anthony Conti and Jack I. Bardon

It is the central purpose of graduate training in school psychology to produce psychologists who function effectively in the schools. It is also incumbent upon practitioners in school psychology to demonstrate their effectiveness to others. In recent years, accountability has become the watchword upon which budgets are planned and staff allocations are made. Training programs increasingly have been asked to demonstrate how training influences practice, and students in training have sought to increase their competence through improved supervisory procedures. Yet, perusal of program descriptions, discussion with school psychology graduates from many training programs, and a review of literature in school psychology suggest that there are few accepted methods to evaluate the results of practice in school psychology. Difficulties with evaluation systems are understandable given that the outcomes of a school psychologist's services depend on such diverse variables as the personality characteristics of the psychologist, the area of the country in which he practices, and the requirements of the specific school situation.

Clair and Kiraly (1971) discussed some of the factors that must be considered when the accountability of school psychological services is established and defined accountability as requiring that behavioral objectives be specified as they relate to the school psychologist's role and that these objectives be quantified. Tomlinson's report (1973) on accountability procedures in the Minneapolis Public Schools appears to be the only detailed study in the literature of specific accountability procedures used to assess the effectiveness of school psychological services.

SOURCE. Reprinted from Psychology in the Schools, 1974, XI, 1, 32-39. By permission of the authors and Clinical Psychology Publishing Co., Inc.

PROBLEMS IN EVALUATION

Training and practice in school psychology involve considerations similar to those in other professional psychology specialities. Berelson (1960) made the point that practices in graduate training are perpetuated precisely because the evaluators of the products are themselves the producers. As Proshansky (1972) has argued, graduate training in general has changed very slowly since its inception. Similarly, graduate training and practice in school psychology have changed slowly. As James (1902) indicated, there has never been a priesthood that initiated its own reforms.

A study be Clair, Osterman, Kiraly, Klausmeier, and Croff (1971) indicated that many school psychology training programs still place greatest emphasis on testing and diagnostic skills. Similarly, a survey of practicing school psychologists showed that the greatest amount of time spent by psychologists in the schools was in testing and diagnosis (Farling and Hoedt, 1971). The area of testing and diagnosis is the easiest for faculty in school psychology programs to evaluate (and even to teach). It is not difficult to determine how accurately a student administers the Wechsler Intelligence Scale for Children or how completely he can score and interpret a Rorschach protocol. Other areas of school psychological work are more difficult to assess, especially those related to consultation. How does one determine the psychologist's effectiveness in relating to children and school staff in useful ways?

Evaluation of consultation skills has been the responsibility of school psychology trainers who, if they are conscientious, observe the trainee in a practicum setting, discuss his work with school staff, and draw conclusions as to the trainee's effectiveness. Too often feedback to the trainee is in the form of a grade for practicum work rather than in constructive recommendations for improved functioning. This form of evaluation is influenced by a myriad of factors such as the perception of the trainee held by the evaluating trainer; relationships of the trainer to school staff, school situational variables; and the distortions in performance that may occur when one is being observed in order to be evaluated. Of course, when a practicing school psychologist seeks feedback from staff, parents, and colleagues, similar distortions may result from the many factors that influence their relationships.

USE OF CONSUMERS

It is the authors' thesis that a more consistent feedback system can be developed for the trainee or the practitioner in school psychology by use of the consumers of psychological services (school staff, parents, and pupils) as evaluators. The idea is not by any means original, nor is it by itself sufficient. Evaluation of teaching effectiveness in colleges and universities invariably includes reports or ratings by students. A questionnaire given to clients, used by a

clinical psychogist in private practice, was recently described
(Lewin, 1973) and reported to be helpful as well as an excellent
public relations tools. While the assessment of behavioral objectives
continues to be an important aspect of the determination of professional effectiveness, there is no assurance that <u>our</u> objectives are the
same as those perceived by our consumers, nor is there assurance that
behavioral outcomes are the sole measures of effectiveness. The
addition of consumer evaluation to our repertoire of professional
activities holds promise for enriching knowledge of our efforts as
well as providing a new dimension in psychologist-consumer relationships.

What follows, then, is a series of three scales to be completed
by the consumers of school psychological services, to be used by
psychologists who are interested in determining the outcomes of their
professional efforts. The scales represent a tentative proposal for
such evaluation and are not inclusive of all areas in which ratings
may be appropriate. Material from this article may be used by any
who desire to do so. The only request the authors make is that scale
modifications and the results of usage be shared with them.

Concerns for the judicious use of these scales include (a) that
appropriate procedures be established to ensure confidentiality for
those who complete the scales; e.g., all forms might be sent to a
central office for filing and periodically turned over to the school
psychologist, and (b) that information obtained in the university setting be shared in constructive ways with the trainee who is being
evaluated.

RATING SCALE A

<u>Projected use</u>: In the evaluation of the school psychologist's written
communication.

<u>Projected users</u>: All those who receive written communication from the
school psychogist.

<u>When Completed</u>: Immediately after reading a written communication.

INSTRUCTIONS: Your reactions to the report you just read would be
appreciated. Please complete those rating scales and questions which
apply to the report, and return them to . . . . It is not necessary to sign your name.

1. The general context of the report (but not the recommendations):
   a. seemed sensitive to this problem situation

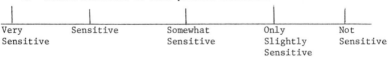

Very	Sensitive	Somewhat	Only	Not
Sensitive		Sensitive	Slightly	Sensitive
			Sensitive	

Comment:

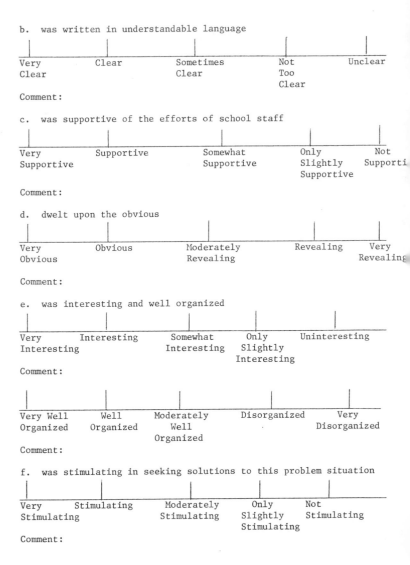

b. was written in understandable language

Very Clear	Clear	Sometimes Clear	Not Too Clear	Unclear

Comment:

c. was supportive of the efforts of school staff

Very Supportive	Supportive	Somewhat Supportive	Only Slightly Supportive	Not Supporti

Comment:

d. dwelt upon the obvious

Very Obvious	Obvious	Moderately Revealing	Revealing	Very Revealing

Comment:

e. was interesting and well organized

Very Interesting	Interesting	Somewhat Interesting	Only Slightly Interesting	Uninteresting

Comment:

Very Well Organized	Well Organized	Moderately Well Organized	Disorganized	Very Disorganized

Comment:

f. was stimulating in seeking solutions to this problem situation

Very Stimulating	Stimulating	Moderately Stimulating	Only Slightly Stimulating	Not Stimulating

Comment:

g. was useful in understanding the problem situation

Very Useful	Useful	Moderately Useful	Only Slightly Useful	Not Useful

Comment:

2. The recommendations made in this report may be described as:

a. helpful in establishing a solution to this problem situation

Very Helpful	Helpful	Somewhat Helpful	Only Slightly Helpful	Not Helpful

Comment:

b. easily applicable to the specific problem situation

Very Applicable	Applicable	Somewhat Applicable	Only Slightly Applicable	Not Applicable

Comment:

c. specific to this situation

Very Specific	Specific	Sometimes Specific	Somewhat General	Very General

Comment:

d. clearly stated

Very Clear	Clear	Sometimes Clear	Not Very Clear	Unclear

Comment:

3. Did the psychologist discuss the report and recommendations with
    you?

                              Yes   No
Comment:

4. Was such interpretation (if it occurred) helpful?

                    Yes   No

Comment:

5. Did the psychologist consult you before writing the report?

                    Yes   No

Comment:

6. Did the psychologist consult you in the development of the
   recommendations?

                    Yes   No

Comment:

7. Rate the total report as to its usefulness:

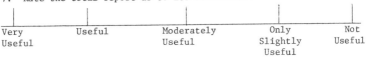

Very	Useful	Moderately	Only	Not
Useful		Useful	Slightly	Useful
			Useful	

Comment:

8. Suggestions for improvement:

RATING SCALE B

<u>Projected use</u>: In the evaluation of the school psychologist's verbal
communication.

<u>Projected users</u>: School staff, parents, high school pupils and
others using the school psychologist as a consultant.

<u>When completed</u>: At various times following personal consultative
contact with the school psychologist.

INSTRUCTIONS: Your reactions to consultation services would be
appreciated. Please complete those rating scales which apply to your
recent contact with them . . . . . . Return them to . . . . . Your
ratings are to be made without personal identification unless you
choose to sign your name.

1. The psychologist may be generally described as:
   a. sensitive to the problem situation

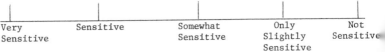

Very	Sensitive	Somewhat	Only	Not
Sensitive		Sensitive	Slightly	Sensitive
			Sensitive	

Comment:

b. easy to understand

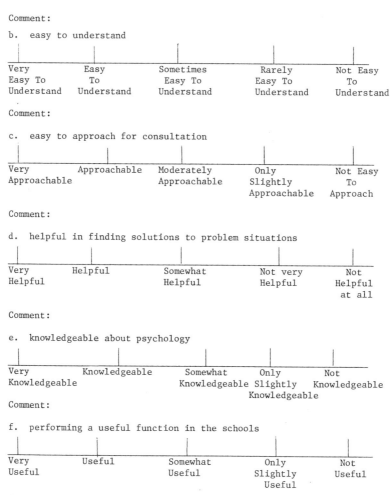

Very | Easy | Sometimes | Rarely | Not Easy
Easy To | To | Easy To | Easy To | To
Understand | Understand | Understand | Understand | Understand

Comment:

c. easy to approach for consultation

Very | Approachable | Moderately | Only | Not Easy
Approachable | | Approachable | Slightly | To
| | | Approachable | Approach

Comment:

d. helpful in finding solutions to problem situations

Very | Helpful | Somewhat | Not very | Not
Helpful | | Helpful | Helpful | Helpful
| | | | at all

Comment:

e. knowledgeable about psychology

Very | Knowledgeable | Somewhat | Only | Not
Knowledgeable | | Knowledgeable | Slightly | Knowledgeable
| | | Knowledgeable |

Comment:

f. performing a useful function in the schools

Very | Useful | Somewhat | Only | Not
Useful | | Useful | Slightly | Useful
| | | Useful |

Comment:

2. Additional comments and suggestions for improvement:

RATING SCALE C

<u>Projected use</u>: In providing the psychologist with information about how he is perceived by pupils with whom he works.

<u>Projected Users</u>: Pupils seen by the psychologist for testing, counseling, or any other services.

<u>When completed</u>: At various times following personal contact with the school psychologist.

<u>Special note</u>: With early elementary school children it may be necessary to use the teacher or an older child as a facilitator in completing this scale.
INSTRUCTIONS: Your reaction to school services would be appreciated. Please complete those rating scales and questions which apply to your recent contact with . . . . Return it to . . . . .
. . . . . It is not necessary to sign your name.

1. Rate the school psychologist on the following:

a.

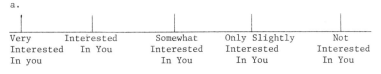

Very	Interested	Somewhat	Only Slightly	Not
Interested	In You	Interested	Interested	Interested
In you		In You	In You	In You

Comment:

b.

Very	Easy to	Sometimes	Rarely	Not Easy
Easy To	Talk to	Easy To	Easy to	To Talk To
Talk To		Talk To	Talk To	

Comment:

c.

| Very | Helpful | Sometimes | Rarely | Not |
| Helpful | | Helpful | Helpful | Helpful |

Comment:

84

d.

Very	Understanding	Sometimes	Rarely	Not
Understanding		Understanding	Understanding	Under-
				standing

Comment:

2. Would you like to meet with this person again?

                         Yes   No
Comment (why):

3. What did you like most about this person?

4. What did you like least about this person?

5. Did meeting with this person make you uncomfortable?

                         Yes   No
Comment (why):

References

Berelson, B. Graduate education in the United States. New York:
    McGraw-Hill, 1960.
Clair, T.N., Osterman, R., Kiraly, J., Kausmeier, R., & Croff, M.
    Practicum and internship experiences in school psychology;
    recent trends in graduate training. American Psychologist,
    1971, 26, 566-574.
Clair, T.N., & Kiraly, J., Jr. Accountability for the school
    psychologist. Psychology in the Schools, 1971, 8, 318-321.
Farling, W.H., & Hoedt, K.C. National survey of school psychologists.
    Washington: U.S. Department of Health, Education and Welfare,
    1971.
James, W. The varieties of religious experience. New York: Longmans
    Green, 1902.
Lewin, M.H. Consumerism in the private office. Professional Psycho-
    logy, 1973, 4, 109-110.
Proshansky,H. For what are we training our graduate student?
    American Psychologist, 1972, 27, 205-212.
Tomlinson, J.R. Accountability procedures for psychological services.
    Psychology in the Schools,1973, 10, 42-47.

A FOLLOW-UP INVESTIGATION OF FAMILIES REFERRED TO OUTSIDE AGENCIES

Anthony P. Conti

Summary: A follow-up study was conducted to determine the outcome of 254 referrals made by 47 school psychologists in New York and New Jersey. The referrals represented randomly selected cases in which the recommendation was made to the families of elementary school children to use services external to the school setting. Evaluation of referral outcome was determined in light of the reason prompting the referral recommendation. Explanations for the outcome of referrals summarized in this investigation were advanced and the limitations of this study noted.

When the school psychologist encounters a child whose needs cannot adequately be satisfied within the school setting his role becomes one of referral agent. Operating in this capacity he recommends, usually to the family of the child in question, the use of community resources and agencies offering services which he feels can best suit the unique needs of its child.

The role of school psychologist as a referral agent has been described extensively in literature related to the specialty (Cutts, 1955; Gray, 1963; Bardon, 1964). In addition, studies have identified that other school personnel have designated the referral role as an important one for school psychologists (Perkins, 1964; Roberts & Solomons, 1970). Finally, the few studies which deal with the actual practices of school psychologists indicate that a great deal of time is invested in the performance of the referral function (Blanco, 1970; Farling & Hoedt, 1971). In spite of the emphasis this role has received (in schools as well as other psychological specialities) few, if any, attempts have been made to evaluate it systematically.

SOURCE. Reprinted from Journal of School Psychology, 1973, 11, 3, 215-223. By permission of the author and publisher. Copyright 1973 by the Journal of School Psychology, Inc. Published by Behavioral Publications, New York.

This investigation proposes to determine the outcome of referrals made to families to use resources external to the school setting. It was reasoned that knowledge of outcome is essential for referral agents in evaluating the effectiveness of the referral process. This investigation procedure follows that of a pilot study (Conti, 1971) and represents a more complete attempt to determine the outcome of referrals made to external resources by school psychologists.

METHOD

Area Studied. Geographically the area selected for this study consisted of suburban sections of New York and New Jersey. Rosen, Kramer, Redick & Willner (1968) have indicated that these two states rank highly in the number of referral resources available per 1,000 population. Schools in suburban sections of these states seemed more likely to possess the financial potential for employment of qualitatively and quantitatively adequate pupil personnel workers. Further, suburban schools have access to treatment facilities provided in nearby cities as well as facilities structured on a county-wide basis.

A list of school systems meeting the criteria of being suburban and having a pupil enrollment of from 3,000 to 15,000 (systems of this size seemed more likely to employ full-time school psychologists) was compiled from data gathered by Sietsema, Mongello, & Montague, (1971). From this list 75 districts in New York and 75 districts in New Jersey were selected randomly.

Selection of Participating School Psychologists. The random procedure used to select school districts insured the random selection of school psychologists within districts. A letter, return form, and stamped envelope were mailed to the chief school psychologist in each district. The letter briefly explained the purpose of the study and requested the participation of school psychologists who: (1) were currently employed full time as school psychologists and who were employed full time in the district during the previous 1970-71 school year (to enable follow-up on cases referred a year to six months earlier and to insure that an adequate number of referrals were made in 1970-71 to enable valid random selection of cases referred), and (2) held permanent certification in school psychology in New York and New Jersey (to insure minimum competency and some acquaintance with the external referral process). The letter explained that the study carried the endorsement of the Rutgers University School Psychology Program and the New York and New Jersey State Departments of Education.

Sixty-eight school psychologists in 49 school districts returned the appropriate form offering participation.

Correspondence to Participants. The 68 psychologists offering participation were then mailed a cover letter, instruction sheet, six case data summary forms, and a stamped return envelope. This material was piloted on a group of 15 school psychologists not included in the study sample. The cover letter briefly reviewed the purpose of the study and requested the names and addresses of participants to enable follow-up on incomplete information. The instruction sheet detailed procedures for case selection and data form completion; it requested that each participant return the case data forms prior to December 1, 1971. The case data summary form was developed on the basis of a rationale of the progression of the referral process (Conti, 1971). The form tapped information on 35 variables in the referral process, the child and family referred, and the outcome of the referral.

Case Selection. Each psychologist was asked to select six cases he referred (working alone or in conjunction with other school personnel) to services outside of the school setting. Case selection was structured according to the following criteria: (1) that the child in each case was an elementary (grades K-6) student and not in special education classes at the time of referral; (2) that the cases randomly be selected according to the first initial of the child's last name (The psychologist was instructed to select cases in which the last name of the child began with the letter H and complete the appropriate number of data forms. If the criteria of six cases was not met by using this letter he was asked to select cases in which the child's lase name began with the letter D. If the criteria of six cases was not met by using these two letters he was asked to proceed to use the following letters in the order shown until six data forms were completed; H D F A I E C B G Z Y J K L U W T S M O R N P Q V X)[2]; and (3) initial referral to an outside resource was made by the school psychologist between 9/70 and 6/71.

The final criterion of follow-up to referrals made originally between 9/70 and 6/71 insured that this study would represent a follow-up of cases referred from six months to one year earlier. It was reasoned that contact with, and/or use of, a recommended service had enough time to occur within six months to a year. Extension of the follow-up period to beyond a year might have introduced other factors, e.g., subject attrition rate, changes in the status of the original referral.

Follow-up. Of the 68 school psychologists offering participation 18 returned data forms as requested by December 1, 1971. A hand-written letter to the remaining 50 resulted in the return of forms from 29 additional participants.

Quality Control. To determine if cases were selected according to the established criteria and data forms completed in an unbiased manner six randomly selected participants were interviewed by phone.

[2]This order was determined by using a table of random numbers (Dayton, 1970).

A series of ten questions was devised to establish the method of case selection and form completion. The results of this procedure suggested that not all participants may have followed instructions closely and that some bias toward the selection of referrals with positive outcome may have occurred.

RESULTS

Of the 47 school psychologists submitting data, 24 practiced in New York State and 23 practiced in New Jersey. Eleven participants held doctorates, four held specialist degrees, and 32 held master's degrees. The reported range of years' experience in employer districts was from two to 20 years; average length of employment was 7.1 years.

Of the 269 case data forms returned by participants, 15 forms failed to meet specified criteria.[3] The remaining 254 forms were separated into various categories of referrals to counseling and other resources according to the type of service(s) desired in making the recommendation for referral to the family. Further classification of the forms into categories of other and counseling referrals was conducted on the basis of information on the outcome of the referral. Contact, as an outcome, was defined as attendance in at least an initial interview with the recommended service.

Table 1
Frequency and Percent of Total for Outcomes
of Referrals Made to Counseling Services

Category	Frequency	Percent of Total
Families who contacted and continued beyond five sessions	63	47%
Families who contacted and continued beyond three sessions	5	4%
Families who contacted but terminated after initial interview or diagnostic work up	33	25%
Families who did not contact	31	24%
Total	132	100%

[3] Some participating psychologists did not complete all six forms requested.

89

Table 1 delineates the categories established for outcome of referrals made to counseling services and provides frequency and percent of the total for each designation.

Table 2 delineates the categories comprising other referrals based upon service desired and outcome; offering frequency and percent of total for each designation.

Table 2
Frequency and Percent of Total
For Services Desired and Outcomes
of Referrals Made to Resources Other
Than Those Providing Counseling

Category	Frequency	Percent of Total
Neurological/Medical:		
Families who contacted.	64	52%
Families who did not contact.	12	10%
Educational Diagnosis/Supplemental Instruction:		
Families who contacted.	20	16%
Families who did not contact.	6	5%
Psychiatric Diagnosis:		
All families contacted.	8	7%
Special School Placement:		
All families contacted.	12	10%
Subtotal: Families who contacted	104	85%
Subtotal: Families who did not contact	18	15%
Total	122	100%

The first two categories in this table include referrals made to neurologists or other medical specialists (excluding psychiatrists) for diagnosis and/or treatment (in many cases medication to control a behavior disorder was described as the desired treatment).

The third and fourth categories include referrals made to educational specialists, such as developmental optometrists, reading clinics, learning disabilities specialists, hearing and speech clinics etc.

For category five it will be noted that all of the reported referrals were made exclusively in New Jersey. This may be explained by the classification system established under the Rules and Regulations Pursuant to Title 12A, Chapter 46 of the New Jersey Statutes (June 24, 1970). Each school district in New Jersey is required legally to identify and classify exceptional children under these Rules and Regulations.

While the type of referral described in category six was not exclusive to either state it will be noted that all families contacted the recommended services. This phenomenon may be explained as a function of the compulsory education laws maintained in New York and New Jersey.

<h2 style="text-align:center">DISCUSSION</h2>

In evaluating the outcome of referrals to external resources in this investigation one criterion for successful referral was determined to be whether contact (attendance at an initial interview) was made by the family referred. Roberts and Solomons (1970) have argued that once contact is made the family referred is no longer the responsibility of the referral agent. After contact the referral resource has the responsibility of offering some service to the family or of referring it elsewhere. If this reasoning is accepted and contact is used as the sole criterion for evaluation, then the results of this study suggest that (given certain circumstances) referral of families by school psychologists to counseling services is relatively effective, with 76% of those referred initiating contact. Referral to services other than those providing counseling is also quite effective, with 85% of those referred initiating contact.

In the case of referrals made to resources other than those providing counseling the criterion of whether or not contact took place may be adequate in evaluating referral outcome, mainly because the purpose underlying such a referral was examination and diagnosis of a medical or educational nature. In most cases reported examination and even treatment could be accomplished in the contact session with minimal follow-up. Accordingly, if contact took place it is reasonable to assume that the purpose of the referral was accomplished. However, in the case of referrals made to counseling services contact is only an initial step in accomplishing the purpose underlying the referral recommendation. The complete purpose in such a referral is for counseling to occur. Accordingly, the evaluation of the outcome of referrals made to counseling resources is incomplete if contact is used as the sole criterion.

The school psychologist as researcher is in a difficult situation when attempting to judge the success or failure of counseling for a case in which he has acted as referral agent. Accordingly, ratings of improvement or prognosis would not be valid criteria with which to evaluate referrals to counseling services. Continuance as a measure of evaluation of counseling referral outcome is a logical choice (Krebs, 1971) as this factor is the only objective treatment variable significantly associated with ratings of improvement for adult (Luborsky, Auerbach, Chandler, & Cohen, 1971) and child (McDermott, Harrison, Schrager, Khlins, & Dickerson, 1970) counselees. In this study continuance past the initial interview or the diagnostic workup was selected as a basis for further evaluation of counseling referral outcome. In this investigation 51% of the families referred to counseling services made the recommended contact and continued to accomplish the purpose of the referral.

It can be inferred that when the purpose of the external referral in this study was counseling, then that purpose was achieved only slightly more than half of the time. In contrast, referrals to resources other than those providing counseling appeared more likely to achieve their intended purpose. This conclusion confirms the results of the pilot study which indicated that referrals to counseling services were far less likely to achieve their purpose than referrals to other resources (Conti, 1971). Obviously, these results may be explained by the differences in referral reasons and by the influence of related variables such as ease in justifying the referral of the family; stigma attached to counseling and contact with "mental health" workers; and potential time, transportation, and financial commitments of families referred (See Conti, 1972, for an analysis of the influence of these variables).

It is obvious that the two types of referrals are very different and as such need to be conducted in different manners by referral agents. In order to insure successful counseling referrals, factors influencing families who fail to contact the recommended service, or who contact but fail to continue, need to be explored more fully from the viewpoint of the school psychologist (and school as referral agent), the family referred, and the recommended counseling facility. Research is needed to determine how the ambiguity of the referral recommendation, the stigma of counseling contact, the availability of counseling resources (in terms of time, transportation, and cost), the sociological and psychological characteristics of families referred, and the myraid of variables associated with the operation of the recommended service influence whether or not contact is made and continuance observed.

It is necessary to note that the results of this investigation may be biased in such a way as to present a more positive picture of the outcome of external referrals than the one which exists in the majority of situations. An important factor contributing to this bias is that information for this study was obtained from "cooperative" school psychologists only. This procedure may hold a tendency toward the creation of an unrepresentative sample in terms of the entire population of school psychologists within the area studied. For example, a school psychologist asked to participate in this research might well have declined to cooperate if he was aware of many unsuccessful referrals. Similarly, a psychologist might have agreed to cooperate if he was aware of many successful external referrals. The procedure of using only cooperative psychologists, while necessary under the circumstances, holds inherent a tendency toward a positive bias, i.e., successful external referrals.

This bias has been reinforced, albeit deliberately, by the selection of geographical areas for study which contained better than the national average number of external resources (Rosen, 1965). In an area where external services are greater in number and perhaps better qualitatively, successful external referral is more probable than in areas lacking numerous external resources. Similarly, where referral agents are better trained and possess adequate experience successful external referrals are more likely. In this research school psychologists were required to meet certain minimum standards in order to participate. One criterion for participation was permanent New York or New Jersey state certification as a school psychologist. The maintenance of this standard indicates that the participants in this study may have been better trained than school psychologists practicing but lacking permanent certification in these states. Also, the participants may have been better trained than many school psychologists in other states not requiring the certification of school psychologists or maintaining qualifications for certification at a lower level than New York or New Jersey (Gross, Bonham, & Bluestein, 1966).

Further, the psychologists participating in this research held an average of slightly more than seven years of experience in their employer school districts; thus, the participants were experienced school psychologists who had sufficient time to develop a good working knowledge of the quantity and quality of external services in their respective areas.

In summary, the participants in this research can be described as highly motivated, practicing in areas where better than the national average number of external resources existed, well-trained, and possessing adequate experience as school psychologists and within employer districts. It may be concluded that this research was conducted under the best possible circumstances. Generalizations from the results of this study to situations lacking a fair number of referral resources, or motivated, well-trained, and experienced school psychologists should be done cautiously.

An additional factor, possible creating further bias in the direction of successful external referrals, came to light during the completion of the quality control phase of this study. Two of the six school psychologists interviewed selected cases to be included in this investigation from memory and then entered files to gather necessary information. The remaining four psychologists reportedly went to files to select cases and gather necessary information. All six participants reported that they used the randomized alphabetical procedure specified for case selection. However, in those instances where memory was relied upon to select cases, factors relating to selective perception may have had an influence. Accordingly, there may have been a tendency (conscious or unconscious) on the part of participants to recall and include cases in which referral efforts were successful. While a review of cases submitted by the two psychologists who had reportedly selected cases from memory failed to demonstrate an uneven distribution of successful or unsuccessful referrals, the influence of selective perception on the part of all participants cannot be ignored.

In light of these variables as suggested by previous research summaries (Rosenthal & Frank, 1958; Bandura, 1969), external referrals in general may be much less successful than the results of this investigation indicate. In conclusion, it may be necessary for psychologists at this point in time to question the worth of external referral as it effects children, parents, personnel, and institutions. It may be time to develop alternative procedures for leading clients to treatment or treatment to clients.

References

Bandura, A. Principles of behavior modification. New York: Holt, Rinehart, and Winston, 1969.

Bardon, J.I. Problems and issues in school psychology - 1964. Proceedings of a conference on new directions in school psychology. Journal of School Psychology, 1964, 3 (2), 1-45.

Blanco, R.F. Fifty recommendations to aid exceptional children. Psychology in the Schools, 1970, 1, 29-37.

Conti, A.P. A follow-up study of families referred by school psychologists to resources outside of the schools. Unpublished doctoral dissertation, Rutgers University, 1972.

Conti, A.P. A follow-up study of families referred to outside agencies. Psychology in the Schools, 1971, 8 (4), 338-341.

Cutts, N.E. (Ed.) School psychologists at mid century. A report of the Thayer conference on the functions, qualifications, and training of school psychologists. Washington, D.C.: American Psychological Association, 1955.

Dayton, C.M. Design of educational experiments. New York: McGraw-Hill, 1970.

Farling, W., & Hoedt, K. National survey of school psychologists. Washington, D.C.: U.S. Department of Health, Education, and Welfare, 1971.

Gray, S. The psychologist in the schools. New York: Holt, Rinehart, and Winston, 1963.

Gross, P., Bonham, S., & Bluestein, V. Entry requirements for state certification of school psychologists: A review of the past nineteen years. Journal of School Psychology, 1966, 4 (4), 43-51.

Krebs, R. Using attendance as a means of evaluting community mental health problems. Community Mental Health Journal, 1971, 9 (1), 72-77.

Luborsky, L., Auerbach, A., Chandler, N., & Cohen, J. Factors influencing the outcome of psychotherapy: A review of quantitative research. Psychological Bulletin, 1971, 75 (3), 145-185.

McDermott, J., Harrison, S., Schrager, J., Khlins, E., & Dickerson, B. Social class and child psychiatric practice: The clinician's evaluation of the outcome of therapy. American Journal of Psychiatry, 1970, 126 (7), 75-80.

Perkins, K. School psychology: From identification to identity. Journal of School Psychology, 1964, 2 (1), 7-16.

Roberts, R., & Solomons, G. Perceptions of the duties and functions of the school psychologist. American Psychologist, 1970, 25 (6), 544-549.

Rosen, B., Kramer, M., Redick, R., & Willner, S. Utilization of psychiatric services by children: Current status, trends, implications. Washington, D.C.: U.S. Government Printing Office, 1968.

Rosen, J. Mental health. Public Health Reports, 1965, 80 (2), 122-123.

Rosenthal, D., & Frank, J. The fate of psychiatric clinic outpatients assigned to psychotherapy. Journal of Nervous and Mental Diseases, 1958, 127, 330-343.

Rules and Regulations Pursuant to Title 18A, Chapter 46, New Jersey Statutes (June 24, 1970), Title 6, Chapter 28, New Jersey Administrative Code.

Sietsema, J., Mongello, B., & Montague, J. Educational directory 1970-71 public school systems. Washington, D.C.: U.S. Government Printing Office, 1971.

Eric Hatch and Jerry Lynch

One of the most persistent problems confronting a school psychologist is that of effective communication with everyone in his
school system. His inability to see various school personnel at all
times to communicate thoughts and information is both realistic and
frustrating.

School psychologists are not trained as news reporters, but
due to the necessity of reaching many professionals within a district,
publishing a psychological newsletter might be a new skill a school
psychologist could consider adding to his repertoire. The concept
of a newsletter is certainly nothing new, but the use of one by the
local school psychologist can be a very advantageous tool for functioning to his fullest potential. Such a newsletter, presently
being published four times a year by the senior author in a rural
school district, has proven very successful. Among the many things
it provides are the following:

Information. A newsletter is an excellent vehicle for trans-
mitting current references to journal articles or books which teachers might otherwise not have a chance to discover. Toward that end
we have established a psychological lending library whereby teachers
may borrow, via interoffice mail, any journal or book referred to in
an issue of the newsletter. Occasionally, an extremely pertinent
article from a professional journal is published in toto in the
newsletter.

Informative articles can be both formal and informal. For
example, a recent issue of the newsletter addressed some of the
legal questions involved in the dissemination of psychological reports alongside a rather humorous article by the psychological
team's social worker entitled, "It's Not All Just Drinking Coffee."

SOURCE. Reprinted from Journal of School Psychology, 1973, 11, 3,
256-257. By permission of the author and the publisher. Copyright
1973 by the Journal of School Psychology, Inc. Published by Behavioral Publications, New York.

Accountability. Through the use of the newsletter, the school psychologist has the opportunity to tell all personnel in the district what he has done, what he is doing, and what he plans to do. As a result, the role model he has defined for himself soon becomes known to those who wish to use his services. A newsletter also helps to eliminate the sometimes insidious "grapevine" and also provides incentive for the psychologist to follow through on his stated plans. Teachers may discover that their goals are similar to that of the school psychologist, a fact which is not always apparent where continual communication is difficult.

Modeling. A psychological newsletter helps teachers learn to regard psychological matters as things which can be discussed "out in the open" as opposed to the "hush-hush" aura still prevalent in many school districts. This is particularly important in a district previously unaccustomed to psychological services.

There is nothing fancy about the format of such a newsletter. The important things are the dissemination of information and the enhancement of teachers' familiarity with names, programs, and ideas. To date we have had an overwhelming positive response from all who have been receiving our newsletter (including teachers, principals, board of education members, and other school districts). We are no longer the strange faces that jump in and out of schools with our "bag of tricks" but instead are familiar "faces" even though our countenances may not always be gazed upon directly. Although not looked upon as a panacea to a school psychologist with a heavy work load, a newsletter can possibly serve to lessen the burden and eliminate the communication gap which so many of us seem to have experienced at one time or another.

PSYCHOLOGICAL REPORTS: AN ALTERNATIVE TO TRADITIONAL METHODOLOGY

William M. Erwin and Thomas M. Cannon, Jr.

Traditionally psychologists and other professionals have relied almost solely on the written report as the major vehicle to provide feedback to their source of referrals. Although most written reports seldom are longer than three pages they are frequently a challenge to compose and distribute and sometimes a chore to study for the person who requested the evaluation. A damaging criticism of written reports is that there is often a significant delay between the examination and the receipt of the written appraisal by the teacher or other interested school personnel. It is partially in response to this criticism that this article is directed. It describes a program that uses tape-recorded staff conferences in which both of the authors have participated.

The authors used audio tape-recorded staffings in a university-sponsored clinic that evaluated elementary and junior high school age children who were thought to have some type of learning disability. The tape-recorded staffings were used to provide rapid feedback to teachers and counselors so that recommendations could be implemented immediately. A tape recording of 10 to 15 minutes duration can cover much more material, can elaborate more extensively, and can incorporate the opinions of several resource people without the loss of the separate identities of the staffing people, and does not require the immediate secretarial assistance of the written report procedure. In actual practice, the clinic also furnished the referring school or agency a follow-up written report some time after the child had been evaluated. So, while the tape recordings did not eliminate the energy expenditure of writing reports, they did provide swift feedback and allowed the written reports to follow at a more convenient time. The remainder of the paper briefly describes the clinic program with additional comments on the advantages of using taped recordings of staff meetings.

SOURCE. Reprinted from Psychology in the Schools, 1973, X, 4, 404-406. By permission of the authors and Clinical Psychology Publishing Co., Inc.

The clinic operated for two to three half-day periods each week. During each half-day the number of children who were seen ranged from two to six; the usual number of children was three or four. The staff consisted of two psychologists, two educational diagnosticians, and occasionally some supplementary assistance by an advanced undergraduate or graduate student. The student help was used to administer some of the routine testing tasks. The secretarial staff consisted of part-time undergraduate students.

During the first 2 hours of each session the children were rotated to each of the four primary specialists so that each child was seen by each professional staff member. Psychometric activities of the team members normally incorporated the usage of the Draw-a-Man Test (Harris, 1963), the Developmental Test of Visual-Motor Integration (Beery, 1967), a shortened administration of the Rorschach (1942), the Vocabulary Subtest of the Wechsler Intelligence Scale for Children (Wechsler, 1949), the Wide Range Achievement Test (Jastak & Jastak, 1965), selected portions of the Durrell Analysis of Reading Difficulty (Durrell, 1955), the San Diego Quick Assessment (LaPray & Ross, 1969), and selected tasks designed to measure cognitive development according to Piaget's theory (Phillips, 1969). The final hour was spent in staffing, at which time each child was discussed. Each team member offered his impressions of each child, and a moderator summarized the group's impressions and recommendations for each child. The counselor, principal, or teacher who brought the children to the clinic was encouraged to participate in the staffings and was invited to ask questions or to make comments if he wished. Occcassionally a parent also visited the clinic with the group and was allowed to sit in on the staffings and to ask questions.

One of the team members operated the two tape recorders. Two machines were required, since one tape stayed with the examining group while the other was returned to the referring school. The moderator introduced the tape with the team identification, professional roles of team members, date of audio taping, place of audio taping, client's name, client's age, client's grade, and client's home school. Next, the reason for referral was reviewed carefully. This often was a problem because referral explanations frequently were vague and general. The team members then alternated with brief presentations in their respective areas of expertise. The format for reporting was not immutable, and deviation from the regular routine was accepted freely whenever it seemed appropriate. Team members also felt free to ask questions or to seek clarification of points from other team members.

Normally the team moved from the introduction of the audio tape through the following general areas:
  1. Behavior during examination.
  2. Ability of the child to absorb and utilize visual or spoken

instructions and to express himself motorically and verbally.
3. General mental ability both in terms of an estimated potential and a functioning level.
4. Achievement level in the essential academic areas with specific deficits explicitly noted.
5. Social skills and social maturity level.
6. Personality appraisal as it related to the educational problems and needs of the child.
7. Summation of the team's impressions of the child.
8. Educational remedial recommendations.
9. Educational setting behavioral management suggestions.
10. Recommendations for future reexaminations or for further referrals.

In summary, tape-recorded staffings possessed three main advantages: (a) feedback to school personnel was more rapid than with the written report, (b) more information was transmitted, and (c) the tape-recorded staffing was more informal and more personal than a written report.

The major disadvantages of the taped staffing were twofold: (a) cost of the initial investment, and (b) storage of the audio tapes. Certainly the economic factor is an important consideration. In many cases, however, tape-recording equipment is already available and the only extra expense would be the purchase of audio tapes or cassette cartridges. It is also possible that other factors may offset the initial purchase price of audio tapes and recording equipment. For instance, the more efficient utilization of secretarial help may be a compensating factor, since the secretary can type the follow-up reports at a more leisurely pace because the recommendations already have been given to the school system.

The storage of audio tapes can present a problem, particularly when space is limited. However, after several years in the file, tapes or cassettes may be recycled for use with another student, as reports more than 2 years old rarely are of any practical value. In any case, the original test data could be kept by the clinic for reference long after the tapes have been used again for another student.

The departure from written report procedures described in this paper frequently evokes resistance in teachers, administrators, and counselors. Some administrative levels may regard written reports as supporting proof for placement decisions, while taped reports are seen as too novel to be acceptable. In no way do the authors recommend that the tape-recorded staffing universally replace the written report. However, as an adjunct or alternative to the written report method, the authors do feel that staffing by audio tapes and cassettes is a very useful technique that could be employed profitably by many agencies.

References

Beery, K.E. Developmental Test of Visual-Motor Integration. Chicago:
    Follett Educational Corporation, 1967.

Durrell, D.D. Durrell Analysis of Reading Difficulty. New York:
    Harcourt, Brace & World, 1955.

Harris, D.B. Children's drawings as measures of intellectual maturity:
    a revision and extension of the Goodenough Draw-A-Man Test.
    New York: Harcourt, Brace & World, 1963.

Jastak, J.F. & Jastak, S.R. The Wide Range Achievement Test.
    Wilmington, Del.: Guidance Associates, 1965.

LaPray, M., & Ross, R. The graded word list: quick guage of reading
    ability. Journal of Reading, 1969, 12, 305-307.

Phillips, J.L., Jr. The origins of intellect: Piaget's theory. San
    Francisco: Freeman, 1969.

Rorschach, H. (Transl. by P. Lemkau and B. Kronenburg.) Psycho-
    diagnostics: A diagnostic test based on perception. Berne:
    Huber, 1942 (1st German ed., 1921; U.S. distributor, Grune &
    Stratton.)

Wechsler, D. Manual for the Wechsler Intelligence Scale for Children.
    New York: Psychological Corporation, 1949.

Thomas N. Fairchild

The purpose of all of the accountability techniques described in this section is to help school psychologists provide substantive evidence regarding their effectiveness; and consequently, to help them justify their presence in the schools. Therefore, it is extremely important that the school psychologist synthesize all of the account- ability data he or she has collected. This information should then be organized into a meaningful written report for dissemination to building principals, building staff, supervisors, the director of pupil personnel services, and the superintendent of schools. This is most easily accomplished through the SCHOOL PSYCHOLOGICAL SERVICES YEARLY REPORT.

The SCHOOL PSYCHOLOGICAL SERVICES YEARLY REPORT should consist of the following sections: SERVICES PROVIDED, EVALUATION OF SERVICES, and GOALS.

The SERVICES PROVIDED section should communicate the types of activities that the school psychologist was engaged in during the past school year. In his SCHOOL PSYCHOLOGICAL SERVICES YEARLY REPORT, this writer included a list of all the students which had been eval- uated. These students were listed by building. The purpose was to show the size of the school psychologist's caseload and roughly give an indication of the number of individual students which he or she might be able to serve on a yearly basis. However, with the recent passage of the Family Rights and Privacy Act, listing students names would be unacceptable. It may be useful to list the numbers of students assessed according to grade levels.

The most appropriate way to communicate the types of services provided is to share in this section the yearly summary of the daily log.

SOURCE. Thomas N. Fairchild. Unpublished article.

The EVALUATION OF SERVICES section will vary considerably, and the content will depend upon whatever accountability information the school psychologist had gathered as a means of evaluating his effectiveness. The results of follow-up questionnaires, time-lapsed data, accountability interviews, in-service evaluations, agency referral follow-ups, etc. would be documented in this section.

The GOALS section should include a list of the goals that the school psychologist had identified at the beginning of the school year, and some evidence regarding how well the goals had been accomplished during the year.

In order to provide the reader with a greater appreciation of the SCHOOL PSYCHOLOGICAL SERVICES YEARLY REPORT, the writer has included two sample yearly reports which were written while being employed as a school psychologist. (The names of specific buildings have been deleted and letters included in their place). The samples are intended to allow you to see how the accountability data might be organized into a meaningful written report which can be shared with administrators and staff. Feel free to adopt the format or to adapt it. If it does not meet your needs design your own SCHOOL PSYCHOLO-GICAL SERVICES YEARLY REPORT form. It is of paramount importance, however, that you share your accountability data. Unless it is shared, substantive evidence will not be provided regarding your effectiveness, and little change will be affected in the attitudes of educators who believe school psychologists are "frills", or in the minds of educators who perceive school psychologists as ineffect-ive. In order to promote school psychological services, collect accountability information and share it.

YEARLY REPORT

School Psychological Services

August 21, 1972 - June 1, 1973

Thomas N. Fairchild
July 30, 1973

104

TABLE OF CONTENTS

I. SERVICES PROVIDED

II. EVALUATION OF SERVICES

III. GOALS

APPENDIX

*Deleted because of confidentiality

YEARLY SUMMARY OF DAILY LOG
(1972-1973)

School Psychological Services	Number of Hours	Number of Time
ASSESSMENT		
Administration and scoring of formal and informal tests	109.25	13.3
Report writing	98.00	11.9
Consulting other professionals regarding a student	34.00	4.1
Diagnostic interviews with students	25.00	3.1
Interview with counselors, principals, and social workers	22.25	2.7
Teacher interviews	11.75	1.4
Observational techniques	10.50	1.2
Parent interviews	9.00	1.1
Reviewing cumulative records	6.00	.7
INTERVENTION		
Indirect Intervention		
Parent consultation	49.00	5.9
Teacher consultation		
Recommendations based on contact with student	28.50	3.5
Recommendations made without student contact	12.00	1.4
Consulting with counselors, principals and social workers	22.50	2.7
In-service presentations	19.50	2.4
Staffings	6.50	.8
Direct Intervention		
Counseling	65.00	7.9
EVALUATION		
Follow-up conferences to determine efficacy of intervention		
Conferences with parents	18.00	2.2
Conferences with teachers	17.00	2.1
Conferences with counselors, principals, and social workers	10.75	1.3
Research on efficacy of school psychological services		
Recording monthly summary of daily log	18.50	2.3
Follow-up questionnaires	16.00	1.9
Time elapsed data	3.00	.4
In-service evaluation	3.50	.4
Role and function	3.00	.4

Final Report	8.75	1.1

ADMINISTRATION

Travel	50.25	6.1
Review of mail and copyreading psychological reports	33.75	4.1
Miscellaneous (unable to categorize)	31.00	3.8
Supervision of practicum student	25.25	3.1
Preparation for testing and conferences	21.00	2.5
Attendance at meetings	14.00	1.7
Professional development	9.00	1.1
Public Relations	6.25	.7
Correspondence	2.25	.3

YEARLY TOTAL

Psychological Service	Number of Hours	Percent of Time
ASSESSMENT	326.25	39.7
INTERVENTION	203.00	24.8
EVALUATION	98.50	12.0
ADMINISTRATION	192.75	23.5
TOTAL	820.50	100.00

1971-1972 Mean number of hours per referral = 7.61
1972-1973 Mean number of hours per referral = 7.21

RESULTS OF FOLLOW-UP QUESTIONNAIRE

TABLE 1

COMBINED DATA FOR BOTH TEACHERS AND PARENTS
FOR SCHOOL YEAR   1972-1973

(DATA COMPARED TO DATA FROM 1971-1972)

1971-1972 School Year

Number of students followed-up	48
Number of questionnaires distributed	63
Number of respondents	52
Percentage return	83%

1972-1973 School Year

Number of students followed-up	52
Number of questionnaires distributed	74
Number of respondents	51
Percentage return	69%

			1971-72	1972-73
(1)	Did you have a better understanding of the child as a result of your discussion with the psychologist?	YES	73%	84%
		NO	19%	14%
		NOT APPLICABLE	8%	2%
(2)	Were recommendations realistic and/or practical?	YES	87%	94%
		NO		2%
		NOT APPLICABLE	13%	4%
(3)	Were the recommendations of the psychologist effective?	YES	44%	57%
		NO	2%	6%
		NOT APPLICABLE		2%
		CANNOT BE ASCERTAINED	54%	35%
(4)	Were you able to carry out the recommendations of the psychologist?	YES	79%	90%
		NO		4%
		NOT APPLICABLE	21%	6%

RESULTS OF FOLLOW-UP QUESTIONNAIRE

TABLE 2

COMBINED DATA FOR BOTH TEACHERS AND PARENTS
FOR FALL AND SPRING SEMESTERS

Fall Semester		Spring Semester	
Number of students followed-up	26	Number of students followed-up	26
Number of questionnaires		Number of questionnaires	
distributed	38	distributed	36
Number of respondents	23	Number of respondents	28
Percentage return	61%	Percentage return	78%

(1) Did you have a better understanding of the child as a result
of your discussion with the psychologist?

YES	(22) 96%		(21) 75%
NO	(1) 4%		(6) 21%
NOT APPLICABLE	(0) 0%		(1) 4%

(2) Were recommendations realistic and/or practical?

YES	(21) 91%		(27) 96%
NO	(0) 0%		(1) 4%
NOT APPLICABLE	(2) 9%		(0) 0%

(3) Were the recommendations of the psychologist effective?

YES	(11) 53%		(17) 61%
NO	(0) 0%		(3) 11%
NOT APPLICABLE	(1) 4%		(0) 0%
CANNOT BE			
ASCERTAINED	(10) 43%		(8) 28%

(4) Were you able to carry out the recommendations of the
psychologist?

YES	(21) 92%		(25) 89%
NO	(1) 4%		(1) 4%
NOT APPLICABLE	(1) 4%		(2) 7%

TABLE 3

TEACHER DATA FOR THE FALL
AND SPRING SEMESTERS

Fall Semester   Spring Semester

Number of students followed-up	26	Number of students followed-up	26
Number of questionnaires distributed	19	Number of questionnaires distributed	19
Number of respondents	11	Number of respondents	18
Percentage return	58%	Percentage return	95

(1) Did you have a better understanding of the child as a result
    of your discussion with the psychologist?

YES	(11)	100%	(13)	72%
NO	(0)	0%	(4)	22%
NOT APPLICABLE	(0)	0%	(1)	6%

(2) Were the recommendations realistic and/or practical?

YES	(11)	100%	(17)	94%
NO	(0)	0%	(1)	6%
NOT APPLICABLE	(0)	0%	(0)	0%

(3) Were the recommendations of the psychologist effective?

YES	(6)	55%	(12)	67%
NO	(0)	0%	(2)	11%
NOT APPLICABLE	(0)	0%	(0)	0%
CANNOT BE ASCERTAINED	(5)	45%	(4)	22%

(4) Were you able to carry out the recommendations of the
    psychologist?

YES	(10)	91%	(15)	83%
NO	(1)	9%	(1)	6%
NOT APPLICABLE	(0)	0%	(2)	11%

110

RESULTS OF FOLLOW-UP QUESTIONNAIRE

TABLE 4

PARENT DATA FOR THE FALL
AND SPRING SEMESTERS

Fall Semester		Spring Semester	
Number of students followed-up	26	Number of students followed-up	26
Number of questionnaires distributed	19	Number of questionnaires distributed	17
Number of respondents	12	Number of respondents	10
Percentage return	63%	Percentage return	59%

(1) Did you have a better understanding of the child as a result of your discussion with the psychologist?

YES	(11)	92%	(8)	80%
NO	(1)	8%	(2)	20%
NOT APPLICABLE	(0)	0%	(0)	0%

(2) Were the recommendations realistic and/or practical?

YES	(10)	83%	(10)	100%
NO	(0)	0%	(0)	0%
NOT APPLICABLE	(2)	17%	(0)	0%

(3) Were the recommendations of the psychologist effective?

YES	(6)	50%	(5)	50%
NO	(0)	0%	(1)	10%
NOT APPLICABLE	(1)	8%	(0)	0%
CANNOT BE ASCERTAINED	(5)	42%	(4)	40%

(4) Were you able to carry out the recommendations of the psychologist?

YES	(11)	92%	(10)	100%
NO	(0)	0%	(0)	0%
NOT APPLICABLE	(1)	8%	(0)	0%

111

RESULTS OF FOLLOW-UP QUESTIONNAIRE

TABLE 5

COMMENTS ELICITED FROM TEACHERS (T) AND PARENTS (P) FOR
FALL AND SPRING SEMESTERS

Fall Semester

(T)   Suggestions are practical and easily applied. Follow-up procedures
      and interest are appreciated.
(T)   I wish they could be seen by you more often.
(T)   I would like to thank you for your excellent services. I can see so
      much improvement in the child which you tested. Your recommendations
      were very helpful and effective. Thank you.
(P)   We feel you have done a fine job. Thank you for your help.
(P)   We think it is going to need more time.
(P)   With the help of the school psychologist I feel I better understand
      my child and I have developed a closer relationship with my child.
(P)   Is doing very good work advising child to help her in the subjects
      she is low in.
(P)   Child has advanced rapidly since the test and visits with the psychologis
(P)   Thank you for all of your help.
(P)   We were unable to obtain any information other than what we already
      knew and were working on previously.

Spring Semester

(T)   The recommendations confirmed exactly my evaluation but this was a
      tremendous stepping stone for turning the child around. We could
      convince him he wasn't "dumb" because the psychologist had tested
      him. We had an overnight miracle from underachiever to an average
      of at least one 100 per day.
(T)   Sincere thanks for all you do in such a limited time.
(T)   Need for continued contact and additional recommendations. Psychologist
      is a real person and therefore encouraging to search and work with.
(T)   I have noticed marked improvement in Jeff since his referral. His
      attitude has improved considerably and he has been more conscientious
      about completing assigned work. I feel that if we as teachers, can
      remain conscious of Jeff's need to go at his own pace, at his own level,
      he will continue to achieve.
(P)   We are very grateful for all the help and interest in our child.
(P)   Wonderful help to our child and we were very grateful.
(P)   I did appreciate the opportunity to talk with you. Since our meeting
      was only last week I haven't had much chance to put into practice your
      suggestions in regard to helping her but feel they will be of benefit.

112

IN-SERVICE EVALUATION
(Fall Semester)

PURPOSE

In the Fall Semester of the 1972-1973 school year in-service presentations were scheduled at three elementary schools. In-service meetings were scheduled for the purpose of explaining and discussing the psychological procedures, psychological tests used for assessment, and psychological reports. Topics were presented in the sequence outlined above. In each instance the time expired before adequate attention could be devoted to teachers' understanding of psychological reports.

RESULTS

After the presentation and discussion, teachers were presented with a brief questionnaire to indicate whether or not they had a better understanding of procedures, psychological tests, and reports. The responses for each school are recorded below

School	Teachers Present	Number and percentage of teachers responding that they have a better understanding of psychological:		
		Procedures	Tests	Reports
A Elementary School	11	(10) 90%	(9) 81%	(6) 54%
B Elementary School	14	(13) 93%	(7) 50%	(4) 29%
C Elementary School	21	(19) 91%	(19) 91%	(13) 62%

PURPOSE OF IN-SERVICE PRESENTATION
(Spring Semester)

Occasionally, a child's behavior warrants a referral to an outside agency for recommendations regarding medication as an appropriate intervention strategy. Often teachers do not have an adequate understanding of the type of child who would profit from cerebral stimulant medication, or of the expected effects of properly prescribed medication on the child's behavior. Therefore, it was decided to offer an in-service presentation that would provide the teachers with a better understanding of cerebral stimulant drugs and their effectiveness when dealing with the learning disabled or behavior disordered children. Dr. Hunter Comley presented a slide presentation and lecture on the characteristics of children requiring cerebral stimulant drugs, as well as, an explanation of the effects of the medication on the children's behavior. A discussion period followed the presentation. The reactions of the teachers to the presentation were extremely favorable, as suggested by the results of the in-service evaluation forms.

113

RESULTS OF IN-SERVICE EVALUATION
(Spring Semester)

Twenty-eight teachers from A Elementary School and C Elementary School were given evaluation forms to complete regarding the in-service presentation. The results are as follows:

In response to the item, "Was the information presented to you today primarily new information? (Do you feel you learned something?)," 15 teachers responded yes and 2 responded no.

In response to the item, "Do you feel that this in-service presentation was of value to you as a teacher in dealing with the kind of child discussed?" 23 teachers responded yes, and 3 responded no.

Attitudes towards use of cerebral stimulant drugs for children with behavior and/or learning problems prior to the presentation were generally favorable (22 teachers responded in this manner). Of these 22, eight indicated that their attitudes had been further strengthened and supported. Teachers indicated that their already positive attitudes had been strengthened and they had developed a greater understanding of this type of child which w improve their handling of a child with these problems.

Of the remaining six respondents, the attitudes of five were generally unfavorable, and one teacher was neutral. It is noteworthy to mention that the attitudes of all six of these teachers changed in a positive direction as a result of the in-service presentation.

Comments regarding the in-service were also elicited from the teachers. There responses were:

"Found the broad characteristics interesting and informative."

"It was a good review for me."

"An extremely interesting and appropriate topic much in need of open discussion and understanding."

"This was one of the best and most informative in-service meetings we've had."

"Very interesting. I hope I can deal with this child in a more patient understanding way."

"Very good presentation of conduct and medication for unstable child. Thank you very much."

"Would like a longer period which would begin earlier in the afternoon and be over at 3:30 p.m."

"This was the best in-service meeting this year and for the past several years."

114

"Presentation was quite interesting due to manner of the speaker. Enjoyed his unique use of cartoons in making his point."

"It was interesting and profitable."

"Very interesting presentation. I'm sure we could all relate to 'Dennis the Menace,' which made the understanding of this problem easier."

"I found this program extremely interesting and stimulating. I feel it is important for teachers, who spend so much of the waking hours with the children, to be aware of these problems in children."

Teachers were also extremely interested in following up on this topic with greater emphasis on handling these children in the classroom. They also recommended the presentation for a Home-School meeting; hoping that parents would gain a greater understanding of this type of child.

TIME ELAPSED DATA

TABLE 6

DATA FOR 1972–1973 SCHOOL YEAR
GROUPED ACCORDING TO INDIVIDUAL SCHOOLS

In order to ascertain how effective a school psychologist is, one criterion that should be measured besides the efficacy of recommendations, is the immediacy of feedback after the initial referral has been made. In an attempt to do this, data has been collected regarding:

Factor I – The number of school days that elapse between the date the referral is made (date on referral form) and the first contact with the child.

Factor II – The number of school days that elapse between the date of the first contact with a child and the date the primary referral source receives meaningful feedback.

Factor III – The number of school days that elapse between the date the child is referred until the date that the primary referral source receives meaningful feedback regarding appropriate intervention strategies.

MEAN NUMBER OF DAYS ELAPSED

	Factor I	Factor II	Factor III
A Elementary School	4.44	10.94	15.38
B Elementary School	5.76	9.61	15.38
C Elementary School	13.41	11.94	25.41
Other Elementary Schools	7.25	13.50	20.75
D High School	10.37	22.50	32.87
E High School	3.00	15.20	18.20

GOALS 1972-1973

SCHOOL PSYCHOLOGICAL SERVICES

GOAL I   Accountability for psychological services biannually.

> Objective A Provide a summary of daily log to indicate services offered and proportion of time devoted to the various services.   Yes
>
> Evaluate A Summary of log distributed to Director of Pupil Personnel Services, and Coordinator of School Psychological Services.   Yes
>
> Objective B Hold conferences with elementary school principals to elicit feedback regarding the efficacy of services, and suggestions for improvement.   No
>
> Evaluate B A report of the conference will be given to the Director of Pupil Personnel Services and Coordinator of School Psychological Services.   No
>
> Objective C A follow-up questionnaire will be disseminated to parents and teachers to ascertain how effective recommendations have been.   Yes
>
> Evaluate C Data compiled from the questionnaire will be presented to the Director of Pupil Personnel Services and the Coordinator of School Psychological Services.   Yes

GOAL II   Increase the number of in-service presentations

> Objective A Develop and disseminate a questionnaire that would elicit what type of information the teachers consider desirable.   Yes
>
> Evaluate A Questionnaire distributed.   Yes
>
> Objective B Schedule a minimum of two in-service presentations for the 1972-1973 school year on preferential topics revealed from the questionnaire.   Yes
>
> Evaluate B Record of in-service presentations.   Yes
>
> Objective C Develop and disseminate a questionnaire following in-service to ascertain the usefulness of the presentation   Yes

Evaluate C   The results would be included in the
              biannual report to the Director and
              Coordinator.   Yes

GOAL III   Expand the usefulness of the daily log to include the
           time factor. One criterion of an effective school
           psychologist should be the immediacy of feedback after
           an initial referral has been made.

           Objective   Incorporate a form to log referral dates,
                         evaluation dates, and conference dates.
                         The length of time elapsed between the
                         date of referral and first contact and
                         conference with primary referral source.
                         This will give some indication of how
                         soon the teacher gets meaningful feed-
                         back regarding a pupil after the initial
                         referral.   Yes

           Evaluate   The resulting data will be included in the
                        biannual report to the Director of Pupil
                        Personnel Services and the Coordinator
                        of School Psychological Services.   Yes

GOAL IV   Improve the Effectiveness of Recommendations. At the time
           the questionnaire was disseminated last year 54% of the
           respondents were unable to ascertain whether or not the
           recommendations had been effective.

           Objective   Recommendations will be stated in behavioral
                         objectives whenever possible. This should
                         improve the effectiveness of recommendations
                         and increase and add responses on the ques-
                         tionnaire.   Yes

           Evaluate   Fewer than 54% should respond "cannot be
                        ascertained at this time."   Yes

GOAL V   Involve more school personnel in the decision-making
           process. Last year I was only involved in one staffing
           of a pupil.

           Objective   Devote a greater percentage of my time to
                        staffings.   Yes

           Evaluate   The yearly summary of the daily log should
                        reveal the percentage of time devoted to
                        staffings. This should exceed last years
                        total (.4%).   Yes

APPENDIX

CEDAR RAPIDS COMMUNITY SCHOOLS
Department of Pupil Personnel

During the semester many referrals were received from parents and teacher
Large caseloads prohibited me from working directly with a child; therefc
my primary mode of intervention has been to make recommendations based up
an individual assessment of the student. In order to ascertain how effec
I have been in providing help to you, I would appreciate your response to
items below.

Please do not include your name or the child's name on the form.

Thank you for your cooperation.

                                        Sincerely,

                                        Thomas N. Fairchild
                                        School Psychologist

(1) Did you have a better understanding of the child as a result of
     your discussion with the psychologist?

              YES_____   NO_____   NOT APPLICABLE_____

(2) Were recommendations realistic and/or practical?

              YES_____   NO_____   NOT APPLICABLE_____

(3) Were the recommendations of the psychologist effective?

              YES_____   NO_____   NOT APPLICABLE_____

              CANNOT BE ASCERTAINED AT THIS TIME_____

(4) Were you able to carry out the recommendations of the psychologist?

              YES_____   NO_____   NOT APPLICABLE_____

Other comments or suggestions would be appreciated:

Follow-Up Questionnaire

Fall In-Service
Presentation and Informal Discussion of
Psychological Tests, Procedures, and Written Reports

1. As a result of the presentation and discussion, I have a better understanding of:

_____psychological tests
_____procedures
_____psychological reports
_____all of the above
_____none of the above

2. _____I am more confused than ever.

3. _____Sorry, I was sleeping.

Regarding Recommendations

1. _____ Prefer recommendations to be specific, yet allow the teacher
to determine how she wants to utilize her time.

2. _____ Recommendations should be specified in specific behavioral
objective terms. The psychologist, teacher, and other
specialists can write up objectives together. Decisions
will be made regarding material, who will work with child,
what will be accomplished, and when follow-up will occur to
determine efficacy of the intervention.

Follow-Up Questionnaire
SPRING IN-SERVICE

Was the information presented to you today primarily
new information? (Do you feel you learned something?)   YES   NO

Do you feel that this in-service presentation was of
value to you as a teacher in dealing with the kind of
child discussed?   YES   NO

Prior to today's meeting, what was your general attitude
toward the use of cerebral stimulants for children with
behavior and/or learning problems?

                    generally favorable
                    generally unfavorable
                    strongly opposed
                    no opinion

After hearing today's discussion, has your attitude changed
any?   YES   NO

If YES, in what way?

_____

_____

We would appreciate any comments or suggestions you would care to make
concerning this in-service meeting or any future programs.

YEARLY REPORT

School Psychological Services

1973-1974

Thomas N. Fairchild
June 4, 1974

123

TABLE OF CONTENTS

*Deleted because of confidentiality

124

RESULTS OF FOLLOW-UP QUESTIONNAIRE

<u>Teachers</u>   <u>Parents</u>

No. of questionnaires distributed 66   No. of questionnaires distributed 81
No. of questionnaires returned   48   No. of questionnaires returned   41
Percentage return   73%   Percentage return   51%

(1) Did you have a better understanding of the child as a result of your
     discussion with the psychologist?

         YES   (45) 94% | (35) 85%
         NO   (2)   4% | (5)   12%
         NOT APPLICABLE   (1)   2% | (1)   2%

(2) Were recommendations realistic and/or practical?

         YES   (41) 89% | (34) 87%
         NO   (2)   4% | (5)   13%
         NOT APPLICABLE   (3)   7% | (0)   0%

(3) Were the recommendations of the psychologist effective?

         YES   (30) 64% | (30) 73%
         NO   (2)   4% | (3)   7%
         NOT APPLICABLE   (4)   9% | (0)   0%
         CANNOT BE |
            ASCERTAINED   (11) 23% | (8)   20%

125

COMMENTS FROM QUESTIONNAIRES

<u>TEACHERS</u>:

"Tom was extremely helpful in his suggestions about this boy. He regularly checked with us as to his progress. He was very easy to work with and showed a genuine concern. He conscientiously checked on this student, himself. He is an asset to our school."

"More suggestions on types of rewards would be helpful. For instance, points."

"The recommendations were realistic, but little effect was seen by student's progress."

"Your genuine concern for each child serves as a catalyst in motivating teachers to follow suggestions."

"Continual follow-up is needed to assist classroom teacher."

"We have found Mr. Fairchild does the following:

1. Establishes good rapport with parents and teachers.
2. Does much preliminary work prior to conference.
3. Good follow through."

"More follow-up with teacher and child."

"I think you've done a great job!"

"Tom Fairchild - you're a most down to earth and practical person. Your evaluation of child and willingness to share impressions with teachers and parents has been a great benefit to all concerned."

"I am very happy to have Tom as psychologist. He listens to what I have to say and acts as quickly as he can on the problem. He makes many suggestions and really takes the time to explain the child's problem to me. I feel he has good rapport with parents at a conference."

"This child has profited greatly from our discussions and as a result of our referrals. He is now doing well and much better adjusted. This referral has contributed much to the child's well being."

"This testing was done on parents' request to determine if Jay should start kindergarten this year. It has proved to be a wise choice in starting him."

<u>PARENTS</u>:

"I appreciated learning more about my child's problem and what to do to help. Thank you."

"Do not agree that what he said is true. I think just a slow learner but will see in time."

"As an answer to number three 'almost yes.' We can definitely see a move in the right direction not only in her but also her parents. I am really glad to have had the opportunity to see the problem from your perspective rather than ours as parents. I feel the visit was very beneficial to us. Thank you for your time with our daughter and us."

"Child was supposed to have been watched, and a report given us on his behavior. So far we have heard nothing."

"I can now see where part of Mike's problem comes from me. We have a long way to go to help Mike learn what no is. I can see at home by giving him more responsibilities he feels more important and behaves better. I think our meeting with Dr. Fairchild has helped us understand the problem and is making for a happier home."

"We would appreciate more communication with the school."

"I did better on my own than with any of the psychologist's recommendations."

"More time is needed to really know the results."

"We had a behavior problem and our suggestions on how to correct it have really helped."

"Our discussion with the psychologist helped clarify our understanding of the problem and still all unreasonable fears, helping us to deal with the problem in a calmer, more rational way. Only time can tell the effectiveness but without the psychologist, we'd still be groping in the dark with fear."

"The methods for stimulating my child were effective for a time. However, it was physically impossible for him to continue being stimulated because of a medical problem. This was tho, the first time we were able to motivate him. All problems are solved because of this first beginning. Thank you very much."

"We have noticed a definite good change in Charles at this time. We are very happy we followed your advice."

"We'd just like to say thanks for all your help."

"Helping this mother set up some behavior mod at home was most effective and carried over in the school. Thanks."

127

"Helped me change my behavior to deal more effectively with the child's behavior."

"More of an understanding from Dr. Walter Block, Dr. Kazam Fathie and the Mayo Clinic in Rochester."

TIME ELAPSED DATA

The following is a record of the number of school days that elapses (on the average) from the time a student is referred until the time the referral source receives meaningful feedback regarding intervention strategies. It is recorded separately from each school excluding the high schools.

A Elementary School	24.29
B Elementary School	31.00
C Elementary School	18.00
D Elementary School	28.37
E Elementary School	38.31

Inspection reveals that considerable time was elapsing this year before persons were getting feedback. Some factors that were partially responsible for this unfortunate time lapse were:

1. Too large a caseload; consequently an unusually high number of referrals. The time lapse at E Elementary School was related to the fact that the examiner could not provide that school with more service time.

2. Some of the delay at D Elementary School can be attributed to the principal assuming the responsibility for scheduling conferences. As a result, they were frequently not scheduled when planned.

3. The B Elementary School time lapse was affected by the first grade team who made up a list of students to be seen during the fall semester. None of the students were priority cases. The teachers simply wanted information regarding ability, etc. Consequently, students seen late in the fall had extremely long time lapses.

*I feel it is crucial to point out that much of the effectiveness of school psychological services relies on the immediacy of feedback. In order that this might be accomplished, psychologists need to be given more realistic caseload assignments so that the amount of time elapsing before the psychologist gets to see the referred student is drastically reduced.

SCHOOL PSYCHOLOGICAL SERVICES

GOALS (1973-74)

Was Goal
Accomplished?
(circle)

GOAL I   COMMUNICATIONS

Objective 1   Schedule at least 1 conference with   Yes   No
each elementary principal during the
school year for the express purpose
of eliciting feedback regarding the
efficacy of school psychological
services.

Evaluate 1   Report of conferences will be
included in the Final Yearly Report.

Objective 2   Adopt Psychologist's Active Cases   Yes   No
(PAC) follow-up procedure in order
to evaluate efficacy of recommendations.

Evaluate 2   Results of follow-up will be recorded
in the Final Yearly Report.

GOAL II   TEACHING PROCESS

Objective 1   Provide 2 in-service presentations   Yes   No
during the school year.

Evaluate 1   Data will be available in Final Report.

Objective 2   Meet with small groups of teachers   Yes   No
for informal discussion regarding
classroom problems.

Evaluate 2   A record of contact will be available in my daily log.

GOAL III PROFESSIONAL GROWTH

Objective 1   Keep abreast of current develop-   Yes   No
ments in the field of school
psychology and special education
by reading selected articles in
the following journals: Journal
of School Psychology, Psychology
in the Schools, Exceptional Children.

Evaluate 1   Personal statement.

Objective 2   In order to improve efficacy in   Yes   No
dealing with management problems
in the home, I will read the
following books:
Children: The Challenge
Logical Consequences
Parent Effectiveness Training

130

	How to Parent
Evaluate 2	Personal statement.

Objective 3	Attend at least 1 workshop or convention related to professional interest.	Yes No
Evaluate 3	Approved application for travel.	

ADDITION TO THE GOALS

In defense of my lack of completion of Goal I and Goal II, I would like to not the other comparable activities took place.

COMMUNICATIONS
Although the PAC was not used, I did continue to use my own personal method of following up students to evaluate the efficacy of recommendations I have made.

TEACHING PROCESS
Two in-service presentations were not provided to teachers as I had planned, but I was responsible for co-leading two PRISM in-service sessions for school psychologists. I also assumed responsibility for supervising a school psychology practicum student from the University of Iowa.

DETERMINING THE EFFECTIVENESS OF THE SCHOOL PSYCHOLOGIST'S ROLE

Accountability encompasses more than just methods for evaluating one's personal effectiveness. Accountability, in the writer's opinion, also involves determining the efficacy of various school psychological services delivery systems. School psychologists need to determine if certain service models are more effective than others. In order for school psychology to grow as a profession, and in order for school psychologists to grow as professionals, they need to determine the appropriateness and utility of various service models.

Investigators have attempted to do this using a variety of approaches. Gilmore and Chandy have documented teacher's perceptions of school psychological services using both structured interview and questionnaire formats. Tyler and Fine conducted a rather sophisticated comparison of two modes of school psychological consultation. A subjective description of the transition of school psychological services from a clinical model to a consultation model is discussed in the Briggs article. More objective comparisons of delivery systems are available in the Fairchild article, and the Waters article. Fairchild compared and evaluated the effectiveness of two models of school psychological services -- the diagnostician model and the consultation model. The two models were compared on the following two variables: immediacy of feedback; and the effectiveness of the recommendations. In Waters article, data was gathered on an entire school psychological services department which had shifted from a psychometric model to a consultant model. The effectiveness of the new service model was evaluated by distributing questionnaires to school personnel to solicit their feedback.

School psychologists should become actively involved in evaluating the appropriateness of various school psychological service models in order that they might ascertain which service model is most effective for their setting.

TEACHERS' PERCEPTIONS OF SCHOOL PSYCHOLOGICAL SERVICES

George E. Gilmore and Jean Chandy

Summary: Teachers from two schools responded to a structured
interview designed to reveal their perceptions of the roles and
functions of school psychologists-psychometrists. Responses of
teachers grouped according to degree of teaching experience and
amount of contact with school psychologists or psychometrists were
compared on five sets of variables pertaining to the psychologist's
role and functions. Results illustrate that teachers view the
psychologist as a specialist in emotional problems whose major diagnostic procedure is testing, who recommends treatment but does little
himself. Statistical analysis indicates that both the factors of
teaching experience and contact with psychologists differentiate
between teachers' perceptions of the school psychologist's functioning. Teacher recommendations for change in psychological services
are outlined.

The role and functions of the school psychologist have recently
been subject to scrutiny (Fifield, 1967; Mumford, 1970; Shaw, 1967;
Wolman, 1967). One central hypothesis emerging from such examination
is that the school psychologist's work is substantially affected by
the way in which other school personnel perceive his role. It is
suggested that such perceptions determine the organization of a
psychological service, the training and qualifications of its personnel, the types of problems referred, to whom the referral is made,
and the diagnostic and treatment procedures conducted (Baker, 1965;
Fine & Tyler, 1971; Handler, Gerston, & Handler, 1965; Styles, 1965).

Investigators have studied the views of teaching personnel in
different ways, examining their perception of the school psychologist's (a) training and competencies, (b) role functions, and (c)
usefulness. Styles (1965) found that teachers credited the school

SOURCE. Reprinted from Journal of School Psychology, 1973, 11, 2,
139-147. By permission of the authors and the publisher. Copyright
1973 by the Journal of School Psychology, Inc. Published by Behavioral Publications, New York.

psychologist with more intensive expertise in clinical psychology and more thorough knowledge of severe emotional disturbance than was warranted by actual training. Roberts' (1970) teachers felt that school psychologists required more training in educationally oriented problem areas and that psychologists should become more involved in all functions, especially as therapist, mental hygienist, and educational programmer. With respect to actual and desired role functions Lucas and Jones (1970) found that teachers of mentally retarded children would like the psychologist to engage in more psychotherapy, while the psychologist considered this the least important aspect of his role.

Previous studies used questionnaires. Return rate of questionnaires varied considerably, from 94% to 40%. Such variation suggests that responses reported may be of a biased sample. The wide range of teacher responses reported in some studies indicates the necessity of differentiating the perceptions and attitudes of various teacher groups.

This study concerns itself with teacher perceptions of what school psychologists actually do, their competencies, and teachers' recommendations for change. Another goal of this study was to discover whether teachers grouped on two dimensions (degree of contact with psychologists and amount of teaching experience) and had different views on the school's psychological services. Previous research presented a somewhat ambiguous picture - Baker (1965) stated that teachers' opinions of the effectiveness of psychological services declined after use, while the work of Lucas and Jones (1970) suggested that teachers having more contact with psychologists rated the services higher. Another important variable on which teachers differ is teaching experience. Though in general it has been suggested that younger, less experienced teachers are more open to help (Iscoe, Pierce-Jones, Friedman, & McGehearty, 1967). Baker (1965) found that there was more co-action between more experienced teachers and psychologists and the psychologists involved older faculty more than younger teachers in the diagnostic and treatment activities.

PURPOSES

In conjunction with the several studies noted above, this work attempted to delineate how teaching personnel perceived school psychological services. Recognizing the complexity of this general question, answers to six more specific questions were sought. As teachers perceive it:

1. In relation to what types of problems would teachers request help from the school's psychological services?
2. What diagnostic procedures are psychological personnel likely to use?

3. What are the types of treatment likely to occur?
4. How are these treatments put into effect?
5. What skills do the school's psychological personnel have, compared to the average teacher?
6. What changes in school psychological services would teachers recommend?

PROCEDURES

Two schools took part in this investigation, one serving a largely black population in what is economically one of the poorer sections of the school district, the other serving a lower middle-class white population. One is an elementary school with grades 1-6, while the other serves upper elementary students - grades 4-6. According to official records the schools do not differ significantly in the frequency with which they use psychological services. Each had a master's level psychometrist, experienced in both classroom teaching and psychometry. Each spent half a day a week in the schools under study. Both schools used the services of psychological consultants about half a day per week.

Information was gathered through the use of structured interviews conducted individually with participants by the principal investigator. It included five open-ended questions which allowed teachers considerable freedom to describe their perceptions of the school's psychometrists and psychologists, followed by twenty-six specific questions which required teachers to select a single response on a five-point scale. Questions were read to the teacher and both verbal and multiple choice responses were recorded by the interviewer. Interview time averaged 25 minutes.

RESULTS

While the voluntary nature of participation was emphasized both to the school principals and to the individual teachers, there was 100% participation in one school (N=19) and 93% in the other (N=14).

For statistical analysis of the findings, six sets of variables and two sets of teacher groups have been defined. Teacher participants were consecutively grouped on two dimensions, according to the number of years of teaching experience (4 years or less=inexperienced, 5-9 years=moderately experienced, 10 years or more=experienced) and according to the frequency per year which they report using psychological services (never=no contact, 1-3 times=moderate contact, 4 or more times=high contact). The first five variable sets which include a series of specific questions are: Set I, Type of Child-Learning Problem; Set II, Diagnostic Activities; Set III, Types of Treatment;

Set IV, Treatment Management; Set V, Psychologist-Psychometrist
Skills, Variable Set VI, Teachers' Recommendations, is based on a
post hoc coding of responses to a single open-ended question.

Perceptions of the Total Group. Table 1 presents the mean
results obtained for the total group on individual items in each of
the five sets of variables. Examination of Set I suggests that
teachers want psychologists to be involved more often in problems
related to the emotional and behavioral domains, retardation, and
low achievement than with the intellectually gifted child and those
with out-of-school problems. Teachers believe that a child's problems should be moderately severe before seeking the help of a school
psychologist.

Empirical data describing teachers' views of the diagnostic
process (Table 1, Set II) indicate that teachers feel that psychologists test children a good deal and that all other diagnostic activities rank second to this primary work. Psychologists observe children in the classroom less frequently than they engage in any other
diagnostic work, according to teachers. Comments indicated that a
month elapses before action is taken on referral.

As illustrated in Table 1, Set III, teachers feel that there is
no difference in frequency with which six relatively distinct treatments result from the intervention of the school psychological personnel. Teachers indicate that psychologists most frequently just give
written or verbal recommendations and rarely will be actively involved
in treating the child either in conjunction with the teacher or independently.

Teachers have rather definite ideas about the skills of psychologists (Table 1, Set V). Comparing these personnel to the "average
teacher," they suggest that psychologists are much more expert about
children's emotional development, know less than the average teacher
about teaching in general or about classroom management, and are
somewhat more skillful in understanding children's abilities.

Table 1

Perception of Psychologists-Psychometrists
Means and SDs of Total Group (N=33)[1]

Variable	Mean	SD
Set I. Type of Child Learning Problem		
1. Children with apparent emotional problems	3.8	1.12
2. Bright low achievers	3.4	1.05
3. The intellectually retarded	3.8	1.00

4.	Children who present classroom behavioral problems	3.8	1.19
5.	Intellectually gifted children	2.5	.89
6.	Children who manage school adequately with out-of-school problems	2.8	1.18
7.	How serious should a problem be before involving psychologists	3.1	1.15

Set II. Diagnostic Activities of Psychometrists and Psychologists

8.	Study the child's cumulative folder	3.2	1.31
9.	Discuss the problem with the teacher	2.9	1.36
10.	Discuss the problem with the school principal	2.6	1.36
11.	Observe the child in class	2.1	1.32
12.	Administer psychological tests	3.8	1.13
13.	Talk with child's parents or family	2.4	1.34

Set III. Types of Treatment

14.	Curricular change	3.6	1.15
15.	Behavioral control techniques for use in the classroom	3.5	1.02
16.	Transfer of child out of regular classroom	3.1	.93
17.	Special in-school treatment (e.g., speech-therapy, resource room)	3.9	.77
18.	Referral of child to some out-of-school agency	3.7	.99
19.	Referral of parents to counseling	3.3	1.03

Set IV. Treatment Management

20.	The psychologist will just make recommendations	4.1	.95
21.	The psychologist will work with the teacher in developing and carrying out some treatment	2.4	1.27
22.	The psychologist will actually conduct treatment	1.9	1.15

Set V. Psychologist-Psychometrists Skills Compared to the Average Teacher

23.	Knowledge about teaching	2.6	1.16
24.	Knowledge about emotional development	4.5	.70
25.	Management of classroom behavior	3.2	1.03
26.	Understanding children's abilities	3.6	.77

---

[1]Responses to items coded on a 5-point scale (1=low, 5=high). In Set I, scale reflects desirability of involvement of psychologist in activities described; in Set II-IV, scale reflects likelihood of psychologist's doing or prescribing activities described; in Set V, scale reflects relative amount of knowledge.

Comparisons between Groups. A discriminant analysis procedure (Cooley & Loehnes, 1962) was used to compare group responses to sets of variables. This procedure indicated whether profiles of groups across a set of items were similar or different. If such initial analysis indicated that groups responded in a significantly different fashion to such sets, an analysis of variance was utilized to determine whether groups differed significantly in their responses to specific items. Duncan's multiple-range test was utilized to compare group means on individual items. Tables 2 and 3 present group means on variable sets found significant by discriminant analysis procedure.

Comparisons by Years of Teaching Experience. A comparison of the responses of teachers grouped by level of experience indicates that novices and veterans have significantly different perceptions of Treatment Management ($p < .05$). With somewhat less confidence it can be suggested that they differ in their views of the Types of Treatment which are likely to occur ($p < .10$). Comparing group means it is found that inexperienced teachers expect just recommendations more often than experienced teachers ($p < .05$). Those with a moderate amount of teaching experience expect just recommendations more often than do either inexperienced or experienced teachers ($p < .05$). Conversely, teachers with a moderate amount of experience expect the psychologist to actually conduct treatment less often than do experienced teachers ($p < .05$).

Concerning the types of treatment likely to result from the psychologist's involvement, experienced teachers predict the transfer of a child out of the regular classroom more often than their inexperienced colleagues ($p < .05$), while they predict the use of classroom behavioral techniques more than moderately experienced and inexperienced teachers.

Comparison by Use of Psychological Services. Grouped according to the frequency to which they have utilized psychological personnel, we find that teachers differ in their responses to only one variable set - Set II, Diagnostic Activities ($p < .001$). The main factor distinguishing groups is whether they have or have not had contact with psychologists: differences do not fall along a continuum of contact. Teachers with no psychologist contact credit them with studying cumulative records, discussing the problem with the teacher, observing the child in the class, and talking with the child's parents more than do teachers who have worked with psychological personnel ($p < .05, .05, .001, .001$). (See Table 3.)

138

Table 2
Discriminant Analysis and Analysis of Variance

| Item | Mean | | | F-Ratio |
	Inexperienced (N = 13)	Moderately Experienced (N = 9)	Experienced (N = 11)	
Set III[a]				
14	3.23	3.78	3.91	1.14
15	3.23	3.22	4.18	3.64*
16	2.54	3.33	3.54	4.62*
17	3.77	4.11	4.00	.53
18	3.46	3.89	3.91	.73
19	3.23	2.89	3.73	1.72
Set IV[b]				
20	4.23	4.89	3.36	9.95**
21	2.15	1.89	3.00	2.27
22	1.84	1.33	2.54	3.07*

[a]Discriminant Analysis: F-Ratio = 1.73

[b]Discriminant Analysis: F-Ratio = 2.38*

* $p < .05$

** $p < .01$

Teachers' Recommendations. Teachers were asked what changes they would recommend in the school psychological services. More than 85% of the participants made multiple recommendations. The percentage of teachers offering six somewhat distinct types of recommendations is reported in Table 4. Thirty-six percent of the teachers specifically requested that their school be assigned a full-time psychologist. The theme which was most consistently voiced in conjunction with this recommendation was not speed of services but a wish for consistent and long-term involvement of psychological personnel. One third of the teachers strongly recommended that the time between referral and psychologist's involvement be drastically reduced. In striking correspondence with professional writings they suggested that if psychological personnel could not become involved with school problems as they occurred, their effectiveness was seriously hampered. An equal number of teachers suggested a variety of changes in "treatment procedures." Some teachers asked for more recommendations; others discouraged the use of recommendations because they were usually either "outdated" or impractical for the classroom setting.

139

Teachers suggested that psychometrists and psychologists become
more directly involved with teacher and child (and perhaps family)
in planning and effecting any treatment. Almost 25% of the
teachers simply requested more teacher-psychologist contact. A
smaller but significant proportion of teachers recommended an increase in the percent of parent-psychologist contacts. In summary,
these recommendations indicate that teachers want more psychological
services and desire some change in the methods characteristic of
school psychological services-especially as such methods affect the
treatment of child learning problems.

Table 3
Discriminant Analysis and Analysis of Variance

| Item | Mean | | | F-Ratio |
	No Contact (N = 8)	Moderate Contact (N = 13)	High Contact (N = 12)	
8	4.25	3.08	2.58	4.70*
9	3.88	2.46	2.75	3.09*
11	3.50	1.46	1.75	9.47**
13	3.88	2.08	1.67	10.96**

* $p < .05$
** $p < .001$

Table 4
Teachers' Recommendations

	Recommendation	Percent of Respondents Recommending
1.	The school to be assigned its own staff psychologist	36
2.	Reduction of time between referral and action	33
3.	Changes in treatment procedures and/or recommendations	33
4.	An increase of teacher-psychologist contact	25
5.	An increase in parent-psychologist contacts	18
6.	Modification of diagnostic procedures	15

DISCUSSION

Perhaps the most important summarizing statement generated by these findings is that it is inappropriately deceptive to discuss teachers' perceptions of school psychological services in terms of the average teacher. The two simple groups (by number of years of experience and by degree of past use of psychological personnel) utilized in the present analyses illustrate that teachers have quite varied and diverse perceptions of the school psychologist. In part, this reflects the diversity of viewpoints in the literature of what the school psychologist's role is and ought to be. More importantly, the differences between groups suggest that teachers' perceptions of the psychologist change as a result of their experience, both as teachers and as personnel working with psychologists.

There is some support of Baker's (1965) findings that more experienced teachers report greater teacher-psychologist contact than less experienced teachers. In this study the veteran teachers expected more than mere recommendations and credited the psychologist with actually conducting the treatment more than did less experienced teachers. It may be that veteran teachers have more skills in using the psychologist effectively, or that psychologists feel that they can draw upon the teaching expertise of the veteran.

Another important finding is that teacher perceptions grouped by degree of use of psychologists differ significantly on the basis of whether they have used a psychologist or not rather than varying on a continuum. It is noted that teachers with no experience with psychological personnel have a more roseate view than teachers with experience, in keeping with Baker's (1965) findings that the confidence placed in the psychological services by teachers actually showed a slight decline once the service had been rendered.

There is also concurrence with earlier research that teachers see the psychologist as more competent in dealing with emotional problems and less competent in classroom management. This view of school psychologists as more emotional-problem oriented than either training programs or supervisors would allow (Kirschner, 1971) suggests a major discrepancy in role perception. The apparent incongruity between the demand for more contact, on the one hand, and low rating of psychologists' helpfulness once contact has been established, on the other, offers a hypothesis: such dissatisfaction does not refer to psychological services per se but to the current emphasis on diagnosis rather than on intervention.

Implications. This study has three limitations: the small sample; the fact that an interview procedure, even structured, allows for unmeasured experimenter effects; and the survey was conducted in a single school district. Therefore, the findings can be generalized only with great caution. However, the results of this study are of enough significance to provide implications for both the practitioner and the trainer. The psychologist in the schools must recognize that such services are being offered to educational personnel who entertain set views about him which indeed affect his functioning.

An analogous message is appropriate for those involved in the training of school psychologists. Furthermore, such trainers need to recognize that teachers are in part calling for what is typically labeled "consultation," but more consistently they are asking that school psychologists stretch their present involvement from diagnosis to actual involvement in the design and conduct of intervention.

References

Baker, H.L. Psychological services: From the school staff's point of view. Journal of School Psychology, 1965, 3, 36-42.
Cooley, W.W., & Loehnes, P.R. Multivariate procedures for the behavioral science. New York: John Wiley & Sons, 1962.
Fifield, M. The role of school psychology in public education. Psychology in the Schools, 1967, 4, 66-68.
Fine, M.J., & Tyler, M.M. Concerns and directions in teacher consultation. Journal of School Psychology, 1971, 9, 436-444.
Gross, F.P., & Farling, W.A. An analysis of case loads of school psychologists. Psychology in the Schools, 1969, 6, 98-100.
Handler, L., Gertson, A., & Handler, B. Suggestions for improved psychologist-teacher communication. Psychology in the Schools, 1965, 2, 77-81.
Iscoe, I., Pierce-Jones, J., Friedman, S.T., & McGehearty, L. Source strategies in mental health consultation: A brief description of a project and some preliminary results. In E. Cowen, E.A. Gardner, & M. Zax (Eds.), Emergent approaches to mental health problems. New York: Appleton-Century-Crofts, 1967, Pp. 307-330.
Kirschner, F.E. School psychology as viewed by the supervisor of school psychological services. Journal of School Psychology, 1971, 9, 343-346.
Lucas, M.S., & Jones, R.L. Attitudes of teachers of mentally retarded children toward psychological reports and services. Journal of School Psychology, 1970, 8, 122-130.
Mumford, E. Promises and disaffections in mental health programs in schools. Psychology in the Schools, 1970, 7, 20-28.
Roberts, R.D. Perceptions of actual and desired role functions of school psychologists by psychologists and teachers. Psychology

in the Schools, 1970, 7, 175-178.

Shaw, M.C. Role delineation among the guidance professions, Psychology in the Schools, 1967, 4, 3-13.

Styles, W.A. Teachers' perceptions of the school psychologists' role. Journal of School Psychology, 1965, 3, 23-27.

Wolman, T.G. Implications of social change for school psychology. Psychology in the Schools, 1967, 4, 68-70.

EDUCATORS DESCRIBE THE SCHOOL PSYCHOLOGIST

George E. Gilmore and Jean M. Chandy

A general, two-pronged hypothesis characterizes theoretical and empirical literature concerned with the school psychologist's role (Bardon, 1963; Fifield, 1967; Mumford, 1970; Shaw, 1967; Wolman, 1967). In brief, it is suggested that the school psychologist's functioning is affected by his own self-definition (Dansinger, 1969; Gross & Farling, 1969; Knowles & Shertzer, 1968; Roberts, 1970) and by the role functions allocated to him by varied personnel: state boards of education (Baker, 1965; Lucas & Jones, 1970), university faculty (Barclay, 1965; Rudnick & Berkowitz, 1968), and school administrators and supervisors (Kitschner, 1971). Several studies assume that the views of teachers are of prime significance. Investigators usually ask how the teacher views the psychologist's competencies, appropriate role, and usefulness (Baker, 1965; Roberts, 1970; Styles, 1965). The wide range of teacher responses reported in these studies indicates the necessity to differentiate the perceptions and attitudes of various teacher groups.

The present study examines the perceptions of varied teacher groups, as well as those of psychologists and school administrators (principals). The effects of school size and economic status of the school on perceptions of the psychologist's role are evaluated. A previous study (Gilmore & Chandy, 1973) contrasted responses of teachers classified on two dimensions: amount of teaching experience and frequency of professional contacts with school psychologists. Comparisons were made on five sets of variables: (a) type of learning problem that merited referral; (b) diagnostic activities of psychologists; (c) types of treatment; (d) treatment management, and (e) psychologists' skills. Not surprisingly, this survey of a small number of teachers ($N = 33$) indicated that psychologists are viewed as specialists in emotional rather than academic problems with relatively less skill in classroom management, whose major

SOURCE. Reprinted from Psychology in the Schools, 1973, X, 4, 397-403. By permission of the authors and Clinical Psychology Publishing Co., Inc.

diagnostic procedure is testing, who recommended treatment but
do little themselves. There was some support of earlier research
(e.g., Baker, 1965) in that experienced teachers reported that they
had been involved to a greater degree by the psychologist in diagnosis and management than did newer teachers and that teachers with
less experience with psychological personnel expected more psychologist involvement in treatment than did teachers more experienced
in the use of psychological personnel.

The initial study has several limitations. The sample, while
examined intensively (97% responded to an individual interview),
was small. The participants represented only two schools within
a large, multifaceted school district, and the structured interview
procedure allowed for an undetermined experimenter effect. The
sample selected precluded comparisons according to the economic
status of the school. Several significant groups, such as principals and psychologists, were not included, hence no examination
could be made of discrepancies in role perception of the several
types of school personnel involved.

A major goal of the present study was to obtain more representative and generalizable data, as well as to study the effects of
additional factors. There also was a need to replicate earlier
research that presented a somewhat ambiguous picture. For example,
while one study (Styles, 1965) reports that teachers experienced
with psychological services rate these services higher, other
studies (Baker, 1965; Gilmore & Chandy, 1973) suggest that favorable perception declines after usage. In addition to the five
variable sets listed earlier, three variable sets were employed.
These sought answers to the following questions: (a) Is the
psychologist seen mainly as a tester or as one who possesses a
broader range of skills in the psychoeducational domain? (b) How
serious should a problem be before psychologists become involved?
(c) How helpful to themselves and to the child do teachers find the
psychologist?

METHOD

Sample
     Nine schools took part in this investigation; four qualify as
Title I schools and are located in economically depressed sections
of the district. The remaining five schools are located in the
middle-class or upper-middle-class sections of the district. Schools
range in size from 260 to just under 800 students. Eight-seven percent of the faculty (92 Title I teachers and 100 non-Title I teachers),
7 of the 9 principals, and all 12 of the district's school psychologists completed the questionnaire (Total N = 211).

145

Instrument

Data were obtained through the use of a questionnaire that was group-administered to the faculty of each school. The instrument contained 37 multiple choice questions, each of which used a 5-point scale and allowed for anonymity (see Appendix A). Administration time averaged 15 minutes.

Procedure

Teacher particiapnts were grouped consecutively on two dimensions: according to the number of years of teaching experience (4 or less = inexperienced; 5 to 9 years = moderately experienced; 10 or more years = experienced). Secondly, teachers were grouped according to the degree to which they reported the use of psychological services (never = no contact; 1 to 3 time per year = moderate contact; 4 or more times per year = high contact). Schools were grouped according to (a) socioeconomic status (Title I or non-Title I) and (b) size (large = above, and small = below the median size of 590). Finally, responses of participants were compared according to their role as principal, teacher, or psychologist.

A discriminant analysis procedure (Cooley & Lohnes, 1962) was used to compare group responses to the eight variable sets. This procedure indicated whether profiles of groups across a set of items were similar or different. An analysis of variance was performed on those group responses that were significantly differenct. Group means on individual items were compared by means of t-tests.

RESULTS

When in the following summary of results the differences between three groups are noted, the relevant statistics (t-score, degrees of freedom, and probability level) will be reported in the order in which such multiple comparisons are described.

Comparisons by Teaching Experience

Teachers of varying experience agree on the type of child who most needs psychological referral - the behavioral problem - and on the degree of psychologist involvement in treatment - very little. While they perceive the psychologist's diagnostic work similarly in most respects, their views of one diagnostic activity, namely testing, are clearly different. The moderately experienced and veteran teachers more often than newer teachers expect the psychologist to test ($t = 2.33$, $df = 85$, $p < .05$; $t = 2.88$, $df = 117$, $p < .01$) and to talk with the principal in response to a referred problem ($t = 2.17$, $df = 86$, $p < .05$; $t = 2.01$, $df = 117$, $p < .05$). Teaching experience affects perception of type of treatment likely to occur as a consequence of the psychologist's involvement.

146

New teachers expect less curricular change than do their moderately experienced colleagues (t = 2.17, df = 85, $p<.05$). Similarly, veteran more often than novice teachers anticipate that the psychologist's involvement will result in the referral of parents to some counseling service (t = 2.30, df = 117, $p<.05$). Both moderately experienced and veteran teachers expect that the psychologist will recommend that a child be placed outside of the regular classroom more often than do their novice colleagues (t = 2.18, df = 85, $p<.05$, t = 2.25, df = 117, $p<.05$). In contrast, newer teachers expect the utilization of special in-school programs, such as language learning laboratories, more often than do either moderately or highly experienced teachers (t = 2.38, df = 85, $p< .05$, t = 2.31, df = 117, $p<.05$). Finally, the moderately experienced compared to veteran teachers more frequently perceive the psychologist as helpful to the child (t = 2.34, df = 113, $p<.05$) and to teachers (t = 2.32, df = 113, $p<.05$).

Comparisons of Teachers According to Prior Use of Psychologists
    Teaching experience itself apparently is unrelated to the way in which the psychologist is used; however, prior use of the psychologist is found to be a significant factor that affects the teachers' perception of the psychologist in the specific role of test administrator vs. the more general role of psychoeducational consultant. Both moderate- and high-psychologist-contact teachers are more likely than those with no contact to view the psychologist in the less restrictive role (t = 2.02, df = 99, $p<.05$; t = 4.22, df = 89, $p<.001$). Similarly, high-contact teachers are more likely than those with only moderate contact to consider the psychologist as a consultant rather than simply as a test administrator (t = 2.75, df = 117, $p<.01$). Teachers who vary in prior psychologist contact also differ in their evaluation of the services rendered. Those with no psychologist contact consider the psychologist a greater help to children than do either moderate- or high-contact teachers (t = 1.99, df = 99, $p<.05$; t = 2.28, df = 89, $p<.05$).

Comparison by School Characteristics
    As measured by the present instrument, school size does not affect a faculty's perception of psychological services. In contrast, the socioeconomic status of the school is found to be of major significance. While the diagnostic procedures followed by the psychologist are seen to be the same by the staffs as Title I and non-Title I schools, the types of intervention expected to result differ. Personnel and Title I schools have lower expectations that psychological involvement will result in parental referral (t = 2.68, df = 157, $p<.01$), curricular change (t = 2.60, df = 157, $p<.01$), or the implementation of behavioral control procedures (t = 4.55, df = 157, $p<.001$). Teachers in the Title I schools feel that the psychologist knows less about emotional development (t = 2.03, df = 157, $p<.05$) or classroom management (t = 2.24, df = 157, $p<.05$), and they view the psychologist as a tester rather than as

147

a consultant more than do non-Title I teachers (t = 2.66, df = 157, $p < .01$). In simple terms, these findings indicate that the faculties at schools of measurable lower SES attribute fewer and more restricted skills to the school psychologist.

Comparison of Teachers, Principals, and Psychologists

Principals and psychologists view the psychologist as a consultant more frequently than do teachers (t = 2.30, df = 164, $p < .05$; t = 2.71, df = 170, $p < .01$). Psychologists feel that a school problem need only be mild, while more teachers suggest that it should be at least relatively serious before psychological personnel become involved (t = 2.63, df = 170, $p < .01$). Psychological personnel credit themselves more frequently than do teachers with studying cumulative folders (t = 2.44, df = 170, $p < .05$) discussing problems with teachers, (t = 2.83, df = 170, $p < .01$) and understanding a child's emotional development (t = 2.47, df = 170, $p < .05$).

Compared to teachers, both principals and psychologists attribute more knowledge to the psychologist concerning classroom management (t = 2.77, df = 164, $p < .01$; t = 2.00, df = 170, $p < .05$) and the understanding of children's abilities (t = 2.88, df = 164, $p < .01$; t = 2.05, df = 164, $p < .05$). However, principals and teachers feel that the psychologist is more knowledgeable about teaching than do the psychologists themselves (t = 2.94, df = 164, $p < .01$; t = 2.49, df = 170, $p < .05$).

DISCUSSION

Results from the two studies generally concur; however, several findings illustrate statistically significant differences in the larger study that emerged only as trends in the earlier work. While it is possible that the interview procedure allowed more personal in-depth information to emerge from the initial study, the more representative sampling and anonymity of respondents encourage discussion and recommendations to be based essentially on these findings.

Experienced teachers have higher expectations for interventions which, while more varied, are also more traditional. Such tradititional interventions frequently involve exclusion of the referred child from the regular classroom or school. Newer teachers are looking for more novel interventions, such as the use of in-school and in-class services. This contemporary-traditional dimension is also suggested in terms of teachers' understanding of assessment. It is the veteran teacher who most frequently looks for the psychologist with test kit in hand.

When the responses of the several teacher groups to the eight variable sets are compared, more differences are found in the variable set labeled "types of treatment" than in any other set. These findings strongly suggest that while the psychologist's data-gathering

148

procedures may vary little as he works with different groups of teachers (e.g., experienced or inexperienced), what he does with his findings is influenced substantially by the personnel with whom he works (e.g., any treatment whatever, in- or out-of-class interventions.

An important conclusion may be drawn from this study: the frequency with which teachers contact psychologists is positively related to their functioning, both as examiners and as psychoeducational consultants. Those who know psychologists are prepared to employ them in both roles. However, support is given to the findings of earlier studies (Baker, 1965; Gilmore & Chandy, 1973) in that even limited teacher-psychologist contact deflates the value attributed to psychological personnel. The incongruence with the Styles (1965) study may be explained by the fact that his sample consisted of special education teachers, who because of their training may have had more success in understanding and implementing the psychologist's recommendations than did regular classroom teachers, who served as Ss in the other studies.

It is clear that principals and psychologists attribute greater utility and skills to the psychologists than do teachers. This agrees with earlier findings that teachers attribute less skill in classroom management to the psychologist than does the psychologist himself (Roberts, 1970). Since the majority of problem-solving encounters are teacher-psychologist, these findings have some operational implications. The psychologist either can attempt to bolster his abilities in the eyes of teachers or, perhaps more productively, take the teachers' perspective seriously and approach school problems with a recognition of the teacher as a genuine colleague with educational expertise that the psychologist himself may not enjoy.

The differences perceived by Title I and non-Title I teachers are worthy of note. The results indicate that psychologists make different kinds of treatment recommendations depending upon the economic status of the population that is being served. There are no data available to answer the question: are such differences appropriate to the varied populations, or are they the consequence of differences in funding, bias, or prejudice, or, more simply, a result of the difficulty that psychologists encounter when they are working within differenct cultures?

Three major recommendations emanate from these studies. (a) Psychologists, teachers, and principals would profit from short-term joint training programs designed to communicate both complimentary and contradictory needs, expectations, and skills. Some support for this is noted in that recently trained teachers seem more ready to use the newer assessment and intervention procedures that are being introduced into the system by psychologists. (b) The data presented in the bulk of studies should encourage future research to turn from the study of perceptions to the study of actual psychologist behaviors. (c) Obviously, the apparent effect of the economic status of a school population on psychoeducational interventions merits intensive study.

APPENDIX A
A Questionnaire Designed to Assess Teacher Perceptions of Psychological Services

INSTRUCTIONS: For each of the following questions circle one response which best fits you or your view of school psychological services. Psychological services is really a broad term including many diverse roles and personnel but for this study school psychological service refers only to the activities of psychometrists, school psychologists, and school psychology interns.

1. What is your usual professional activity in schools?
   (a) teacher, (b) principal, (c) visiting teacher, (d) resource teacher, (e) counselor, (f) psychometrist, (g) other (please describe).

2. If you are a teacher, please indicate the grade or grade levels you are teaching this year.
   (a) grade 1, (b) grade 2, (c) grade 3, (d) grade 4, (e) grade 5, (f) grade 6, (g) other (please describe briefly).

3. How long have you worked in education either as teacher, administrator, or specialized personnel?
   (a) 1 year or less, (b) 2 or 3 years, (c) 4 or 5 years, (d) 5 to 10 years, (e) more than 10 years.

4. How long have you worked in the . . . . Independent School District?
   (a) 1 year or less, (b) 2 or 3 years, (c) 4 or 5 years, (d) 5 to 10 years, (e) more than 10 years.

5. How often during the past year (1971-1972) have you used the psychologist or as a psychologist have your services been used mainly to have a child tested or evaluated?
   (a) never, (b) occasionally, (c) about half of the time, (d) usually, (e) always.

6. How often during the past year (1971-1972) have you used the psychologist or as a psychologist have your services been used mainly as an advisor or consultant who did not test the child? (Use response scale given for Question 5).

150

7. In the following question six different kinds of child-learning problems are described. For each type of problem check one response which indicates how strongly you feel that such children should be referred for school psychological services. Check one of the following responses for each description; (a) Yes, such children should always be referred to the school psychometrist or psychologist, (b) such children should usually be referred, (c) sometimes they should be referred, sometimes not, (d) such children should only be referred rarely, (e) no, such children should not be referred to the psychometrist or psychologist.

    I.   Children with apparent emotional problems. For instance, children who seem to be extremely anxious or show unreasonable fears.

    II. Children who seem to be bright enough but are just not achieving well academically.

    III. Children who appear to be retarded or very slow.

    IV. Children who present serious behavioral problems in class. For instance, the child who causes a ruckus in the room that is disturbs other children.

    V. The intellectually gifted child who very quickly masters the learning expected for a child his age.

    VI. Children who are managing school adequately, but have serious problems outside of school. For instance, the child who is having trouble with his family or in his neighborhood.

8. With which of the following kinds of children can the school psychometrist or school psychologist be most helpful? (I) emotionally troubled children, (II) low achievers, (III) the retarded, (IV) behavior problems, (V) intellectually gifted, (VI) children with out-of-school problems.

9. How serious would you say a child's problem should be before it is a good idea to involve someone from the school's psychological services? (a) quite severe, (b) just serious, (c) moderate, (d) less serious, but noticeable, (e) mild.

10. Once a request has been made, how long will it be before some action is begun by the school psychometrist or psychologist? (a) less than two weeks, (b) between two weeks and a month, (c) about 2 months, (d) about a semester, (e) more than a semester.

11. When attempting to deal with a child's problem the psychometrist or psychologist may do a variety of things. How much would you estimate that they do each of the following (use the following response scale: (a) very little, (b) a little, (c) somewhat, (d) a good deal, (e) very much):

      I.   Study the child's cumulative record?
     II.   Discuss the problem with the child's teacher?
   III.   Talk with the school principal?
    IV.   Observe the child in the classroom?
     V.   Administer psychological tests to the child?
    VI.   Talk with the child's parents or family?

12. Compared to the average teacher (use one of the following responses for each: (a) much less than the average teacher, (b) somewhat less than the average teacher, (c) about as much as the average teacher, (d) somewhat more than the average teacher, (e) a good deal more than the average teacher).
      I.   About how much do psychometrists and psychologists seem to know about teaching?
     II.   About how much do they seem to know about emotional development?
   III.   About managing classroom behavior?
    IV.   About understanding children's school abilities?

13. Below are listed six different treatments which sometimes result from having used the school psychological services. Please check how likely it is that each treatment will occur (use the following response scale: (a) very likely, (b) likely, (c) perhaps, (d) unlikely, (e) very unlikely).
      I.   Design a curricular change for an individual or group of children.
     II.   Develop behavioral control techniques for use in the classroom.
   III.   Transfer the child from the regular classroom.
    IV.   Use some special treatment service, such as speech therapy or a resource room or learning laboratory.
     V.   Refer the child to some outside agency such as a pediatrician or the child guidance clinic.
    VI.   Recommend counseling or some other treatment for the parents.

14. The psychometrist may simply recommend some treatment for a child, may join in with the teacher in giving such treatment, or may conduct the treatment herself. (Use the following response scale for each item: (a) always, (b) usually, (c) sometimes, (d) rarely, (e) never).
      I.   About how often will the psychometrist just make a verbal or written recommendation?
     II.   How often will she join the teacher in developing and carrying out some treatment for the child?
   III.   About how often does the psychometrist actually conduct the treatment of the child herself?

15. Generally speaking how helpful to children are the school psychological services?
    (a) very helpful, (b) helpful, (c) slightly helpful, (d) no help, (e) detrimental.

16. How helpful are these services to the teachers, administrators and other personnel? (Use response scale given in Question 15).

References

Baker, H.L. Psychological services: from the school staff's point of view. Journal of School Psychology, 1965, 3, 36-42.

Barclay, J.R. Descriptive, theoretical and behavioral characteristices of subdoctoral school psychologists. American Psychologist, 1971, 26, 257-280.

Bardon, J.T. Mental health education: a framework for psychological services in the schools. Journal of School Psychology, 1963, 1, 20-27.

Cooley, W.W., & Loehnes, P.R. Multivariate procedures for the behavioral sciences. New York: John Wiley, 1962.

Dansinger, S.S. A five year follow-up study of Minnesota school psychologists. Journal of School Psychology, 1969, 7, 47-53.

Fifield, M. The role of school psychology in public education. Psychology in the Schools, 1967, 4, 66-68.

Gilmore, G.E., & Chandy, J. Teachers' perceptions of school psychological services. Journal of School Psychology, 1973, 2, 140-147.

Gross, F.P., & Farling, W.A. An analysis of case loads of school psychologists. Psychology in the Schools, 1969, 6, 98-100.

Kirschner, F.E. School psychology as viewed by the supervisor or school psychological services. Journal of School Psychology, 1971, 9, 343-346.

Knowles, R.T., & Shertzer, B. Attitudes toward the role of the psychologists and the counselor in the secondary school. Journal of School Psychology, 1968, 7, 40-47.

Lucas, M.S., & Jones, R.L. Attitudes of teachers of mentally retarded children toward psychological reports and services. Journal of School Psychology, 1970, 8, 122-130.

Mumford, E. Promises and disaffections in mental health programs in schools. Psychology in the Schools, 1970, 7, 20-28.

Roberts, R.D. Perceptions of actual and desired role functions of school psychologists by psychologists and teachers. Psychology in the Schools, 1970, 7, 175-178.

Rudnick, M., & Berkowitz, H. Preparation of school psychologists: for what? Psychology in the Schools, 1968, 5, 53-59.

Shaw, M.C. Role delineation among the guidance professions. Psychology in the Schools, 1967, 4, 3-13.

Styles, W.A. Teachers' perceptions of the school psychologists' role. Journal of School Psychology, 1965, 3, 23-27.

Wolman, T.G. Implications of social change for school psychology. Psychology in the Schools, 1967, 4, 68-70.

THE EFFECTS OF LIMITED AND INTENSIVE SCHOOL PSYCHOLOGIST-TEACHER CONSULTATION

Milton M. Tyler and Marvin J. Fine

Summary: Effects of two modes of school psychological consultation were examined against four main outcomes: (1) changes in teacher understanding of the child, (2) the direction of the changes in teacher understanding of the child, (3) teacher satisfaction with consultation, and (4) teacher follow-through on psychologist's recommendations. The two consultative modes were differentiated by the amount of time and by the length and elaboration of the psychological report. Eight school psychologists alternated in acting out the different consultative modes, plus a control condition, with a total of 120 teachers who had referred children. Data were obtained through paper and pencil questionnaires completed pre- and postconsultation by teacher and psychologist. The results strongly supported the intensive over the limited consultation, and any consultation over no consultation.

Effective school psychological consultation has been viewed by many as being closely associated with the teacher's response to the service. Actual changes in teacher attitudes, understanding, or behavior may be the objectives of the consultation. But even if the objectives are more narrowly defined in terms of changes in pupil behavior, the teacher is often the change agent and also the individual most integral to enhancing or defeating implementation of a program initiated by others. Despite the importance of the teacher, the factors within a psychologist-teacher consultation that increase teacher receptivity have remained primarily speculation and opinion.

A study by Kaplan and Sprunger (1967) did attempt to investigate the consultation variable of time spent with the teacher. Its results failed to discriminate between the conditions of more and less time spent, but did support that either of their consultative

SOURCE. Reprinted from Journal of School Psychology, 1974, 12, 1, 8-16. By permission of the author and the publisher. Copyright 1974 by the Journal of School Psychology, Inc. Published by Behavioral Publications, New York.

conditions led to positive changes in the teacher over the condition of no consultation. Unfortunately the Kaplan and Sprunger study was limited in several important respects, including differentiation of the two treatment conditions.

This study is in part a replication of aspects of the Kaplan and Sprunger study, but it has also broadened the scope of inquiry. On a relatively pragmatic level four research questions were posed:

1. Does psychological consultation lead to a change in teacher understanding of the child?
2. If change occurs, does the teacher's understanding of the child become more or less like the psychologist's?
3. To what extent are teachers satisfied with psychological consultation?
4. Does the teacher actually follow through with the psychologist's recommendations?

These four questions actually deal with the outcomes of consultation and as such are dependent variables. The independent variables in this study were two consultation modes that were differentiated primarily in two ways: the amount of time spent with the teacher and the length and elaboration of the report. Eight hypotheses, expressed in null form, were postulated and these will be presented under analysis of data.

METHOD

Participants. Eight Kansas school psychologists agreed to participate in the study as field workers. Each psychologist was to use the next 15 referrals meeting the criteria of the child's not being a special class candidate. This procedure led to the involvement of 120 different teachers and 120 different children. Each teacher and child was involved only once.

Treatments. The term "consultation" has been given varied meanings in the psychological literature and there is no consensus as to common definition. The position assumed in this study was that any professional encounter between psychologist and teacher that required the psychologist to apply his technical skills toward the resolution of some problem could be termed a consultative experience. The actual procedures followed in this study were variations on the referral-child study-report paridigm and were approximations of Caplan's case-centered consultation (Caplan, 1970).

The two consultative treatments employed were labeled the intensive and limited modes. The intensive consultation consisted of (a) a 15- to 24-minute preassessment psychologist-teacher contact, (b) a 30- to 40-minute interpretive, postassessment contact, and (c) a

psychologist's report of at least three double-spaced typewritten
pages detailing the psychologist's findings and itemizing specific
recommendations. This report was submitted at the time of the final
contact. The limited consultation consisted of (a) a five- to ten-
minute preassessment conference, (b) a ten- to 15-minute interpretive, postassessment conference, and (c) a one to one and one-half
page summary report which included a nonelaborated listing of
recommendations.

Aside from the specifications of the two consultative modes,
each school psychologist was free to use whatever diagnostic, interview, or observation procedures he wished. Since cases were randomly
selected and the study focus was on teacher-psychologist interaction,
the actual workups were not deliberately controlled.

A control group was also included and will be discussed in the
next section.

Procedure. Each psychologist was instructed to alternate
sequentially the assignment of referral cases to the two treatment
conditions and to the control group, as the cases were received.
This insured randomization of assignment. Each teacher was then
sent a modified 57-item form of the S.R.A. Youth Inventory (Remmers,
1951) to complete and return on the referred child. This instrument
was used in the Kaplan and Sprunger study (1967) and was found appropriate for eliciting teacher perceptions of a child. The instructions
to each teacher stated that the child was selected to be a part of a
study. The teacher was then asked to complete the inventory from
the viewpoint of the child.

Following the completion of the inventory the psychologist pro-
ceeded to act out the predetermined consultation with that teacher.
It was estimated that each consultation would cover approximately a
two-week period. At the termination of consultation the teacher was
asked again to complete the modified S.R.A. Inventory and also an
eight-item questionnaire that focused on such things as teacher satisfaction with the time spent by the psychologist, teacher estimate
of the psychologist's helpfulness, and teacher beliefs as to the
psychologist's interest. Each of the eight items was rated on a
five-point scale.

The control teachers were sent the S.R.A. Inventory after they
were initially identified and again after a two-week period, but
they had no contact with the psychologist during the duration of the
study. The teacher instructions for completing the Inventory the
second time were similar to the first occasion. While it might be
anticipated that the control teachers would be frustrated by having
to complete the Inventory a second time without having received any
service, there were no reported difficulties and a high percentage

of the Inventories were returned. An effort was made to offer the control teachers psychological services as soon as possible after the two-week lapse.

Following his workup of the referred child, the psychologist also completed the S.R.A. Inventory. In every case the Inventory was completed from the point of view of the child and therefore represented an indice of teacher and psychologist understanding of that child.

One week after termination of consultation the psychologist visited the teacher to discuss the implementation of his recommendations. Then the psychologist completed a five-point rating scale on the extent of teacher implementation of the recommendation.

Eleven of the total of 120 teachers failed to complete their questionnaires adequately and those data were deleted from the study. For most of the analyses the sample was composed of 36 teachers in the limited consultation group, 35 teachers in the intensive consultation group, and 38 teachers in the control group. On the last analysis requiring psychologist rating of the teachers, the total sample of 40 teachers per consultation group was used, since this data had been obtained satisfactorily in total from the participating psychologists.

ANALYSIS AND RESULTS

The concern of the first three hypotheses was simply whether the different treatments would relate to quantitative changes as measured by the S.R.A. Inventory. A change was noted if from pre- to post-inventory an item was added or deleted.

One-way analysis of variance (Guilford, 1965) was used to test null hypotheses one through three which state that there will be no difference in change scores between limited, intensive, and control groups, pre- to posttest scores on the S.R.A. Inventory.

Hypotheses one through three:

1. There will be no significant difference in the quantity of change of teacher understanding of the child between groups of teachers receiving limited psychological consultation and no psychological consultation.

Table 1
Pre- to Posttreatment Change Score Data

Group	Intensive (N=35)	Limited (N=36)	Control (N=38)
X	19.77	15.63	10.54
SD	7.36	7.12	4.03

2. There will be no significant difference in the quantity of change of teacher understanding of the child between groups of teachers receiving intensive psychological consultation and no psychological consultation.

3. There will be no significant difference in the quantity of change of teacher understanding of the child between groups of teachers receiving limited and intensive psychological consultation.

This means and standard deviations of change scores for the intensive, limited, and control groups are presented in Table 1.

The F value of 17.99, significant at the .01 level, indicated that differences existed among the three groups (see Table 2).

To test for differences between means, the Tukey test for gaps (Myers, 1966) was applied. As shown in Table 3, differences between means for all groups were significant beyond the .01 level.

Since the mean differences were significant between the limited and control groups, the intensive and control groups, and the limited and intensive groups, hypotheses one, two, and three were all rejected at the .01 level of confidence.

The next three hypotheses were concerned with the direction of change in the S.R.A. ratings. To obtain the relevant data, first the teacher pretreatment S.R.A. Inventory was compared with the psychologist's S.R.A. Inventory and the number of agreements were noted. This procedure was repeated with the teacher posttreatment S.R.A. Inventory. The "t" test analysis then focused on examining the differences between pre- and posttreatment agreement scores for the experimental and control groups.

Hypotheses four, five, and six:

4. There will be no significant differences between the pre- and post-consultation teacher-psychologist agreement in

understanding of the child of the teachers receiving limited consultation.

Table 2
Analysis of Variance of SRA Change Scores
for Limited, Intensive, and Control Groups

Source of Variation	Sums of Squares	Df	Mean Square	F
Treatment	1,495.60	2	747.80	17.99**
Within Treatment (error)	4,241.03	102	41.58	
Total	5,736.63	104		

** $p < .01$

Table 3
Tukey Analysis of Differences between Means for the
Limited, Intensive and Control Groups

Group	Control	Limited
Limited	5.09**	
Intensive	9.23**	4.14**

** $p < .01$

5. There will be no significant differences between pre- and postconsultation teacher-psychologist agreement in understanding of the child of the teachers receiving intensive consultation.

6. There will be no significant difference between the change of positive agreement with the psychologist's understanding of the child of teachers receiving the limited and intensive consultations.

The results of related t test (Guilford, 1965) analyses between teacher pre- and postconsultation S.R.A. agreement scores with psychologist S.R.A. scores for both the limited and the intensive groups are presented in Table 4. The t value for the limited group was .89, indicating no significant difference in change scores from pre- to posttesting. This permitted the acceptance of hypothesis four. The intensive group, however, changed significantly from pre- to posttesting. The t value of 2.29 for the intensive group was beyond the .05 level of confidence, which required rejection of hypothesis five.

The results of the unrelated t test analysis between agreement gains scores of the limited and intensive groups is shown in Table 5.

The obtained t value of 1.96 failed to reach significance at the level of confidence, leading to the acceptance of hypothesis six.

Table 4
"t" Test Analysis of Teacher-Psychologist SRA
Agreement Scores, Pre- and Postconsultation

Group	Agreement Scores				t
	Preconsultation		Postconsultation		
	$\overline{X}$	S.D.	$\overline{X}$	S.D.	
Limited (N = 36)	28.83	7.52	31.09	8.83	.89
Intensive (N = 35)	30.80	9.75	35.29	11.39	2.29*

*p<.05

Table 5
Analysis of Agreement Gains Scores

Group	Limited (N = 35)	Intensive (N = 36)	t
$\overline{X}$	2.26	4.49	1.96
SD	3.99	5.38	

An additional concern of the study was to examine teacher attitude toward the school psychologist in relation to limited and intensive consultation. An eight-item instrument was accordingly designed to determine teacher's attitudes concerning the two modes of consultation.

The median test (Siegel, 1956) was used to test null hypothesis seven.

Hypothesis seven:

161

7. There will be no significant difference regarding satisfaction with psychological consultation among groups of teachers receiving limited and intensive consultation.

Each subject's total score for all eight questions was first derived and analyzed with the Median test. The analysis yielded a chi square value of 17.34, which for one degree of freedom exceeded the critical value at the .01 level of confidence, and accordingly hypothesis seven was rejected. These results indicated that the teachers receiving intensive consultation were more satisfied with the psychologist's services than were teachers receiving limited consultation.

In addition, the Kilmogorov-Smirnov two-sample test (Siegel, 1956) was employed to examine differences between the limited and intensive groups on each of the eight questions of the instrument. These data are summarized in Table 6.

Analysis of the teachers' responses on all questions except question 4 yielded K values sufficiently high so that the differences found between the intensive and limited groups' scores on these questions were significant statistically at the .01 level of confidence. On question 4 there was no statistical significance between intensive and limited group scores.

Both the overall analysis and the analysis by question yielded highly significant differences between the limited and intensive groups' scores regarding their satisfaction with the school psychologists' services. These results indicate that teachers receiving intensive consultation were generally more satisfied with the school psychologists' services than were the teachers of the limited group.

The final concern of the study was to examine the extent of teacher follow-through of psychologists' recommendations in relation to the mode of consultation. Each of the eight school psychologists rated each of their participating teachers in the limited and intensive groups one week following the interpretive conference. The teachers were rated on a five-point scale ranging from no implementation of psychologists' recommendations through maximum implementation.

Hypothesis eight:

8. There will be no significant difference between the extent of follow-through on psychologists' recommendations between groups of teachers receiving limited and intensive consultation.

162

Table 6

Kolmogorov-Smirnov Two-Sample Test of Differences
between Intensive and Limited Group Scores of
Teacher Satisfaction with Psychologists'
Services by Question

Question	K Value[1]
1. The school psychologist's interest in my problems	K = 12**
2. The school psychologist's interest in my point of view regarding the referred child	K = 11**
3. The helpfulness of the psychologist regarding my understanding of the child	K = 10**
4. The helpfulness of the psychologist's written report	K = 5
5. The amount of time spent in conference with the psychologist	K = 19**
6. The helpfulness of the psychologist's recommendations	K = 9**
7. The applicability of the psychologist's recommendations	K = 11**
8. The psychologist's overall helpfulness	K = 11**

**$p < .01$

[1]All of the significant K values were in favor of the intensive group.

A summary of the school psychologists' ratings of the degree of teacher implementation of psychologists' recommendations for both the limited and the intensive groups is shown in Table 7.

Table 7

Ratings of Teacher Follow-Through
on Psychologist Recommendations

Scale Value	Limited	Intensive
5	11	12
4	10	15
3	9	7
2	6	6
1	4	0

163

The Mann Whitney U technique (Siegel, 1956) yielded a U value of eight, which failed to reach the level of significance required to reject hypothesis eight at the .05 level of confidence. Therefore hypothesis eight was accepted.

The findings were generally in favor of the intensive over the limited contacts between psychologist and teacher. In relation to the intensive experience, teachers changed more in their understanding of the child and significantly in the direction of greater agreement with the school psychologist. Also, the teacher indicated greater satisfaction with the intensive experience.

As to the fourth question on teacher follow-through, it is interesting to note that while statistical significance was not obtained, the data quantitatively were supportive of the intensive mode of consultation. Also, each of the consultation modes seemed to have led to rather substantial teacher follow-through. The findings of no significant difference between the two consultation modes and the rather substantial follow-through by both groups need some qualification.

Since the psychologists were responsible for the ratings, the possibility of bias definitely exists. These psychologists were aware of which teachers were in the respective consultation groups and possibly were inclined to favor the intensive mode. A counter bias, however, would likely have been the psychologist's desire to see substantial teacher follow-through regardless of consultative mode. Even if the psychologists attempted to control their personal biases, the teachers may have had some reluctance to communicate a lack of good follow-through. A more objective means of assessing teacher behavior ought to be utilized in future studies to bypass the potential biasing of reports by involved psychologists and teachers

Literature regarding the characteristics of a facilitative relationship contributed toward attempts to explain the several findings of this study. Certainly, the psychologist's willingness to spend the amount of time with the teachers necessitated by the intensive mode of consultation was valued by them, as shown by their response to the teacher questionnaire on satisfaction with psychological services. A productive direction for future research may be to examine more closely the nature of a facilitative relationship between psychologist and teacher. Such factors as the psychologist's theoretical orientation to service and the extent to which the teacher perceives his possessing Rogers' (1959) facilitative characteristics could be studied and would bring some theoretical bases to an otherwise pragmatically studied area.

As stated earlier, this study was in part a replication of the Kaplan and Sprunger (1967) study. Its findings will be reviewed as they relate to the current study. Kaplan and Sprunger found that both the limited and intensive modes of consultation led to significant changes in teacher understanding of the child, but that there was no significant difference in change of understanding between the two treatment groups. The current study also found that both limited and intensive consultation led to significant changes in teacher understanding of the child; however, a significant difference was obtained between the treatments, with the intensive group revealing significantly greater changes over that of the limited group.

Another finding of the Kaplan and Sprunger was that both modes of consultation led teachers to view the child significantly more as the psychologist viewed him. Significant difference in this change of agreement with the psychologist were not obtained between treatment groups. The current investigation obtained somewhat different findings. The intensive group did change significantly in the direction of the psychologist's understanding of the child, while the limited group did not change significantly in this direction.

This study supported the basic thesis of the Kaplan and Sprunger study that school psychological consultation does have an impact upon the teacher. But this study seemed to be showing greater discrimination in results as related to the two treatments. One criticism levied against the Kaplan and Sprunger study was its difficulty in really implementing two separate treatments. The reported findings were interpreted as giving support to this criticism, since greater control over differentiation of treatment was a characteristic of the current study.

References
_____

Caplan, G. Theory and practice of mental health consultation. New
    York: Basic Books, 1970.
Guilford, J.P. Fundamental statistics in psychology and education.
    New York: McGraw-Hill, 1965.
Kaplan, M., & Sprunger, B. Psychological evaluations and teacher
    perceptions of students. Journal of School Psychology, 1967,
    5, 287-291.
Myers, J.L. Fundamentals of experimental design. Boston: Allyn
    and Bacon, 1966.
Remmers, H.H. S.R.A. Youth Inventory. Chicago: Science Research
    Associates, 1951.

Rogers, C.R. Significant learning: In therapy and in education. *Educational Leadership*, 1959, 16, 232-242.

Siegel, S. *Nonparametric statistics for the behavioral sciences.* New York: McGraw-Hill, 1956.

TRANSITION IN SCHOOL PSYCHOLOGICAL SERVICES: A CASE STUDY

Chari H. Briggs

Summary: This article describes the transition of delivery of
school psychological services from primarily a clinical model to one
of consultation. It identifies existing conditions facilitating
change, analyzes problems, and suggests solutions. New services
arising from the changed perception of how a psychologist functions
are discussed.

Much has been written to support the contention that the clinical model of intensive individual psychological study is not the
most appropriate one for the practice of school psychology (Bardon,
1968; Cardon & Efraemson, 1970; Kennedy, 1971; Tomlinson, 1972).
Developmental, preventative, and consultation models offer greater
viability for dealing effectively with the problems presented to
school psychologists. This report will illustrate how a primarily
clinical model of school psychological services in a public junior
high school (grades 7-9) was modified within the time span of a
year to primarily a consultation form of operation.

In a recent article Williams (1972) elaborates the wide-ranging
and flexible roles school psychologists can adopt under the consultation model. He identifies and elaborates four role dimensions
on which consultants will vary: (1) the use of substantive material
in the area of consultant expertise, (2) the consultant as a person,
(3) the consultant as a model of coping effectiveness, and (4) the
consultant as facilitator. These dimensions were found to be both
relevant and important in the situation to be described.

SOURCE. Reprinted from Journal of School Psychology, 11, 1, 88-92,
1973. By permission of the author and the publisher. Copyright 1973
by the Journal of School Psychology, Inc. Published by Behavioral
Publications, New York.

Conditions existing in this school of more than 1,700 students did much to facilitate the transition of the role of the psychologist. For example, the school was in its third year of organization on a team basis. In this instance the concept of "team" was an interdisciplinary one in which one teacher each of mathematics, science, English, and social studies shared the same 110 to 120 students. There were five such teams at each of the three grade levels. Teachers of music, art, health, physical education, home economics, industrial arts, and foreign languages were not part of the team arrangement. The team also included a guidance counselor and administrator. Each team met around a conference table three times a week for about 45 minutes a session. The purposes of these meetings were to facilitate communication among members, increase joint planning, and to exchange information about students that would enable teachers to find approaches and techniques to help realize the school philosophy of individualizing instruction. Winicki (1972) describes similar meetings as consultation strategies to increase the competence of consultees by freeing and supporting their unrecognized talents and resources. Team meetings were, therefore, a ready-made vehicle for the psychologist to use as consultant.

Another feature which aided the change to a consultation model was a guidance department which was remarkably free to seek advice and professional opinion from a psychologist. In dealing with school problems, the consultant used substantive material (Williams, 1972) whenever she felt such information existed or could be translated into relevant form. The respect these counselors gave to one with a doctorate and the reciprocal respect given by the psychologist for their experience and expertise contributed to a minimum of professional jealousies between counselors and psychologist. Finally, members of the administration ranged from laissez faire in their attitudes to being actively supportive of psychological services.

Implementation of the consultation model began in September, 1970, following the transfer of the previous psychologist to another school in the district. The initial problem was to gain visibility for both the psychologist as a person and for the new program in a school with approximately 125 professional staff members. All staff learned about the modified plan for delivery of psychological services at the first faculty meeting of the year. The psychologist presented a personal sketch to the faculty. It was designed to create an aura of easy accessibility, but also to inspire confidence by giving a resumé of educational background and relevant professional interests and experience. The psychologist stressed her intention to be available to teachers and explained the rationale for spending less time than they were accustomed to in direct service to children. Secondly, during the first few weeks of school the psychologist visited team meetings to become further acquainted with the

168

staff and to begin to offer suggestions for solutions to daily problems based on psychological principles. The role of facilitator who draws out and reinforces strengths in the group was also practiced (Williams, 1972). Initially, these visits to team meetings were as "uninvited guest", but soon the psychologist felt accepted as a team member. The third way chosen to gain acceptance and visibility in the school was to fraternize actively with teachers, counselors, and administrators. A basic maxim was never to have coffee or lunch alone, but always to sit at a table with teachers and others and to join their conversations. Frequently they gravitated to concerns about children and the effectiveness of their teaching. On a number of occasions these informal contacts over lunch led to initiation of some professional service to teacher or child. Special attempts to create good working relationships with the five full-time guidance counselors and three administrators were an important part of the program. The psychologist contacted each individually during the first week of school and solicited their ideas for both helpful and innovative ways to utilize psychological services.

Teachers and counselors made all requests for social work and psychological services in written form to the director of pupil personnel, who distributed the request to the specialists providing services in the building in which they originated. Each referral carried with it the traditional expectation that a written report of service provided, based on individual testing sessions in the case of psychologists, would be filed. After the report had been written and read by those concerned with the child, the case became inactive unless otherwise stipulated by the report writer. In initiating a consultation form of service the psychologist encouraged school personnel to seek advice informally and directly, using the formal referral procedures primarily for longer term and more complex situations. Longer term follow-up seemed to be more easily accomplished, when more services were given informally. Seeing the people in the hallways who had previously sought help frequently became a stimulus for follow-up questioning and further consultation. In addition, flexibility in report writing was introduced by making psychological reports on the basis of observations and interviews, including psychological test results if administered. Tests were given only when it was anticipated that they would yield useful information, and not routinely, a practice now in use by a growing number of psychologists who are determining for themselves more flexible styles of operation in dealing with referral problems (Crary & Steger, 1972).

The psychologist made services available to departments and teaching areas of the school where previously none had been either requested or offered. The psychologist's initial meeting in September seems to have been the impetus for many novel requests. In addition, teachers stimulated new requests by sharing their ideas of how they used psychological services with others. Examples of service provided included discussions of child development and child rearing practices in home economics classes; discussion of mental retardation in English classes stimulated by a literature assignment of the experiences and feelings of a young retarded boy; presentation to health classes of what psychology is and what psychologists do, particularly in schools; consultation to the reading specialist regarding cases of poor reading ability; and in-service meetings with teachers who had volunteered to teach the slower learning students with a more applied and activity oriented curriculum.

In a school with such a large student body it is natural to expect that there would be a number of requests for direct service to children on a long-term basis. The clinical model might well predict that the school psychologist (or social worker) should provide them. However, in this metropolitan area such services are available from a nearby community mental health center as well as from private clinics. Therefore, the school psychologist was able to help identify problems needing longer term attention, to work with parents to accept the need for external services, and to provide linkages with community agencies, both by providing referral information to the agencies and feedback to teachers and administrators regarding methods of handling the child in school.

Because of relatively open communication existing between the psychologist and administrators, the psychologist could recommend program modifications as well as make suggestions for new programming. Individual requests for service revealed a number of 12 and 13-year old children who had learning disabilities, (poor reading, spelling, and written expression abilities, frequently accompanied by minor interpersonal problems). No provision for tutorial services were made at the junior high level, although they were available to elementary aged pupils. Requests for a learning disabilities resource teacher led to the funding of such a program, and the psychologist was given free reign to develop a model of operation and to staff it with a full-time teacher and half-time aide. By the conclusion of the school year this had been accomplished, a list of children who could profit from the new service had been developed, and many teachers had been oriented to the new program.

Determination of the effectiveness of this program of school psychological services is primarily subjective, but Barry (1970) suggests that the degree to which goals have been achieved can be practically indicated by whether the consultee again seeks consultation. "Is the consultee satisfied or generally positive in his feelings about the consultant and what he tried to do?" "Do succeeding events reflect the consultation's effectiveness?" By the end of the spring term the building principal, who had previously only tolerated

170

mental health services, had requested and gained approval for an
increase in service for his school from two to three days a week.
This result plus the generally favorable feedback from both staff
and parents to the psychologist and pupil personnel administrator
provide at least some evidence of the success of the consultation
model in this school setting.

References
_____

Bardon, J.I.   School psychology and school psychologists: An approach
    to an old problem. American Psychologist, 1968, 23, 187-194.
Barry, J.R.   Criteria in the evaluation of consultation. Professional
    Psychology, 1970, 1, 363-366.
Cardon, B.W. & Efraemson, M.W.   Consulting school psychology in the
    urban setting: Philadelphia process follow through. Journal
    of School Psychology, 1970, 8, 231-236.
Crary, W.G., & Steger, H.G.   Prescriptive and consultative approaches
    to psychological evaluation. Professional Psychology, 1972, 3,
    105-109.
Kennedy, D.A.   A practical approach to school psychology. Journal
    of School Psychology, 1971, 9, 484-489.
Tomlinson, J.R.   Schools and hospitals: A reply to Bersoff. Profes-
    sional Psychology, 1972, 3, 25-29.
Williams, D.L.   Consultation: A broad, flexible role for school
    psychologists. Psychology in the Schools, 1972, 9, 16-21.
Winicki, S.A.   The case conference as a consultation strategy.
    Psychology in the Schools, 1972, 9, 21-24.

Thomas N. Fairchild

In this study, the traditional diagnostic model of school psycho-logical services was compared with the emerging consultant service model. The study was conducted in an effort to determine the effect-iveness of each model in working with teachers in the elementary grades. The two delivery systems were evaluated by comparing them on two variables: (a) the number of school days that elapse from the time of referral until the teacher receives feedback, and (b) the effectiveness of the recommendations as measured by brief ques-tionnaires. The results revealed that the consultant model with its de-emphasis on the administration of time-consuming tests resulted in more immediate feedback for teachers. Responses to the follow-up questionnaires revealed that the consultant service model was as effective, if not more effective, in the teachers' perceptions, when comparing the effectiveness of the recommended intervention strategies. Although the data are more favorable for the consultant service model, they are not conclusive. Since each model meets some teachers' needs, a merging of these two approaches seems more justi-fiable than abandoning one model in favor of the other.

In recent years, special educators have been critical of key issues in the education of handicapped children: (a) the continuous influence of the medical model (Hammill, 1971; Reger, 1972; Reynolds & Balow, 1972), (b) criteria for special class placement (Garrison & Hammill, 1971; Hammill, 1971), and (c) the efficacy of the special self-contained classroom (Christopolos & Renz, 1969, Dunn, 1968). School psychologists are finding themselves in a precarious position being wedded to the medico-clinical model for their role and function and in executing the responsibility of identifying, testing, and recommending placement of exceptional children.

SOURCE. Reprinted from Psychology in the Schools, 1976, 13, 2, 156-162. By permission of the author and Clinical Psychology Publishing, Co., Inc.

Exhibiting healthy self-criticism, special educators also question the efficacy of traditional categorical delivery systems by advocating alternative systems for the education of children with special needs (Adelman, 1971; Deno, 1970; Hammill & Wiederholt, 1972; Lilly, 1971). Such noncategorical models deemphasize the relevancy of the medical model for special education.

Efforts to mainstream mildly handicapped children into regular classes reduce the need for traditional self-contained classes and diminish the need for diagnosticians to classify and place exceptional children. If psychological services are to survive, it becomes imperative to explore and develop alternative models for school psychological services. Currently, the consultant model has widespread recognition as a viable alternative for psychological services. Meyers (1973) presented an excellent overview of the consultative approaches being used and incorporated them into a consultation model for school psychological services. Waters (1973) surveyed school personnel as consumers of psychological services and concluded that the consultant model was more highly valued than the psychometric model. Current patterns in special education have demanded radical changes in delivering educational services. Also, teachers are more receptive to the consultant model (Waters, 1973); thus, it seems important to evaluate the utility of this model. The purpose of this study then was: (a) to compare the traditional diagnostic model of school psychological services with the emerging consultant service model, and (b) to determine the effectiveness of each model upon teachers.

METHOD

To compare the two service models, the author decided to operate within each model for one-half of the 1972-73 school year. During the fall semester, the traditional diagnostician model was followed; then, at the beginning of the spring semester, a consultant model was adopted. Data were collected in three elementary schools serving first through sixth grade.

A comparison between the traditional diagnostician model and the emerging consultant model required evidence that the writer operated within these two frameworks. Since the diagnostician model presupposes an emphasis on the administration of traditional standardized tests, and, whereas the consultant service model de-emphasizes traditional testing, the two models were compared on this dimension. A record of the frequency of administration of the traditional test battery was kept. The battery included the Wechsler Intelligence Scale for Children, the Wide Range Achievement Test, the Bender Visual Motor Gestalt Test, and the Illinois Test of Psycholinguistic Abilities. The fall and spring semesters would also be compared to data which had been collected during the 1971-72 school year.

173

Evaluation of the efficacy of the two delivery systems would
be accomplished by contrasting the two models on the following
two variables: (a) the amount of time that elapses from the referral
date until the primary referral source receives meaningful feedback,
and (b) the efficacy of the recommended intervention strategies.
These variables were selected because they are certainly the most
crucial. The more immediate the feedback, the sooner recommendations
can be implemented, and the higher the percentage of success, the
more effective the service model.

Time Elapsed Data

The following information was collected for each student
referred -- referral date, first contact date, teacher conference
date, parent conference date, and agency conference date (if an
outside agency was involved). Recording time elapsed data consisted
of counting the number of teaching days that transpired between:
(a) the referral date and initial contact date, (b) the initial
contact date and date of the conference with the major referral
source, and (c) the referral date and conference date with the
major referral source. Data were gathered separately for the fall
and spring semesters.

Efficacy of Intervention Strategies

After each semester had ended, follow-up questionnaires and
stamped, self-addressed envelopes were sent to teachers who had
made referrals requesting help from the school psychologist. The
follow-up questionnaire consisted of the following four questions:
(a) Did you have a better understanding of the child as a result
of your discussion with the psychologist? (b) Were recommendations
realistic and/or practical? (c) Were the recommendations of the
psychologist effective? (d) Were you able to carry out the recommendations of the psychologist? Respondents could check the responses
YES, NO, NOT APPLICABLE, or CANNOT BE ASCERTAINED. The questionnaires
were purposely kept brief in order to maximize the number of returns,
and anonymity was requested in order to encourage objectivity.

RESULTS AND DISCUSSION

Frequency of Administration of Standardized Tests

Table 1 reveals the types of standardized tests administered
during the 1971-72 and 1972-73 school years, as well as the frequency of their use. The data from the 1971-72 school year are presented
to serve as a reference point for the 1972 fall semester, when the
writer operated with the diagnostician service model.

During the 1971-72 school year 48 students had been evaluated
in the three elementary schools selected for this study. A total
of 64 traditional standardized tests were administered to these
students, yielding a mean number of 1.33 standardized tests administered per student. While adhering to the diagnostician service

174

model in the fall of the 1972-73 school year, 19 students were evaluated, and 27 standardized tests were administered for a mean of 1.42 tests administered per student. This mean is comparable to the mean recorded for the 1971-72 school year, and suggests that the writer was continuing to function in a manner consistent with the previous year. While operating within the consultant service model, a concerted effort was made to eliminate the use of standardized tests when a psychological evaluation was requested. Only 7 standardized tests (4 of these were specifically requested by outside agencies) were administered during the spring semester while evaluating 21 students, yielding a mean of .33 per student. This information indicates that the writer was able to discard the diagnostician model during the spring semester.

When comparing the frequency of administration of the various tests, the de-emphasis on standardized testing becomes even more apparent. In the fall, 61% of the students were given the Wechsler Intelligence Scale for Children; whereas, in only 19% of the cases were WISCs administered during the spring semester. The frequency of administration of the Wide Range Achievement Test dropped from 22% to 0%; the number of Bender Visual Motor Gestalt tests declined from 67% to 9%; and administration of the Illinois Test of Psycholinguistic Abilities increased from 0% to 5%.

Table 1.
TYPES OF STANDARDIZED TESTS ADMINISTERED AND
FREQUENCY OF ADMINISTRATION

Standardized Tests	1971-1972 48 Students Evaluated		1972-1973 (Fall Sem.) 19 Students Evaluated	
	Number Administered	Freq. of Administration	Number Administered	Freq. of Administ.
Wechsler Intell. Scale for Children	25	52%	11	58%
Wide Range Achieve. Test	14	29%	4	21%
Bender Visual Motor Gestalt Test	24	50%	12	63%
Illinois Test of Psycholinguistic Abilities	1	2%	0	0%
Total number of Standardized Tests	64		27	
Mean number of stand. tests adm. for each student		1.33		1.42

Table 1. (cont.)
TYPES OF STANDARDIZED TESTS ADMINISTERED AND
FREQUENCY OF ADMINISTRATION

Standardized Tests	1972-1973 (Spring Semester) 21 Students Evaluated	
	Number Administered	Frequency of Administration
Wechsler Intelligence Scale for Children	4	19%
Wide Range Achievement Test	0	0%
Bender Visual Motor Gestalt Test	2	9%
Illinois Test of Psycholinguistic Abilities	1	5%
Total number of standardized tests	7	
Mean number of standardized tests administered for each student		.33

Time Elapsed Information

The time elapsing from the time a teacher requests help until meaningful feedback regarding intervention strategies is received, is a crucial variable upon which to compare the diagnostician and consultant models. The consultant model, with its de-emphasis on time-consuming testing, should result in more immediate feedback than the diagnostician model. Inspection of Table 2 indicates that this is the case.

Table 2.
TIME ELAPSED DATA

	Total Number of Teaching Days Elapsed						
	Fall Semester				Spring Semester		
School	# of Students	Factor I*	Factor II**	Factor III***	# of Students	Factor I	Factor II	Factor III
#1	5	108	115	223	4	64	35	99
#2	7	23	93	116	11	57	104	161
#3	7	30	78	108	6	45	47	92
Total	19	161	286	447	21	166	186	352

176

(Table 2. cont.)

Mean Number of Teaching Days Elapsed

	Fall Semester				Spring Semester		
School	# of Students	Factor I	Factor II	Factor II*	# of Students	Factor I	Factor II	Factor III
#1	5	21.60	23.00	44.60	4	16.00	8.75	24.75
#2	7	3.28	13.28	16.57	11	5.18	9.45	14.63
#3	7	4.28	11.14	15.42	6	7.50	7.83	15.33
Total	19	8.47	15.05	23.52	21	7.90	8.85	16.76

*Factor I - the number of school days that elapse between the date the referral is made (date on referral form) and the first contact with the child.

**Factor II - the number of school days that elapse between the date of the first contact with a child and the date the primary referral source receives meaningful feedback.

***Factor III - the number of school days that elapse between the date the child is referred and the date the primary referral source receives meaningful feedback appropriate intervention strategies.

The mean number of days elapsing between the date of referral and the first contact with the student (Factor I) is comparable for the fall and spring semesters, with a mean of 8.47 days elapsing, and a mean of 7.90 days elapsing, respectively. However, once the psychologist had made contact, the two service models differed greatly in the immediacy with which teachers received feedback. The time that elapsed between the initial contact date and conference date (Factor II) amounted to a mean of 15.05 days per referral during the fall semester. The mean number of days elapsing during the spring semester was reduced to 8.85, while operating within the consultant service model, for a difference of 6.20 school days per referral between the fall and spring semesters. Considering that there were a comparable number of referrals (fall = 19 and spring = 21) both semesters, teachers received feedback in the form of recommended intervention strategies six teaching days sooner when the psychologist provided the consultant service, rather than the diagnostician service. The difference in the time elapsing before teachers receive feedback becomes even more pronounced when the total number of days elapsed is reviewed. Summing all the elapsing days together reveals that 447 teaching days elapsed during the fall semester from the referral dates to the conference dates (Factor III). Even though the two more students were referred during the spring semester, the total number of teaching days elapsed diminished to 352.

177

<u>Efficacy of Intervention Strategies</u>
    The effectiveness of a school psychologist can be assessed most
adequately by determining the effectiveness of recommended intervention strategies. An adequate comparision of the diagnostician
and consultant service models requires data regarding the effectiveness of the two approaches. The two models were compared on this
dimension by examining the results of the follow-up questionnaires
that were disseminated to classroom teachers. Nineteen questionnaires were distributed to teachers after the end of the fall
semester, and nineteen were distributed to teachers after the spring
semester had ended. (Two of the 21 referrals requested during the
spring semester had been made by outside agencies. The psychologist's
involvement required administering standardized tests and forwarding
a written report to the agency. Consequently, these two students
were not followed up because the writer had made no recommendations
to the classroom teachers.) Eleven questionnaires were returned
from the fall follow-up for a return rate of 58% contrasted to a
return rate of 95% in the spring semester with 18 teachers responding. Table 3 presents data for each of the four items on the
questionnaire.

Table 3.
RESULTS OF FOLLOW-UP QUESTIONNAIRE

| | Teacher Data for the Fall and Spring Semesters | | |
| Fall Semester | | Spring Semester | |

(1) Did you have a better understanding of the child as a result
     of your discussion with the psychologist?

Yes	(11)	100%	Yes	(13)	72%
No	(0)	0%	No	(4)	22%
Not Applicable	(0)	0%	Not Applicable	(1)	6%

(2) Were the recommendations realistic and/or practical?

Yes	(11)	100%	Yes	(17)	94%
No	(0)	0%	No	(1)	6%
Not Applicable	(0)	0%	Not Applicable	(0)	0%

(3) Were the recommendations of the psychologist effective?

Yes	(6)	55%	Yes	(12)	67%
No	(0)	0%	No	(2)	11%
Not Applicable	(0)	0%	Not Applicable	(0)	0%
Cannot be			Cannot be		
Ascertained	(5)	45%	Ascertained	(4)	22%

178

Table 3.   (cont.)
RESULTS OF FOLLOW-UP QUESTIONNAIRE

Teacher Data for the Fall and Spring Semesters						
Fall Semester				Spring Semester		

(4) Were you able to carry out the recommendations of the
     psychologist?

Yes	(10)	91%		Yes	(15)	83%
No	(1)	9%		No	(1)	6%
Not Applicable	(0)	0%		Not Applicable	(2)	11%

Responses to question number 1 reveal a reduction in the number
of YES responses, from 100% in the fall to 72% in the spring. This
reduction indicates that many teachers did not have a better understanding of the child after contact with the psychologist operating
as a consultant. The consultant model de-emphasized traditional
diagnostic testing with its focus on searching for intrapersonal
causes of learning and/or behavior problems, and consequently, provides little information regarding underlying causality. The consultant model concerns itself with observable behavior, and the designing and implementation of management techniques to sustain, rein-
force, or extinguish certain behaviors. The above difference was
anticipated due to the differences inherent in the two service
models.

Inspection of responses to questions 2 and 4 suggests that
recommendations were realistic and practical throughout the year,
and most teachers were able to carry out the recommendations of the
psychologist.

In response to question 3, "Were the recommendations of the
psychologist effective?", 55% of the teachers surveyed in the fall
responded YES, while 45% indicated CANNOT BE ASCERTAINED. Respondents in the spring semester replied YES in 67% of the cases, NO
in 11%, and CANNOT BE ASCERTAINED 22% of the time. The fewer
responses of CANNOT BE ASCERTAINED during the spring semester follow-
up would suggest that teachers were better able to make a decision
regarding the effectiveness of the recommendations. The emphasis
on behavioral consultation demands specificity of recommendations.
As recommendations become more specific it becomes easier for the
teachers to evaluate critically whether recommendations are achieving their desired effect or not. This is supported by the increase
in YES responses, and responses recorded in the NO category for the
first time. The greater percentage of YES responses suggests that
teacher follow-up during the spring perceived the psychologist's
recommendations as more helpful even though traditional tests were
not used.

References
_____

Adelman, H.S. Learning problems. In D.D. Hammill & N.R. Bartel
    (Eds.), Educational perspectives in learning disabilities. New
    York: John Wiley & Sons, 1971.
Christopolos, F., & Renz, P. A critical examination of special educa-
    tion programs. The Journal of Special Education, 1969, 3, 371-
    379.
Deno, E. Special education as developmental capital. Exceptional
    Children, 1970, 37, 229-237.
Dunn, L.M. Special education for the mildly retarded -- is much of
    it justifiable? Exceptional Children, 1968, 35, 5-22.
Garrison, M., Jr., & Hammill, D.D. Who are the retarded? Exceptional
    Children, 1971, 38, 13-20.
Hammill, D.D. Evaluating children for instructional purposes. In
    D.D. Hammill & N.R. Bartel (Eds.), Educational perspectives in
    learning disabilities. New York: John Wiley & Sons, 1971.
Hammill, D., & Wiederholt, J.L. (Eds.), The resource room: Rationale
    and implementation. Philadelphia: Buttonwood Farms, Inc., 1972.
Lilly, M.S. A training based model for special education. Excep-
    tional Children, 1971, 37, 745-750.
Meyers, J. A consultation model for school psychological services.
    Journal of School Psychology, 1973, 11, 5-15.
Reger, R. The medical model in special education. Psychology in the
    Schools, 1972, 9, 8-12.
Reynolds, M.C., & Balow, B. Categories and variables in special
    education. Exceptional Children, 1972, 38, 357-366.
Waters, L.G. School psychologists as perceived by school personnel:
    Support for a consultant model. Journal of School Psychology,
    1973, 11, 40-46.

SCHOOL PSYCHOLOGISTS AS PERCEIVED BY SCHOOL PERSONNEL: SUPPORT
FOR A CONSULTANT MODEL

Linda G. Waters

Summary: Questionnaires distributed by 12 school psychologists
to school personnel with whom they had been consulting for six months
were completed and returned by 73 teachers, counselors, and principals. The information provided by the respondents indicated the
frequencies with which the school psychologists engaged in consulting and child study activities, the school personnel's evaluations
of nine different school psychologist skills, and the preferences
of the respondents for the different school psychologist functions
in their schools. The data showed that: (1) school psychologists
were doing more consulting than evaluations of individual children,
(2) school personnel tended to perceive their psychologists as
cooperative, knowledgeable, and skillful, though relatively inef-
ficient and undependable, and (3) school personnel preferred consulting activities to psychometric activities. It was concluded
that the consultant model had been shown to be operative and that
it was more highly valued than the psychometric model by the consumers of psychological services.

Concern with the role of the psychologist working in the public schools has generated much theorizing and experimenting, both
in the field and in training institutions. Pielstick (1970) points
out that the issue is still "lively and unresolved" in spite of
attempts at resolution which he dates from the Thayer Conference
of 1954.

There seems to be a well-developed trend, expressed in the
literature as well as among practicing school psychologists, fav-
oring a consultant model for school psychological services (Madera,
1971). This model emphasizes indirect service (work with teachers
and others who have daily contact with pupils) in preference to

SOURCE. Reprinted from Journal of School Psychology, 1973, 11, 1,
40-45. By permission of the author and publisher. Copyright 1973
by the Journal of School Psychology, Inc. Published by Behavioral
Publications, New York.

individual child study (the "psychometrician" role). Elkin (1963) states that consultation "... is the single most important function which (the school Psychologist) can perform ..." (p. 211). Bergan (1970), in support of the consultant model, holds that "The central task to be accomplished by psychological services in school settings is that of bringing relevant knowledge and techniques from the field of psychology to bear on the education of children" (p. 315). Consultation is seen as the vehicle for accomplishing this.

While psychometric services would seem to be unavoidable for school psychologists, and undoubtedly can have considerable value, several factors weigh against testing as a dominant role feature. Public sentiment against the use of psychological tests, especially for minority group youngsters in the public schools, is rapidly increasing, in some cases resulting in state legislation controlling the use of such tests (Bowers, 1971). Individual testing is very costly in terms of the professional time required and cannot possibly be provided for all the children perceived by their schools as needing it (Kennedy, 1971). Recent research in education calls into question the value of special education classes as preferred placements for children with school difficulties (Lilly, 1970); the need for formal identification of such children has created most of the demand for psychological testing in the school. As special education classes become less popular, school districts will feel less need for psychologists to perform testing functions.

Two fairly recent studies have indicated that individual child study is still the most important function of school psychologists, as far as the school and the psychologists are concerned (Dansinger, 1968-1969; Perkins, 1971). However, Perkins (1971) acknowledges that there remains a pronounced shortage of information regarding just what school psychologists are doing in their schools; Kirschner (1971) contends that "... the views of the consumers of school psychological services have not been adequately represented ..." in research and planning. Tindall (1971) feels that further research is needed regarding the relative efficacy of different role emphasis for school psychologists:

> ... there is little objective data to support emphasis of one role over another. Most psychological services in the schools has grown on the basis of opinion rather than as a result of fact-finding approaches (p. 6).

The study below was a post hoc attempt to provide illuminating data six months after the psychological services department of a large urban school district shifted from a psychometric model to a consultant model.

METHOD

Each school psychologist distributed a short questionnaire to the school personnel with whom he had been working. The questionnaire was to be returned, when completed, to the director of the department of psychological services. A cover letter stressed that the purpose of the evaluations and opinions solicited by the questionnaire was to acquire information regarding the value of departmental services for further planning; respondents were urged to be forthright and objective. They were asked to identify themselves by job title and school, so that strict anonymity was not possible for the principals and school counselors, but was for the teachers.

Questionnaire: The questionnaire was composed of three sections. The first asked the respondent to indicate which of ten listed activities the psychologist had either done at least once, or did regularly or frequently, in the respondent's school. The second section asked for ratings of nine school psychologist skills on a four-point scale ranging from "Less Than Average" to "Superior." The third section was composed of three open-ended items: "What activities, which your psychologist had done in your school, do you consider most valuable?", "What would you like to have the psychologist do more of than he or she presently does?", and "Please add any comments which you feel are relevant to the activities of the school psychologist."

RESULTS AND DISCUSSION

Sample: Twelve school psychologists (M.A. level) distributed the questionnaires. The returned sample consisted of 73 questionnaires, from 31 schools, evaluating 12 school psychologists. The respondents were 16 classroom teachers, 30 counselors, and 27 principals and assistant principals.

School Psychologists' Activities: The relative frequencies of the ten activities listed on the questionnaire are shown on Table 1. The formula for arriving at the "weighted sum" was number of checks plus three times the number of asterisks. On the questionnaire the check response was used to denote "activities the psychologist has done at least once," and the asterisk response denoted activities the psychologist did regularly or frequently in the respondent's school. It was assumed that "regularly or frequently" would imply at least three times the frequency of "has at least once" to most respondents; thus, the asterisk response was assigned a weight of three. While this is arbitrary to some extent, it serves the purpose of indicating the approximate frequencies with which various activities occurred. The figures in Table 1 are neither absolute totals nor frequencies per time unit; rather, they indicate relative amounts of activity or frequencies in each area specified. Table 1 shows that conferences with counselors, teachers, and principals were each taking place with comparable frequency to evaluations of individual children. To this extent, the consultant model was actually being employed.

While no attempt was made in the questionnaire to determine the content of these conferences, it is postulated that even when they related primarily to an individual child, the "client" of the consultation was reaping generalizable information. Data supplied informally by the psychologists indicated that the large majority of the conferences with school personnel concerned general issues, though often a particular problem child might have proved the "entry" for the discussion.

Table 1
Relative Frequencies of School Psychologists' Activities
as Reported by School Personnel

Activity	✓	*	Weighted Sum[1]
Conferences with Counselors	28	38	142
Evaluations of Children	34	32	130
Conferences with Principals	41	29	128
Conferences with Teachers	37	28	121
Classroom Observation	35	19	92
Meetings with Faculty	40	15	85
Conferences with School Nurse	32	13	71
Conferences with Parents	27	12	63
Other	4	6	22
Meetings with PTA	7	0	7

[1]The weighted sums were calculated by adding the number of checks to three times the number of stars. The check signifies "activities the school psychologist has done"; the star "those which he or she does regularly or frequently."

These conferences were consultant functions in that they involved sharing psychological knowledge, both data and theory, with school personnel who work more directly and frequently with the children, thereby helping school personnel to use better their own resources to cope with their daily and extraordinary problems.

Skills Ratings: For each skill listed on the questionnaire, average ratings were computed, assigning a value of three to a rating of "Superior," two to a rating of "Above Average," etc. The averages for all skills, as rated by all respondents and by each respondent group separately, fell within the range from "Above

Average" to "Superior" (although individual ratings did cover the
entire range). This lack of variability in the ratings suggested
a response bias, perhaps related to a halo effect, or perhaps
merely reflecting a cautious or generous nature on the part of the
respondents. In any case, in view of the limited range of average
ratings, they were interpreted relatively rather than absolutely,
in terms of comparisons of the respondent groups and of the rank
orderings of the skills ratings. Table 2 shows the school personnel's evaluations of the school psychologists' skills, rank ordered
for all respondents and for the three respondent groups separately.

Table 2
Rank Orderings of Teachers', Counselors', and
Principals' Ratings of School Psychologist Skills*

Skill	All Respondents	Teachers	Counselors	Principals
Ability to work with others cooperatively	1	1	1	1
Professional knowledge	2	5	3	3
Psychotherapy and Counseling Skills	3	2	8	2
Sense of Responsibility	4	3.5	2	8
Interpretation and use of psychological testing information	5	8	4	5.5
Judgement	6	6	5	4
Helpful communication	7	3.5	7	5.5
Dependability	8	9	6	7
Efficiency and Productivity	9	7	9	9
$\bar{X}$, All Skills	3	4	1	2

*1 indicates highest rating; 9 indicates lowest rating.

All three respondent groups (teachers, counselors, and principals) rated "Ability to work with others cooperatively" highest of
the nine skills listed on the questionnaire. Insofar as the school
psychologist must be accepted in the school before he can be effective in any role, this result is most encouraging and shows some
success for the consultant role.

The relatively low "Dependability" and "Efficiency and Produc-
tivity" ratings reflect in part the effects of several administrative reorganizations which occurred during the three months immediately preceding the distribution of the questionnaires, necessitat-
ing schedule changes and cancellations which were understandably

disruptive to the school personnel (and to the psychologists). It is also possible that the combination of the school psychologists' itinerant status, relative inexperience (the average was 2.5 years), and the newness of the consultant role produced relative inefficiency.

For each respondent group, an average of the ratings on all nine skills was computed; these respondent group averages are rank ordered in the last row of Table 2. School counselors rated the school psychologists highest and classroom teachers rated them lowest, for the average of all skills combined, which might be construed as an evaluation of overall competence or helpfulness. It may be that the anonymity of the teachers in this study, which was not completely possible for the other respondents, enabled them to express less positive evaluations more freely. Also, of the three groups, teachers tend to feel the greatest need for help, insofar as they are faced daily with immediate and often urgent demands both in the classroom and administratively; this may tend to make them both more demanding and more difficult to please.

Open-Ended Items: The responses to the question "What activities ... do you consider most valuable?" lent themselves readily to a comparison of school personnel's feelings regarding psychometric vs. consulting activities. Individual child study was specified by only 25% of the respondents as a most valued activity, whereas 59% specified consulting activities, either in general or specifically (e.g., "meetings with teachers"). (The two response categories were not mutually exclusive; a small number of the respondents specified both.) The marked preference for consultation as opposed to individual child study contradicts the results of Dansinger (1968-69) and Perkins (1971) and suggests that the choice of a consultant model for school psychologists is practical and valuable to the "consumers" of psychological services, as well as theoretically sound.

In their responses to the remaining two open-ended terms, 64% of the respondents indicated that they felt a need for the school psychologist to spend more time in their school. Only 12% indicated a desire for more testing. This latter finding was surprising, but is consistent with the result reported immediately above.

While it may be the case that, once experiencing the consultant relationship, school personnel much prefer it to the more traditional school psychologist as psychometrician, a more cautious interpretation would take into account the specific context of this study. The entire school district was de-emphasizing special education class placement and had plans under way to return many "special education" youngsters to the "regular" classroom.

186

Concurrent with this, the school psychologists were strongly emphasizing working with regular classroom teachers on improving teacher coping skills. These forces may have made it difficult and somewhat "socially unacceptable" for school personnel to express a desire for testing. Nonetheless, it is apparent that the school personnel were to some meaningful extent in support of the consultant model and felt that the psychologists had more to offer in this role than as psychometricians.

CONCLUSION

This survey of 73 school personnel concerning 12 school psychologists is by no means conclusive. However, insofar as the results were discriminating in the comparisons of different skills, different activities, and the perceptions of different school personnel, it is felt that they may be valuable. The most conservative conclusion to be drawn is that school psychologists functioning as consultants can under some circumstance gain the acceptance and appreciation of some portion of the school personnel with whom they work. At best, these results indicate the M.A. level school psychologists can change from an exclusively psychometric role to a consultant model in delivering psychological services and can be accepted and appreciated by school personnel in this role.

References

Bergan, J.R. A systems approach to psychological services. Psychology in the Schools, 1970, 7, 315-319.

Bowers, N.E. Public reaction and psychological testing in the schools. Journal of School Psychology, 1971, 9, 114-119.

Dansinger, S.S. A five-year follow-up survey of Minnesota school psychologist. Journal of School Psychology, 1968-69. 7, 47-53.

Elkin, V.B. Structuring school psychological services: Internal and interdisciplinary considerations. In M.G. Gottsegen and G.B. Gottsegen (Eds.), Professional school psychology. New York: Grune & Stratton, Inc., 1963.

Kennedy, D.A. A practical approach to school psychology. Journal of School Psychology, 1971, 9, 484-489.

Lilly, M.S. A teapot in a tempest. Exceptional Children, 1970, 37, 43-49.

Madera, S.E.K. The school psychologist: A consultative model. Unpublished master's thesis, University of Houston, Houston, Texas, August, 1971.

Perkins, K.J. School psychology: From identification to identity. In F.D. Holt and R.H. Kicklighter (Eds.), Psychological services in the schools. Dubuque: Wm. C. Brown Co., 1971.

Pielstick, N.L.   The appropriate domain of the school psychologist.
    Journal of School Psychology, 1970, 8, 317-319.
Tindall, R.H.   Trends in development of psychological services in
    the schools.   In F.D. Holt and R.H. Kicklighter (Eds.), Psycho-
    logical services in the schools.   Dubuque: Wm. C. Brown Co.,
    1971.

DETERMINING AND IMPROVING THE EFFECTIVENESS OF TRAINING PROGRAMS

As long as we are asking that school psychologist practitioners in the field account for their services, it seems reasonable to require school psychologist trainers to become accountable for their training programs. Competency-based training programs appear to be one vehicle for achieving this goal. If trainers identify the necessary competencies for successful on-the-job functioning, provide experiences which will allow for their development, and design means of determining whether students have achieved these competencies, they can be confident that they are graduating competent professionals.

In developing a competency-based program a decision needs to be made regarding which skills are necessary and relevant for inclusion in the training program. Hunter and Lambert describe the needs assessment activities that they engaged in when gathering information essential to program development. This offers the reader one approach to needs assessment.

The Catterall article describes an excellent competency-based school psychology internship program. Boehm, et al. document competency standards in the area of individual intelligence test administration.

Program evaluation is another aspect of accountability. Martin, et al., discuss an evaluation of their experimental school psychology internship.

Fairchild's article relates to accountability for training programs in a somewhat different manner. His article discusses implications for training programs based on the discrepancies between the skills emphasized in the training programs and the skills actually required for successful on-the-job performance.

NEEDS ASSESSMENT ACTIVITIES IN SCHOOL PSYCHOLOGY PROGRAM DEVELOPMENT

Carol P. Hunter and Nadine M. Lambert

Summary: Needs assessment activities are presented as a basis for gathering information essential to program development, revision, and evaluation. Needs assessment activities include surveys of trends advocated by national authorities and consumers and identification of needs of students and local school systems. These data form the basis for developing program objectives in a sequentially ordered multilevel program.

In developing a competency-based program, how does one determine which skills or competencies are necessary and relevant? Needs assessment activities can guide the collection, selection, and interpretation of information needed in making such decisions.

The needs assessment activities proposed in this paper include three areas of investigation: (1) trends advocated by national authorities, (2) functions deemed important by consumers, and (3) opinions of local trainees, graduates, and consumers.

NEEDS ASSESSMENT ACTIVITIES

During the initial period of transition from the traditional course structure to a competency-based model, considerable effort is devoted to the clarification of the functions of the school psychologist; objectives are based on the competencies and skills necessary to perform these selected functions. The relative importance of the different functions in the school setting is determined.

In order to determine which are the important competencies of the school psychologist (SP), three areas are investigated: (1) the literature is reviewed to determine trends advocated by national authorities, (2) the literature is reviewed to determine functions

SOURCE. Reprinted from Journal of School Psychology, 1974, 12, 2, 130-137. By permission of the author and publisher. Copyright 1974 by the Journal of School Psychology, Inc. Published by Behavioral Publications, New York.

deemed important by consumers, and (3) the local needs are identified by evaluating trainees and graduates, and local consumers are surveyed regarding their needs.

  Trends from Authorities in the Field. The professional identity of school psychology has evolved from struggles to reconcile a variety of points of view in the more than 25 years since APA Division 16 was formed in 1947. Since the 60's, the struggle has become extremely active with several books defining the role of a school psychologist (Bardon & Bennett, 1974; Eiserer, 1963; Gray, 1963; Gottsegen & Gottsegen, 1963; Hirst, 1963; Holt & Kicklighter, 1971; Magary, 1967; Reger, 1965; Valet, 1963; White & Harris, 1961). In addition, many relevant journal articles have been published. Reviewing the perceptions of many of the leaders in the area of school psychology, one sees a number of divergent roles conceptualized. However, there appear to be definite trends toward the future direction and form which school psychology will take. The school psychologist is no longer seen narrowly as a clinical psychologist, therapist, or tester. His competencies must be far broader.

  Some of the trends which must be considered in developing a training program are as follows:

  1. The SP will serve all children in the school (Cutts, 1955; Holt & Kicklighter, 1971; Magary, 1967; Silverman, 1969).
  2. The SP will work frequently with groups rather than individual children and parents and teachers (Footman, 1972; Magary, 1967; Silverman, 1969).
  3. The SP will be involved as an adviser in many more aspects of the total school program including curriculum development (Fifield, 1967; Magary, 1967; Silverman, 1969).
  4. The SP will implement findings from child development and learning, social, and physiological psychology (Silverman, 1969).
  5. The multidiscipline or team approach will continue to be used in solving problems of children and the school system (Silverman, 1969). The SP should know how to handle staffings and guidance committees.
  6. The responsibility of the classroom teacher will be increased with the support of the SP and other specialists in an attempt to keep children in the regular classroom whenever possible. Thus, the SP will be expected to provide help in educational programming and behavioral management.
  7. The SP will de-emphasize his role as test diagnostician and will not administer group tests himself (Bardon, 1965; Magary, 1967; Silverman, 1969). Testing should be centered on intervention planning, not on classification as its sole purpose.
  8. The SP will expand his role in data-oriented problem solving and in doing applied research which is relevant to the needs of the school (Bardon, 1965; Cutts, 1955; Fifield, 1967, Gray, 1963; Reger, 1965; Silverman, 1969).

9. As an objective for school psychological services, the cognitive growth of the child will be fostered (Bower, 1965; Magary, 1967; Silverman, 1969) in conjunction with his affective growth.

10. With the current impetus to develop levels of training in SP at the Vail Conference, 1973, and with defined competencies at each level of training, at least one activity of senior school psychologists will be the supervision of lower-level personnel.

11. The SP's role in early childhood education will be to emphasize prevention and early identification and treatment of potential learning disabilities in preschool and primary children (Bardon, 1965; Footman, 1972; Gross & Farling, 1969; Reger, 1965).

12. The SP will increase his service to culturally disadvantaged children to aid in planning positive stimulation and educational programming which will allow them to fulfill more nearly their potential (Silverman, 1969).

13. The clinical model will be replaced with the consultation model and the SP will function as an expert in psychology and education (Bardon, 1965; Fine & Tyler, 1971; Gray, 1963). The SP's training must include skills in consultation as well as a comprehensive foundation in the behavioral sciences in order to effect behavioral changes in pupils to collaborative work with other educators (Holt & Kicklighter, 1971). This includes consultation to other pupil personnel specialists, teachers, parents, and administrators, and increasing their effectiveness.

14. The reduction in the prevalence of drug abuse and drop-outs (Cassel, 1973) requires the institution of major preventive efforts.

15. The scientific process of decision-making and decision-making in helping relationships (Cassel, 1973) should occupy a high priority among the psychologist's activities.

16. Facilitating the interaction of the child with the educational process (Bardon & Bennett, 1967) as well as the interaction of forces of the community and the school (Reilly, 1968-1969), is a critically important objective of school psychological services. In these efforts, the SP should coordinate all community psychological and service agencies with the school, monitor the referral process, and evaluate follow-up recommendations (Bardon & Bennett, 1967; Fifield, 1967).

17. In-service workshops (Bardon, 1965; Holt & Kicklighter, 1971; Reger, 1965) in child behavior, child development, and interventions to promote the educational experience will be a major responsibility of the SP.

18. The SP will help management personnel specify goals and behavioral objectives for the instructional program as well as other facets of school life (Clair & Kiraly, 1971). For example, California law now requires the establishment of objectives for evaluating teachers and other educators' services.

19. The SP himself should be aware of the ethical and value dilemmas he encounters in his concern for assessing and modifying psychosocial (e.g., interpersonal and organizational relationships) and educational aspects of the school (Medway, 1973) to optimize the school experience for children.

20. Course work, consequently, will need to be designed to include greater emphasis on prescription, remediation, curriculum intervention, behavior modification (Footman, 1972), psychopathology, group management, and change (Holt & Kicklighter, 1971). Field work associated with such course work will require that the SP demonstrate skills in social interaction to maintain effective relations with others, e.g., skills in communication techniques, empathy, and rapport should be demonstrated. The SP must be heard and have something worthwhile to say. More important, perhaps is that the SP must be aware of how others perceive him (Bardon & Bennett, 1967) and seek consultation for himself for his own professional development.

Trends from the Consumers. A review of the literature reporting the consumer's perspective on psychological services illustrates the compatability between role perceptions of school psychology and psychological services needs of the schools. For example, the following services are regularly mentioned as desirable occupations of the SP.

1. The SP should be trained to keep abreast of research in wide areas (Bardon, 1965).
2. The emphasis in service should be at the elementary school level, with special attention to early identification of children with potential problems of adjustment.
3. The SP should spend more of his effort to help teachers understand and intervene appropriately with children (Bardon, 1965).
4. The SP must improve the utility of his recommendations to teachers. Teachers found recommendations useful only about 50% of the time (Baker, 1965; Styles, 1965), and they resulted in perceived changes in less than 43% of cases (Styles, 1965). The relevance of recommendations to individual teacher practice was considered the most important factor in the usefulness of the reports (Mussman, 1964; Rucker, 1967). An important area of conflict and confusion seems to be the psychologists' reports to teachers. Language should be clear and planning should be done cooperatively (Handler, Gerston & Handler, 1965). One report (Lambert, 1973) pointed out that teachers desired reports which provided a practical course of action for follow-up by the psychologist to check on the relevance of the findings for the classroom programs.
5. The SP must increase his proximity to teachers and acquire and maintain effective consultation skills. Styles (1965) found that teachers believed that the most useful information and most workable suggestions came through individual conferences. Lucas & Jones (1970) concluded that EMR teachers who had above median contact with SPs rated SP helpfulness significantly higher than those reporting less contact; however, the results of other studies investigating the effect of contact on acceptance did not support Lucas and Jones' conclusions (Baker, 1965; Gilmore, 1973).

193

6. To achieve these many objectives, the role of the individual school psychologist should be more comprehensive. Supervisors in large metropolitan areas in the United States wanted generalists trained in many functions. While they ranked highest the services of teacher consultation, individual case studies, and in-service training, they also desire evaluation studies of early childhood programs, preventative programs, screening children for placement in special education, counseling parents, liaison agent with community agencies, curriculum consultation, research, and follow-up. The two activities considered "least desirable" were remedial instruction and psychotherapy; some also felt research was relatively "unimportant" (Kirschner, 1971).

7. In questionnaires on the effectiveness of school psychologists, teachers reported them to be less effective in areas involving academics, class placement, and classroom management problems; consequently, they recommended more training in these educationally oriented problems. While the SP has been sharpening his skills of classroom consultation, some teachers believe the SP should still emphasize the functions of therapist and mental health and educational programmer. The SP has had a long-standing objective of promoting mental health and routinely desires updated preparation to deal with emotional and home problems (Roberts, 1970). Nevertheless, there seems to be some discrepancy between teacher and SP views of the extent to which the teacher or psychologist has primary responsibility for the mental health of the child in the classroom.

8. Teachers view the SP as a specialist in emotional problems whose major diagnostic procedure is testing, who recommends treatment but does little himself. When asked for recommendations, 36% of the teachers requested a full-time psychologist at their school; they desired consistent, long-term involvement. They wanted the SP to become more directly involved with teacher and child in planning and effecting any treatment. Twenty-five percent simply asked for more contact. In developing a school psychology training program, it is important to recognize that, in addition to traditional diagnostic work, teachers are requesting consultation and help in classroom planning and in the design and conduct of intervention (Gilmore, 1973; Lambert, 1973).

Following the review of SP functions deemed important by national authorities and consumers, a tentative SP competency scale can be formulated for the training program.

Identifying Local Program Needs. Several procedures are used in obtaining input regarding specific local needs. A Delphi Survey is a suitable method to use for obtaining additional input to aid in competency selection. Reactions can be sought from selected populations such as local consumers, trainers throughout the region, state consultants, trainees or graduates, and practicing SPs through the state SP Association.

Once program competencies have been selected based on the above surveys, the needs assessment process focuses on observing and rating the present interns and previous year's graduates who are employed within the geographical region. They are video-taped, rated on the level at which they have attained each competency on the SP competency scale, and interviewed in order to determine specific behavioral strengths and weaknesses of a large percentage of graduates. All graduates are asked to respond to a program questionnaire which is used to identify additional educational needs and to provide feedback. Dropouts and students excluded from the program are also included in the questionnaire. In addition, the program staff asks employers to rate the interns and graduates and to comment on the needs of the program as they perceive them. A random sample of pupils, parents, teachers, and other staff specialists can also provide evaluation information on the types and levels of services offered by the intern and graduate school psychologist.

Recommendations regarding objectives requiring greater emphasis or the inclusion of new objectives in the training program follow the integration of the information collected in the local needs assessment phase. A realistic criterion of acceptability related to successful job performance for each competency can be established by the program and used for student guidance and development.

DESIGN OF MULTILEVEL SCHOOL PSYCHOLOGY
PROGRAM ON THE BASIS OF NEEDS ASSESSMENT ACTIVITIES

An advisory committee consisting of school district directors of pupil personnel services, practicing school psychologists, representatives of the state school psychological association and the state Department of Education, and graduates and present students, reviews the needs assessment data and the criteria for attainment of the competencies which are developed and establishes a sequential ordering of competencies and levels within competencies. The advisory committee selects courses, field work experiences, and methods for demonstrating competencies which are applicable to the program plans. According to the recommendations of the APA Vail Conference in June 1973, programs should offer multiple levels of training with experiences arranged sequentially. Some models (Arbuckle, 1967; Magary, 1967; Shaw, 1967; Silverman, 1969; Smith, 1962) specify that school psychologists should initially attain a set of core competencies that are generic to pupil personnel services. Certification to work as a psychologist is attained after advanced preparation over and above this generic core level. Other models (Lambert, 1974) provide a sequence of training which includes some of these generic core competencies without the expectancy that the SP first be certified as a counselor or psychological examiner. Still another pattern of multilevel offering is exemplified by the California Professional School of Psychology, which accepts students for doctoral work only after they have achieved the SP credential and have completed three years of work as a school psychologist.

Regardless of the sequence in which the competencies are arranged, the program director, his staff, and the advisory committee normally identify levels of preparation within programs, such as psychological examiner and psychological specialist, or M.A. and Ph.D. levels. It is also important to integrate the sequence of training offered in one institution in such a way that students can move to higher levels of training in the same or other institution if they so desire. Presumably the competencies identified by each local program's needs assessment and program development phases will share a wide base of commonality so that movement to higher levels in the same or different institution will be accomplished with ease.

CONCLUSION

Needs assessment data can guide in the selection of competencies and skills considered essential in the role of the school psychologist. By appraising themselves of trends advocated by national authorities and consumers, as well as by evaluating data provided by local trainees, graduates, and consumers, training program staffs, will have an empirical basis for developing an integrated, multilevel, competency-based training program.

References

Arbuckle, D.S. Counselor, social worker, psychologist: Let's "ecumenicalize." Personnel and Guidance Journal, 1967, 45, 6, 532-538.
Baker, H.L. Psychological services: From the school staff's point of view. Journal of School Psychology, 1965, 3, 4, 36-42.
Bardon, J.I. (Ed.) Problems and issues in school psychology - 1964: Proceedings of a conference on new directions in school psychology. Journal of School Psychology, 1965, 3, 2, 1-14.
Bardon, J., & Bennett, V. Preparation for professional psychology: An example from a school psychology training program. American Psychologist, 1967, 22, 652-656.
Bardon, J., & Bennett V. School Psychology. Englewood Cliffs, N.J.: Prentice-Hall, 1974.
Bower, E.M. Reactions to the conference. Journal of School Psychology, 1965, 3, 2, 36-39.
Cassel, R.N. Types of cases referred and recommended program for school psychology preparation. Professional Psychology, 1973, 4, 377-385.
Clair, T.N., & Kiraly, J. Accountability for the school psychologist. Psychology in the Schools, 1971, 3, 4, 318-321.
Cutts, N.E. School psychologists at mid-century. Washington, D.C.: American Psychological Association, 1955.

Eiserer, P.E. The school psychologist. Washington, D.C.: Center for Applied Research in Education, 1963.

Fifield, M. The role of school psychology in public education. Psychology in the Schools, 1967, 4, 66-68.

Fine, M.J., & Tyler, M.M. Concerns and directions in teacher consultation. Journal of School Psychology, 1971, 9, 4, 436-444.

Footman, G. An analysis of the task and roles of the school psychologist in the State of California. Unpublished doctoral dissertation, University of California, 1972.

Gilmore, G.E. School psychologist: Expectations and perceptions of educational colleagues. Unpublished manuscript, The University of Texas at Austin, 1973.

Gottsegen, M.G., & Gottsegen, G.B. (Eds.) Professional School Psychology, Vol. II. New York: Grune and Stratton, 1963.

Gray, S.W. The psychologist in the schools. New York: Holt, Rinehart and Winston, 1963.

Gross, F.P., & Farling, W.H. An analysis of case loads of school psychologists. Psychology in the Schools, 1969, 6, 98-100.

Handler, L., Gertson, A., & Handler, B. Suggestions for improved psychologist-teacher communication. Psychology in the Schools, 1965, 2, 77-81.

Hirst, W.E. Know your school psychologist. New York: Grune and Stratton, 1963.

Holt, F.D., & Kicklighter, R.H. Psychological services in the schools: Readings in preparation, organization and practice. Dubuque, Iowa: Wm. C. Brown, 1971.

Kirschner, F.E. School psychology as viewed by the supervisors of school psychological services. Journal of School Psychology, 1971, 9, 3, 343-346.

Lambert, N. Teacher perception of school psychologist service activities. Paper presented at the American Psychological Association, Division 16, Pre-Conference Institute, Montreal, August, 1973.

Lambert, N. School psychology at Berkeley, a progress report. Berkeley, University of California, 1974.

Lucas, M.S., & Jones, R.L. Attitudes of teachers of mentally retarded children toward psychological reports and services. Journal of School Psychology, 1970, 8, 2, 122-130.

Magary, J.F. (Ed.) School psychological services: In theory and practice: A handbook. Englewood Cliffs, N.J.: Prentice-Hall, 1967.

Medway, F.J. Toward a model of internally-based change in the schools. Paper presented at the American Psychological Association, Division 16 Convention, Montreal, August, 1973.

Mussman, M.C. Teachers' evaluations of psychological reports. Journal of School Psychology, 1964, 3, 35-37.

Reger, R. School Psychology. Springfield, Ill.: Charles C. Thomas, 1965.

197

Reilly, D.H. Goals and roles of school psychology: A community based model. Journal of School Psychology, 1968-69, 7, 3, 35-37.

Roberts, R.D. Perceptions of actual and desired role functions of school psychologists by psychologists and teachers. Psychology in the Schools, 1970, 7, 175-178.

Rucker, C.N. Report writing in school psychology: A critical investigation. Journal of School Psychology, 1967, 5, 101-108.

Shaw, M.C. Role delineation among the guidance professions. Psychology in the Schools, 1967, 4, 3-13.

Silverman, H.L. School psychology: Divergent role conceptualizations. Psychology in the Schools, 1969, 6, 3, 266-271.

Smith, T.E. An analysis of the role of the school psychologist in the State of California. Unpublished doctoral dissertation, University of Southern California, 1962.

Styles, W.A. Teachers' perceptions of the school psychologist's role. Journal of School Psychology, 1965, 3, 4, 23-27.

Valett, R.E. The practice of school psychology: Professional problems. New York: John Wiley and Sons, 1963.

White, M.A., & Harris, M.W. The school psychologist. New York: Harper and Row, 1961.

A COMPETENCY BASED SCHOOL PSYCHOLOGY INTERNSHIP

Calvin D. Catterall

Most training programs for school psychologists require some
sort of an experience under the direct supervision in a practical
setting called an internship. For the past 12 years the state of
Ohio has been fortunate to have had funding to provide paid internships at the masters-plus/certification level (Smith, 1969; Internship Program in School Psychology, 1969). This intership experience
lasts for a full school year in a school district under the direction
of both an experienced district supervisor and a member of the university staff.

The School Psychology Training Program at The Ohio State University prepares students at both the masters-plus/certification and
doctoral levels. In an attempt to move toward a competency base,
the terminal competencies that all trainees would be expected to
perform by the end of their internship experiences were defined. A
committee, consisting of district supervisors, other school psychologists who had recently completed the training program, interns,
and one member of the university training staff, attempted to define
in behavioral terms a list of abilities that would represent the
minimal level of competency to be performed by a person first enter-
ing school psychology. After the broad competencies were developed,
the committee identified the appropriate criteria, a task made considerably easier because it was possible to rely upon the judgement of
the experienced school psychologists who in their role as district
supervisors have close contact with the interns.

SOURCE. Reprinted from Journal of School Psychology, 1973, 11, 3,
269-275. By permission of the author and the publisher. Copyright
1973 by the Journal of School Psychology, Inc. Published by Behavioral
Publications, New York.

Competencies to be Developed before the End of the Internship

Competency	Intern Demonstrates: Criterion
Testing	Assessment
1. Proficiency in the administration, scoring, and interpretation of the S-B.	1. Administer at least 1 test to individuals at different levels of ability at Preschool/Kindergarten, Grades 1-3, 4-6; Administrations to be checked by District Supervisors. Scores at least 4 consecutive tests with no more than 1 error per test. Identifies strengths and weaknesses and synthesizes observations and test data into total pattern of intellectual/adaptive functioning.
2. Proficiency in the administration, scoring, and interpretation of the WISC.	2. Administer at least 1 WISC at each of following age levels: Grades 4-5, 6-7, 8-9 (checked by District Supervisor Scores at least 4 consecutive tests with no more than 1 error per test. Integrates Verbal and Performance subtest and scale analysis into total assessment of intellectual/adaptive functioning.
3. Proficiency in the administration, scoring, and interpretation of the WRAT.	3. Integrates observation and WRAT test data in assessing student's repertoire of skills used in academic tasks.
4. Ability to administer oral and written reading tests.	4. Selects at least 1 individual readir test; becomes proficient in administerir it; makes recommendations on findings.
5. Ability to administer, score, and interpret human figure drawings.	5. Integrates observations and test dat along with other information into a comprehensive assessment of perceptual/ motor development.
6. Ability to administer, score, and interpret Bender & other visual-motor tests.	6. Integrates observations and test dat into assessment of individual's visual-motor functioning.
7. Ability to administer, score, and interpret the WPPSI.	7. Identifies strengths and weaknesses and sythesizes observations and test da into total pattern of intellectual/adap ive functioning.
8. Ability to administer, score, and interpret existing criterion-referenced tests.	8. Utilizes these tests in determining student's present state of development in various skill areas.

Observation
     Ability to state reasons for doing careful observational study; accurately observing behavior in school setting; and make classroom observations of child to assess individual and group behavior.

     Writes out objectives for doing observational study and methods to be used in 2 different cases. Observes group behavior in at least 4 total classrooms at 4 different age levels using at least 2 different observational/ recording techniques. Observes and records behavior of 4 students to assess their individual and group behavior; attains 80% inter-rater reliability with District Supervisor at least once.

Interviewing
     Ability to interview children, teachers, and adults to secure information.

     Interviews 2 children (1 elementary and 1 secondary) and 2 parents; interviews 4 teachers (Primary, Upper Elementary, Junior High, and Senior High). Effectiveness of interview and relevancy of information judged by District Supervisor.

Review of School Records
     Ability to selectively gather and interpret information available from school records.

     Examines records of 4 students (1 at each of 4 different levels); organizes and outlines relevant educational, medical, and psychological data; relevancy determined by District Supervisor.

Community Resources
     Ability to selectively gather and interpret information available from community resources.

     Indicates procedures followed to get information (i.e., parent permission, etc.); lists relevant information obtained from these resources in at least 5 cases (involving at least 1 direct contact, 1 written communication, and 1 phone contact).

Hypothesis Formation
     1. Ability to establish tentative hypothesis; use assessment data to confirm or reject tentative hypothesis and develop alternative hypothesis when needed.

     1. Lists data or information that supports tentative hypothesis in 3 cases (1 learning and 1 behavior problem). Lists data from further assessment on at least 4 cases that confirms or contradicts tentative hypothesis;

201

2. Ability to present cases to staff meeting to develop further hypotheses.

indicates data to support an alternative hypothesis if needed; adequacy determined by District Supervisor.

2. Presents information and test data for further hypotheses development on 2 cases (1 at beginning and 1 at end of year); adequacy of presentation determined by participating staff.

Planning and Implementing Intervention Strategies

Instructional Strategies

1. Basic knowledge of instructional methods and materials appropraite in basic areas of reading and math.

1. Observes at least 2 instructional programs representing different approaches to teaching of reading and math and identifies (in writing) basic differences therein.

2. Ability to use appropriate remedial techniques in instructional programs for an individual student with a learning problem.

2. Formulates and itemizes practical instructional techniques for modifying students instructional program; practicality judged by District Supervisor.

3. Ability to plan recommendations on classroom structure and instructional process.

3. Formulates and itemizes practical instructional techniques for modifying total classroom; practicality to be judged by District Supervisor.

Behavioral Strategies

Ability to plan and use techniques for effecting behavioral change for individuals and groups.

Formulates objectives, procedures, and means for evaluating behavioral change for an individual and a group. Implements change plan for individual children and for groups; effectiveness determined by degree with which objectives are met.

202

Knowledge of Available Programs

Ability to use standards for state supported special programs to plan for children with physical, learning, and behavioral problems; and employ special procedures for working with culturally disadvantaged.

Identifies and utilized steps to determine eligibility for special educational programs and follows at least 5 cases through to placement. Plans and implements recommendations which are aimed at ameliorating the situational learning difficulties of the culturally disadvantaged.

Utilizing Para Professional and Psychological Support Personnel

Ability to identify, train, and support supplemental personnel and to evaluate the effectiveness of such an intervention strategy.

Identifies objectives for utilizing (at least 3 cases); trains and supports at least 2 supportive personnel; training and adequacy of supervision determined by District Supervisor. Determining the extent to which the intervention involving the use of supportive personnel has led to the desired change based on demonstrated improvement in the student.

Ability to establish working relationships with secretarial staff and to follow established procedures in the Psychological Services Department.

Follows established procedures; effectiveness to be determined by the Department Secretary and the District Supervisor.

Counseling

Ability to implement counseling principles and procedures with individual; use group counseling procedures (with experienced co-leader or under supervisor); and to evaluate the effectiveness of the counseling procedures that have been used.

Counsel with at least 1 student from Elementary, Junior High and Senior High levels for a minimum of 3 sessions; co-leads or conducts under supervisor at least 1 series of group counseling sessions (at least 6 sessions); audio-recorded segments to be evaluated by District Supervisor. Designs and utilized evaluative procedures for measuring the effectiveness of counseling in terms of individual changes for 1 individual or for a group counseling series.

Teachers

Ability to consult with teachers to assist and help find solutions for questions about students and progress; use input from teacher in cooperative development of useful and specific recommendations regarding behavioral skills; and use feedback from teachers in monitoring and/or revising previous plans.

Consultation

Audio tapes 3 teacher conferences 1 at each of 3 levels (Elementary, Junior High and Senior High) which demonstrate ability to communicate and find solutions for student problems. Writes out recommendations worked out cooperatively with 3 teachers; value judged by District Supervisor. Reports/discusses content of follow-up, teacher conferences with District Supervisor.

Parents

Ability to conduct parent conferences, use input from parents, discuss findings and make plans; explain concepts and educational implications of mentally retarded, learning disabilities, etc., as applied to their children; use feedback from parents in monitoring and/ or rebising previous made plans.

Conducts 2 regular and 1 "problem" parent conferences in presence of District Supervisor. Reports/discusses content of at least 2 parent follow-up conferences.

Administrators

Ability to arrange and hold conferences with administrators regarding modification of educational programs.

Arranges and holds at least 1 conference with an administrator in presence of District Supervisor.

Other School Personnel

Ability to consult with other school personnel and assist them to use psychoeducational techniques.

Holds at least 3 conferences with other school personnel and discusses results/progress with District Supervisor.

Community Resources

Ability to consult with community resource personnel about school children's problems and use referral procedures to appropriate community resources.

Shares written notes on 3 cases with District Supervisor on contacts with community agencies; discusses appropriateness of referral with District Supervisor and follows through on at least 2 cases.

204

Evaluation

Ability to evaluate the effectiveness of consultation procedures used.

Discusses the effectiveness of follow through with District Supervisor on at least 2 consultation cases.

Inservice Education

Ability to plan and prepare material, conduct in-service experiences for school personnel, and evaluate efficiency of in-service experiences they have conducted.

Presents in advance to District Supervisor written plans and appropriate materials to be used in in-service program. Conducts or co-conducts an in-service (effectiveness determined by District Supervisor). Plans and conducts an evaluation involving (at a minimum) teacher input; reports results to District Supervisor in writing.

Parent Education

Ability to plan and prepare material, conduct, and evaluate efficiency of parent educational program they have conducted.

Presents to District Supervisor in advance written plans and appropriate materials to be used in a parent education program. Conducts or co-conducts a program (effectiveness of presentation determined by District Supervisor). Plans and conducts an evaluation involving at a minimum input from parents and reports results in writing to District Supervisor.

Relationship-Skills

Ability to work effectively with parents.

Distributes an evaluation form regarding intern's effectiveness in dealing with parents to 5 randomly selected parents with whom trainee has worked.

Ability to work with administrators, teachers, and other school personnel.

Distributes an evaluation form regarding intern's effectiveness to at least 1 administrator, 3 teachers, and 2 other educational personnel.

Ability to work with parents and/or school personnel under stress.

Discusses conferences where parents or school personnel have been under stress with District Supervisor (when applicable).

Ability to work effectively with community resource personnel.

Discusses relationship with community resource personnel with District Supervisor.

Research

Ability to identify and phrase questions in research fashion; conduct a search of the relevant literature; carry out the research; and write up findings.

Identify problem and consults with District Supervisor regarding in-district appropriateness and submits written proposal to University Supervisor for prior approval. Conducts a research study and submits written reports in approved APA Journal style to District and University Supervisors (for evaluation).

Written Communication Skills

Ability to write reports appropriate to problems and people using report.

Develops (with others) an evaluation form to be submitted and completed by in-school personnel who have received their reports; 2 evaluation forms to be completed during Fall, 2 during Winter; all forms returned directly to District Supervisor.

Ability to draw conclusions in a report and to make specific recommendations appropriate to problem and situation.

Submits draft-form, of reports until 5 consecutive reports are judged satisfactory by the District Supervisor.

Ability to write instructional and behavioral management prescriptions.

During Fall proposes and submits 2 prescriptions to District Supervisor for evaluation before sending them to teachers; during last part of school year an evaluation form will be completed by the teacher on at least 2 cases and returned to the District Supervisor.

Ability to exchange information with other professionals.

Submits drafts of communication written to outside professionals for approval of District Supervisor until 2 consecutive communications are judged satisfactory.

206

The Professional School Psychologist

Ability to collect and report data on effectiveness of school psychological activities.	Maintains daily log of activities; summarizes monthly and submits report to District and University Supervisors; maintains records of professional growth in the competencies listed on this form.
Ability to communicate role of and need for school psychologist.	Makes presentation using AV materials(wherever possible) to PTA or other groups.
Ability to prepare vita; apply for positions; interview and gain employment.	Submits a vita to University Supervisor; applies for positions; interviews whenever possible.

Professional Organizations

Joins (whenever possible) local, state, and national school psychology organizations at intern levels; attends and (when appropriate) participates in functions of above organizations.	Submits evidence of support of Professional School Psychology. Attends statewide trainee conference and at least 4 other professional meetings in School Psychology during the year.

DISCUSSION

The list of competencies are being tried out during the 1972-1973 academic year. Even though every effort was made to envision the psychologist's role as much more than a psychometrician, the testing competencies appear to have been stressed considerably more than relationship or consultation skills. Although this effort has helped to improve the program, a great deal of work still needs to be done to perfect it. Since school psychology seems to be changing constantly, a permanent list of competencies will probably never be achieved.

References

Internship program in school psychology. Bulletin No. 2 of the Ohio Inter-University Council on School Psychology. Columbus, Ohio: State Department of Education, 1969.

Smith, D.B. An analysis of doctoral level internships in school psychology. Journal of School Psychology, 1969, 7 (4), 15-26.

BEHAVIORAL OBJECTIVES IN TRAINING FOR COMPETENCE IN THE ADMINISTRATION OF INDIVIDUAL INTELLIGENCE TESTS

Anne E. Boehm, Jan Duker, Maryanne D. Haesloop, and Mary Alice White

Summary: Competency standards are important to school psychology training, and this study demonstrates, in the area of individual intelligence test administration, how competency standards can be implemented. The study sets up behavioral objectives, determines what training is required for specific levels of mastery, and shows what specified training procedures contribute to the achievement of competency.

This paper emphasizes the utility of behavioral objectives in training administrators of individual intelligence tests and reports the results of utilizing such a training procedure.

The accurate use of intelligence tests seems essential for many reasons. The matter of accuracy recently has been brought dramatically to the attention of the public through several lawsuits, one of which charged school psychologists in a northeastern city with the incompetent use of IQ tests, which allegedly led to special class placement for children who were not actually retarded (New York Times, 1970). Whether the allegation that the psychologists involved were "minimally" trained is correct or not, the question of accurate IQ assessment is a crucial one.

In training future administrators of both the Wechsler tests (1949, 1955) and the Stanford-Binet (Terman & Merrill, 1960), as well as other intelligence tests which are individually administered, insuring examiner accuracy is a major goal. For valid and reliable scoring to occur, examiners must receive considerable practice and close supervision during training. Errors which are made during the learning process range from clerical errors to major errors in administration and scoring. One investigation of agreement

SOURCE. Reprinted from Journal of School Psychology, 1974, 12, 2, 150-157. By permission of the authors and publisher. Copyright 1974 by the Journal of School Psychology, Inc. Published by Behavioral Publications, New York.

among psychologists-in-training in scoring WISC protocols at Temple University (Miller, Chansky, & Gredler, 1970) indicated that within this group, the most frequently occurring errors in order of frequency were (1) crediting items after specified cut-off criteria were reached, (2) crediting incorrect responses, and (3) failing to give credit for correct responses. The "Comprehension" and "Vocabulary" subtests were reported as most vulnerable to errors resulting from inappropriate application of scoring criteria. Clerical and computational errors were other sources of difficulty. In a similar study, Warren and Brown (1972) found that even with supervised practice, the accuracy of examiners-in-training failed to improve over the course of a semester. Errors resulted in IQ score changes of from 1-16 points on the WISC and from 1-13 points on the Binet. The frequency of error types, however, differed by the particular test administered.

Miller and Chansky (1972), in a study of agreement in scoring among 64 trained psychologists, found variability in scoring on all the WISC subtests, with the greatest variability occurring on the "Comprehension," "Similarities," "Information," and "Vocabulary" subtests. Furthermore, these investigators found a mean of 2.37 mechanical errors per examiner.

Vital as the question of competent test administration is, little hard data are available as to the amount of training time required to accomplish this goal. A survey by the authors of three major school psychology training programs revealed no explicitly defined criterion level for competency in test administration. Standards for the training of administrators of intelligence tests varied from course to course within these three universities, and differed for the M.A. candidate, the reading specialist, the clinical psychologist, and the school psychologist.

In an earlier study by some of the authors (Boehm, Duker, & White, 1972), a behavioral objective was established which specified that examiners were to make no major scoring errors on two consecutive test administrations. The sources of error considered in evaluating examiner progress toward meeting this behavioral objective are indicated in Table 1.

In four error categories which allowed the deduction of multiple points, each occurrence of the error resulted in a point off until the specified maximum had occurred. In the remaining categories, maximum of one point off was allowed despite the frequency of the error.

In the initial pilot study using this system, eight student examiners participated. All eight students were in a highly selective doctoral program in school psychology, and the Stanford-Binet was the first individual intelligence test taught. Five of these eight students required ten test administrations before they reached the criterion level of two consecutive administrations without major scoring error; two students required nine administrations; one student required eight administrations. The mean was 9.5 administrations. By far the most frequent sources of error involved inaccurate application of correct scoring criteria and the failure to question ambiguous responses. It was not until administration of test number nine that errors were virtually eliminated, and errors sometimes reappeared after an initial administration without errors.

This training experience suggests that with bright, conscientious students enrolled in a doctoral program in psychology (1) approximately eight to ten administrations of the first individual intelligence test learned, with feedback as to errors, are required to attain a criterion of no major errors on two consecutive administrations; (2) major errors will appear after the first successful administration at criterion level; and (3) the most frequent sources of error lie in the incorrect application of scoring criteria and in failure to question ambiguous responses, followed by calculation errors.

Table 1

Sources of Error in Student Administration of
the Stanford-Binet and WISC

Error Source	Points Off
Incomplete Recording of	
Subject's response	(1)
Examiner's questions	(1)
Inaccuracy	
*Calculations	(2)
*Transfer of data	(1)
*Conversion of scores	(1)
Illegibility	(1)
Scoring Errors	
*Inaccurate application of correct criteria	(5)
Failure to score each item	(2)
Administration Errors	
*Ambiguous responses not questioned	(3)
Unnecessary questions asked	(1)
Improper questions asked	(1)
*All appropriate items not administered	(1)
Items not discontinued at proper time	(1)
Figures not drawn in appropriate place (Binet)	(1)
Total possible number of points off for errors	22

*Major errors

In view of these findings, this question then arose: Can time required to achieve competency be shortened through exposing students to practice exercises prior to actual test administration? With the question of shortening the time required to achieve test competency in mind, a series of workbook materials entitled "Guidelines and Exercises for Reducing Scoring Errors on the WISC and the Stanford-Binet Tests" were prepared by the senior author for use in a practicum for mastering psychoeducational assessment skills, including the administration of the Stanford-Binet and the WISC. Prior to actual administration of the first individual intelligence test (Stanford-Binet) and after studying one test manual, the seven students in this course viewed a videotape of a correct administration of the Binet test. During the next class period, students completed the <u>Guidelines</u> exercises for the Binet. Following completion of the <u>Guidelines</u>, the Binet was administered by the seven students to the criterion level of two consecutive administrations without major scoring errors. This criterion was met after eight administrations by two students, nine administrations by four students, and ten administrations by one student, for a mean of 8.8 administrations, compared with the 9.5 administrations required during the prior academic year.

It appeared that these <u>Guidelines</u> attuned the student to potential errors and provided useful practice exercises prior to the actual administration of the Binet, decreasing both the total number of errors made and the total number of administrations necessary in order to attain the bahavioral objective.

A major question raised by these training results 'concerned the applicability of these procedures to a larger, more diversified group of students. Since a course in individual psychological testing is required of students in a number of degree specialities in psychology, it was possible to assess the effectiveness of behavioral objectives with practice exercises and directed practice to a broader, more representative selection of graduate students.

Data were maintained at Teachers College for four course sequences, beginning in 1972-73, which yielded an N of 107 students who were enrolled in a variety of masters and doctoral programs. For directed practice, students were assigned to laboratory sections (maximum of 12 students per section) where laboratory instructors read each test prtocol and recorded the frequency and type of student errors. Over the course of the semester, students studied two of three tests (Stanford-Binet and WISC or WAIS).

Data for these students are presented in terms of the absolute number of errors made across the group per test administration for each test studies (see Tables 2, 3, 4). In addition, the rate of error per test administration was determined in order to examine possible differences among the three tests on the number of errors per administration and the total number of administrations to criterion (Table 5).

A range of four to 11 tests was necessary in order to attain the criterion level of two consecutive administrations without major scoring errors on the Stanford-Binet, although a minimum of six test administrations was required of all students. The mean number of administrations per test to criterion level was 7.9, 7.0, and 7.1 for the Binet, WAIS, and WISC, respectively. The greatest number of test administrations to reach criterion on the Binet is very probably because it was the first intelligence test studied in the course. Errors probably drop out more rapidly on tests learned after the student has mastered one test.

As may be seen for Tables 2, 3, and 4, the most frequent sources of errors were similar for all three tests. These sources included (1) inaccurate application of correct scoring criteria, (2) incomplete recording of subject's responses, (3) failure to question ambiguous responses, and (4) failure to score each item. An additional frequent source of error on the Binet was the failure to discontinue items at proper time.

The effects of item practice and Guidelines exercises and repeated test administrations with written feedback resulted in competent test administration in contrast to the findings of Warren and Brown (1972). By the time students had given eight tests, the mean number of errors had decreased less than .5 per administration for the Binet and WAIS and to 0 for the WISC.

In summary, it appears that behavioral objectives are useful in teaching individualized intelligence test administration to a diversified group of graduate students. Students did attain the level of competency required. Whether or not this competency level will be maintained without appropriate supervision, however, is open to question, a point demonstrated by Miller and Chansky (1972).

It is through the setting of behavioral objectives for such important skills as test administration that our profession will learn what training is required for specified levels of mastery and what specific training procedures contribute to effective professional functioning.

Table 2

Sources of Error* by Number of Test Administrations:

Stanford-Binet (N-107)

Criteria	1	2	3	4	5	6	7	8	9	10	11	Total
Incomplete Recording												
Subject's response	465	419	249	162	62	36	12	18	4	1	0	1,428
Examiner's questions	3	3	2	1	3	1	1	3	0	0	0	17
Inaccuracy												
Calculations	67	59	33	29	22	12	15	5	1	1	0	244
Transfer of data	101	98	17	30	15	19	2	3	0	0	0	285
Conversion of scores	16	22	11	11	5	4	5	2	0	0	0	76
Illegibility	37	10	3	12	4	4	2	0	0	0	0	72
Scoring Errors												
Inaccurate application of correct criteria	211	168	154	133	123	86	33	25	4	0	1	938
Failure to score each item	1417	1259	722	522	169	102	42	32	19	7	0	4,291
Administration Errors												
Ambiguous responses not questioned	228	179	131	108	92	63	36	27	6	7	5	822
Unnecessary questions asked	26	18	40	28	17	28	20	7	5	2	0	191
All appropriate items not administered	117	79	47	31	31	9	17	4	1	0	0	336
Items not discontinued at proper times	489	272	205	158	119	70	30	12	11	6	1	1,373
Figures not drawn in appropriate place	79	69	35	28	14	17	5	2	0	0	0	249
Totals	3256	2655	1649	1253	676	451	220	140	51	24	7	10,382

* Each occurrence of an error was given a score of one.

Table 3

Sources of Error* by Number of Test Administrations:

WISC (N=34)

Criteria	1	2	3	4	5	6	7	8	9	10	11	Total
Incomplete Recording												
Subject's response	29	15	23	9	7	2	2	3	0	0	0	90
Examiner's questions	0	0	0	0	0	0	0	0	0	0	0	0
Inaccuracy												
Calculations	10	4	3	3	4	5	1	0	0	0	0	30
Transfer of data	0	2	1	1	2	2	3	0	0	0	0	11
Conversion of scores	13	4	7	2	3	3	1	0	0	0	0	33
Illegibility	1	0	0	0	1	0	0	0	0	0	0	2
Scoring Errors												
Inaccurate application of correct criteria	81	63	59	62	32	26	14	7	0	0	0	344
Failure to score each item	8	7	3	3	4	2	0	0	0	0	0	27
Administration Errors												
Ambiguous responses not questioned	18	20	24	22	16	4	8	2	0	0	0	114
Unnecessary questions asked	19	7	4	8	5	4	0	1	0	0	0	48
All appropriate items not administered	12	11	6	14	4	3	3	0	0	0	0	53
Items not discontinued at proper time	19	16	16	11	5	7	0	0	0	0	0	74
Totals	210	149	146	135	83	58	32	13	0	0	0	826

*Each occurrence of an error was given a score of one.

Table 4

Sources of Error* by Number of Test Administrations:

WAIS (N=73)

Criteria	1	2	3	4	5	6	7	8	9	10	11	Total
Incomplete Recording												
Subject's response	263	103	73	61	16	5	2	0	0	0	0	523
Examiner's questions	0	0	1	0	0	0	0	0	0	0	0	1
Inaccuracy												
Calculations	26	12	8	5	7	4	2	1	0	0	0	65
Transfer of data	18	11	4	14	1	7	2	1	0	0	0	58
Conversion of scores	9	4	10	4	5	1	3	0	0	0	0	36
Illegibility	18	6	4	1	0	1	0	0	0	0	0	30
Scoring Errors												
Inaccurate application of correct criteria	223	174	146	103	67	37	15	8	7	2	2	784
Failure to score each item	38	29	20	11	4	3	0	0	0	0	0	105
Administration Errors												
Ambiguous responses not questioned	31	25	20	14	12	6	5	3	1	0	0	117
Unnecessary questions asked	7	15	1	4	3	4	1	0	0	0	0	35
All appropriate items not administered	1	0	0	0	0	0	0	0	0	0	0	1
Items not discontinued at proper time	15	5	8	16	4	2	0	0	0	0	0	50
Totals	649	384	295	233	119	70	30	13	8	2	2	1,805

* Each occurrence of an error was given a score of one.

215

Table 5
Rate of Error Per Test Administration Per Test

Test	Stanford-Binet[1]	WAIS	WISC
Number of Tests			
1	30.43	8.89	6.18
2	24.81	5.26	4.38
3	15.41	4.04	4.29
4	11.71	3.19	3.97
5	6.32	1.63	2.44
6	4.21	.96	1.71
7	2.06	.41	.94
8	1.31	.18	.32
9	.48	.11	0
10	.22	.03	0
11	.07	.03	0

[1]Note that the Stanford-Binet was taught first.

References

Boehm, A.E., Duker, J.D., & White, M.A. Behavioral objectives in training for competence in the administration of individual intelligence tests. Unpublished manuscript, Teachers College, Columbia University, 1972.

Boston suit charges harm from faulty I.Q. testing of children. New York Times, 1970.

Miller, C.K., & Chansky, N.M. Psychologists' scoring of WISC protocols. Psychology in the Schools, 1972, 9, 144-152.

Miller, C.K., Chansky, N.M., & Gredler, G.R. Rater agreement on WISC protocols. Psychology in the Schools, 1970, 7, 190-193.

Terman, L.M., & Merrill, M.A. Manual for the Stanford-Binet Intelligence Scale (Form L-M). Boston: Houghton-Mifflin, 1960.

Warren, S.A., & Brown, W.G. Examiner scoring errors on individual intelligence tests. Psychology in the Schools, 1972, 9, 118-122.

Wechsler, D. Wechsler Intelligence Scale for Children, Manual. New York: Psychological Corporation, 1949.

Wechsler, D. Wechsler Adult Intelligence Scale, Manual. New York: Psychological Corporation, 1955.

A TIME ANALYSIS AND EVALUATION OF AN EXPERIMENTAL INTERNSHIP PROGRAM
IN SCHOOL PSYCHOLOGY

Roy P. Martin, James Duffey, and Ronald Fischman

During the 1971-72 academic year, the School Psychology Department
of Temple University contracted with a small suburban school district
to engage in an experimental internship program. The program had two
principle characteristics: a commitment to a consultative model of
school psychology services and an unusually low intern-client ratio.
The low client to intern ratio was obtained by having two doctoral
interns placed in a moderately small elementary school five days per
week for an academic year. The school also had the services of a
part-time guidance counselor and a part-time speech therapist. This
concentration of mental health personnel made possible a commitment
to handling most problems within the confines of the school and
enhanced the possibility that significant quantities of the interns'
time could be devoted to consultative and preventative functions.

This paper is an evaluation of the program. It attempts to
document in detail the types of functions performed by the interns
and the relative quantity of time devoted to each function. It also
evaluates the program from the point of view of the teaching staff of
the school and assesses the effects of the program on the teachers'
conceptions of the optimal functions of mental health professionals.

SUBJECTS AND SETTING

The data reported in this paper concern the internship experience
of two doctoral students enrolled in the School Psychology Department
of Temple University. Both were white males in their late twenties.
They had finished the majority of the requirements for the doctorate
prior to the internship with the exception of the dissertation. One
of the interns (student A) had three years' experience as a junior
high school teacher, but no previous psychological experience other
than certification level practicum experiences. The other intern

SOURCE. Reprinted from Journal of School Psychology, 1973, 11, 3, 263-
268. By permission of the authors and publisher. Copyright 1973 by
the Journal of School Psychology, Inc. Published by Behavioral Publications, New York.

(student B) had functioned as a school psychologist for one year after obtaining state certification, but had no teaching experience. The training of the interns was essentially identical with the exception that one (student A) was enrolled in the Ed.D. doctoral program, while the other was enrolled in the Ph.D. program. Objectively, this meant that student A had been exposed to courses in educational philosophy and theory nor required of student B, while student B had been exposed to roughly an equivalent number of hours in measurement, design, and statistics.

Both interns were placed in one elementary school of a small, suburban school district outside Philadelphia, Pa. The district served a middle- and lower-middle-class population which was about 40% black, with no other significantly large minority cultural or racial groups. The elementary school in which the interns were placed was about 70% black. It served approximately 500 students in grades one through five, with five classes per grade. The staff of the school included 20 classroom teachers and various ancillary personnel including a part-time speech therapist and a part-time guidance counselor.

PROCEDURE

Two general types of data were utilized in the evaluation of the program. The first source was the daily logs kept by the interns. These logs described each activity engaged in during a given day, the time allotted to that activity, and the persons involved in each activity. At the termination of the internship the log entries were categorized into the variables listed in Table 1. The categories utilized were those generally mentioned in role and function descriptions with some additional categories included to cover the activities idiocyncratic to internships.

Table 1
Time Analysis of Functions of Interns

Function	Percentage of Subfunction Time	Percentage of Total Time
Consultation		28.3
Rapport Building	22.0	
Administrative Policy	13.1	
General Classroom	11.4	
Individual Cases	41.7	
Projects	11.8	
Assessment		33.5
Test Administration	36.8	
Observation	11.7	
Interviewing	12.1	
Report Writing	39.6	

Table 1
Time Analysis of Functions of Interns   (cont.)

Function	Percentage of Subfunction Time	Percentage of Total Time
Inservice		13.8
Miscellaneous School Dictated Activity		15.0
Paperwork	45.7	
Errands	23.3	
Meetings	31.0	
Supervision		9.4

The second source of data was a questionnaire administered to the faculty of the school at the termination of the internship. The questionnaire was designed to answer questions relative to the abilities of the interns, the appropriateness of the roles assumed by the interns, and faculty attitudes toward psychological services in general.

RESULTS

One of the primary questions of this study was: How do interns actually function when they serve in a setting with a low intern-client ratio and when the internship was designed to emphasize consultative functions? Data relevant to this question are presented in Table 1. Considering the general categories of consultation, assessment, inservice, supervision, and miscellaneous school-dictated activity, it can be seen that assessment required the greatest amount of time (33.5%). However, this was followed closely by consultation-related activities (28.3%), with miscellaneous school dictated activity (15.0%), inservice (13.8%), and supervision (9.4%) accounting for the remainder of the intern's time. In this categorization, consultation included all one-to-one, or small-group, discussions between the interns and the school staff focused on professional topics of mutual concern. It also connoted reciprocal activity in which the consultant and the consultee were of equal status in the dyad. Consultation was distinguished from inservice activities because in the latter the interaction is between the intern and a large group and is primarily directed by the intern. Assessment included all activities in which the intern's primary purpose was the collection of information.

When each major category is subdivided into more specific functions, the following pattern of results occur. Under consultation, the two activities which took most of the interns' time were contacts with the school staff about specific children, followed by individual contacts with the staff for the purpose of building rapport. Rapport contacts were distinguished from other categories under consultation in that they were not content specific. Consultation with administrators about policy matters, with teachers about

219

general classroom style, and with the staff on specific projects (peer tutoring programs, applications for federal funds, etc.) consumed the remainder of the consultation time.

Under assessment, report writing required the most time, followed closely by test administration and diagnostic activities in a one-to-one relationship with a child. Other types of assessment together accounted for about 24% of the interns' time.

One other piece of data was abstracted from log entries with regard to function: the amount of time spent in all types of paperwork, including writing diagnostic reports, general school paperwork, supervisory paperwork, and scoring test protocals and observations records. Defined in this way, 37.4% of the interns' time was spent in paperwork.

Another issue which is of interest in relation to consultation activity is the relative amount of time spent with various school personnel in this activity. Of the total time in consultation, 3.1% was with the superintendent, 16.7% with the principal, 17.0% with the counselor, 27.7% with teachers, 18.8% with parents, and 11.3% with all others. The large quantities of time spent with the principal and counselor may have been an artifact, in that the interns shared an office with them. This interpretation is borne out when it is observed that the majority of the interaction with these two persons was categorized as rapport related.

The remaining information gathered in this study concerned the evaluation of the internship program by the staff of the school. In this regard it is important first to document the frequency and type of contacts engaged in with the teachers. During the year 15 of the 20 classroom teachers had professional contacts with the interns. Of the five teachers who were not seen, four reported they had no problems of sufficient magnitude to call on the interns, while one stated that the services were not personally offered to her. Each of the teachers who did seek help referred an average of 2.3 students and were seen 4.2 times per child referred. Four teachers requested general help with their classes, and each was seen an average of 6.2 times in relation to these matters.

The 15 teachers who had professional contact with the interns were asked to evaluate the competence of the interns. Ratings were made of four categories of competence on a five-point scale, with one being incompetent and five being highly competent. On technical competence in psychology, ability to get along with others, ability to understand the school and its problems, and general motivation, the mean rankings ranged from 3.9 to 4.4. This indicated strong support for the competencies of the interns. In a related question, the teachers were asked if the fact the interns were students affected their relationships with them. The teachers indicated unanimously that it did not.

The teachers were then asked to state the one area in which the program was weakest. Since many of the teachers did not wish to write their responses, an exact frequency count of responses was impossible. However, the following five responses were made in descending order of frequency: (1) Not enough children were placed in special schools, (2) Mental health staff didn't get to all the children who needed help, (3) Too much "red tape" was involved in the referral process, (4) Mental health staff lacked understanding of the background of the children, and (5) Mental health staff lacked an appreciation of the pressures on classroom teachers.

These responses revealed a substantial degree of frustration with the model of the program. Responses to a further question clarified the reason for this frustration. When asked: What percentage of students in this school do you think need to be referred to an outside agency for special help? The mean response was 48.9%.

The 15 teachers who had worked with the interns during the year were asked to rank several functions of mental health professionals in order of their usefulness to the school. These rankings are presented in Table 2. It can be seen that consultation with teachers was given the highest ranking, followed closely by assessment and referral functions. Interviewing parents was seen as being of moderate importance, while inservice, crisis management, administrative consultation, and research were given low rankings.

Table 2
Ranking of Preferred Psychologist Functions by Teachers (N = 15)

Function	Mean Rank	Rank
Consultation with teachers on general psychological considerations of teaching	2.9	1
Psychological examiner and diagnostician	3.1	2
Source of referrals to remedial agencies outside the school	3.3	3
Interviewer and consultant to parents	4.5	4
Leader of inservice programs for teachers	5.1	5
Manager of children in crisis	5.4	6
Consultant to administration	5.8	7
Researcher in the schools	5.9	8

DISCUSSION

From the point of the training function of the internship, this experimental program was successful. The time analysis revealed that the interns engaged in a wide variety of professional functions, and

the time allotted to each function seemed, in general, to have been
within the range expected at the outset of the program. Also, the
time spent in interaction with school personnel was more evenly
distributed to the variety of personnel than is typical for internships in the authors' experiences. Thus, if the goal of an internship is to provide a situation in which an intern can engage in a
variety of functions and deal intensively with a variety of school
personnel, then the data from this study support the assumption that
these goals will be best met by restricting the intern-client ratio
to perhaps 1 to 250 or 300 students, or 1 to 10 or 15 teachers.

The service function of the program seemed somewhat less successful than the training function, at least to the extent that there
were substantial reservations about the services offered in the eyes
of the consumers of the services. However, the data in this regard
is somewhat contradictory. The teachers ranked consultation with
teachers as the most beneficial function of mental health specialists,
and yet, when asked to give the least adequate aspect of this internship program, a lack of referrals to outside agencies and a lack of
understanding of the problems of teachers were mentioned most often.
The first shortcoming is a function of the consultative emphasis of
the program, and the second points to a problem which the consultative model seeks to deal with most explicitly. The seeming contradic-
tion can, perhaps, be cleared up by considering the following line of
reasoning. The teachers in this school seemed to feel they needed
help and were glad to accept, in most instances, help from the interns.
Thus, consultation was viewed as an important service. However, consultation aims at helping the teacher develop new coping mechanisms
to deal with the problems that face her; this process implies change.
The necessity for change is difficult to accept, and the process of
change is slow. The frustration which inevitably accompanies change
is reflected in teacher statements to the effect that the consultant
did not understand the pressures that are on teachers. This frustration is heightened by the feeling on the part of the teacher that
48.9% of the students in the school need services offered outside the
school. Thus, the teachers seemed to be willing to try to work on
new techniques and to conceptualize classroom problems from a new
perspective, but also seemed to feel that no amount of change on
their part would deal adequately with the quantity of problems that
faced them.

This set of attitudes is not unique to the teachers served by
this internship program; it is pervasive. Teachers often feel that
outside of the school are a large number of agencies who employ
armies of highly trained and competent professionals who can in a
short time remediate most educational difficulties. This attitude
suggests the need for systematic efforts to place in more realistic
perspective the adequacies and inadequacies of remedial service. Perhaps visits to remedial agencies in the area of a given school with a

frank discussion of the limitations of the agency would prove helpful. Another important function for mental health professionals is to outline clearly their personal limitations and the limitations of the mental health field in general. In an effort to gain acceptance in the schools and to become influencial in educational practice school psychologists and other mental health professionals emphasize, and perhaps exaggerate, their powers. This exaggeration is costly in terms of the self-respect of the classroom teacher. Teachers must feel that they are the primary "remedial" force of the society, that as a profession, they are the most able to deal with the great majority of problems, and that the rest of us, though useful, will always be of minimal influence on the great bulk of society.

AN ANALYSIS OF THE SERVICES PERFORMED BY A SCHOOL PSYCHOLOGIST IN AN
URBAN AREA: IMPLICATIONS FOR TRAINING PROGRAMS

Thomas N. Fairchild

The literature is replete with information about the role and
function of a school psychologist, and many divergent points of view
are expressed with regard to the role to which a school psychologist
should subscribe. Rather than provide a discussion of the theoretical
positions that advocate various functions that school psychologists
should be performing, the investigator thought that it would be helpful to determine what services are being provided in the "real world"
of the practitioner. This information would be beneficial to students
in school psychology training programs because it would offer them a
detailed description of the types of activities in which a school
psychologist may find himself involved, as well as the amount of time
allotted for these various services. The data also would have utility as input for school psychology training programs by identifying
the service areas in which school psychologists spend most of their
time and in which they might need more thorough preparation.

METHOD

Procedure
       A daily activities log was developed in order to collect the
necessary data. Services that a school psychologist might perform
were identified, as well as subservices within the larger service
categories. The subservices then were coded to facilitate recording
procedures. While the investigator was working part-time in the
Cedar Rapids Community Schools in Iowa he recorded daily the subservices provided and the amount of time allotted to the performance
of these subservices. During the school year 1971-72 the daily
activities log was used and refined. During the 1972-73 school year
a detailed record was kept that shows the amount of time spent on the
various subservices. Since the investigator had the opportunity to

SOURCE.   Reprinted from Psychology in the Schools, 1974, XI, 3, 275-
281.   By permission of the author and Clinical Psychology Publishing
Co., Inc.

work with all grade levels, K-12, the information represents a cross-section of the activities to which school psychologists may find themselves exposed in the fulfillment of their professional duties within a medium-sized urban and suburban school system.

Recording procedures required coding activities at the completion of each half day, compilation of monthly summaries, and a final yearly summary. The daily log recorded over 800 service hours in pursuance with the investigator's part-time contract. The number of hours and the percentage of the total service time that these hours constituted were recorded for the following service categories: Assessment, Intervention, Evaluation, and Administration. Within the service categories the same data are available for subservice.

RESULTS

Table 1 reveals that the greatest percentage of service time was consumed by the Assessment service category (39.7%). Assessment service is defined by the author as the use of appraisal procedures to locate, identify, and synthesize information into a meaningful report that can be translated into intervention strategies. Intervention service included activities in which the psychologist worked directly with a student or indirectly through other professionals in an effort to improve learning and/or behavior. This service accounted for 24.8% of the school psychologist's total service time. The Evaluation service category required 12% of the total time and included those subservices that involved determination of the efficacy of the Intervention service. The Administration service took 23.5% of the total service time and included traveling to schools, preparing for testing and conferences, supervising, attending meetings and workshops, public relations, and paperwork.

Table 1
The Yearly Total of the Number of Hours
and the Percentage of Time Devoted
to the School Psychological Service Categories

Service Category	Number of Hours	Percent of Time
Assessment	326 1/4	39.7
Intervention	203	24.8
Evaluation	98 1/2	12.0
Administration	192 3/4	23.5
Total	820 1/2	Total 100.0

In Table 2 all of the subservices included within the four service categories of Assessment, Intervention, Evaluation, and Administration are outlined in greater detail. The information reveals the number of hours devoted to each subservice activity during the

225

year, the percent of time spent in relation to the total number of
school psychology service hours, and the percent of time in relation
to the other subservices within each of the four service categories.
Subservices within services categories have been listed in the order
of greatest percentage of time allotted to least percentage allotted.
Administration and scoring of formal and informal tests comprised
approximately one-third (33.5%) of the Assessment service category.
However, when consideration is given to the total time allocated
to school psychological services, this subservice accounted for only
13.3% of the total time. The time devoted to this subservice is much
less frequent than many critics of school psychological services might
suspect. Report writing required close to another one-third (29.9%)
of the Assessment service category, with the final one-third made up
of the following subservices - consulting other professionals about
their interpretation of the assessment results, interviewing students,
teachers, parents and other professionals to elicit meaningful diagnostic information, observational techniques, and reviewing cumulative records.

The Intervention service category was dichotomized into <u>direct</u>
and <u>indirect</u> intervention strategies. Direct intervention denoted
actually working with the student in an effort to improve learning
and/or behavior. The counseling subservice was designated direct
intervention and consumed 7.9% of the total time and nearly one-
third of the Intervention service category time. Indirect intervention strategies comprised the other two-thirds and included those
subservices in which attempts were made to facilitate improvements
in a student's learning and/or behavior indirectly via consultation
with individuals (teachers and parents), small groups (staffings),
and large groups (in-service meetings) with regard to specific intervention strategies.

Table 2
The Yearly Total of the Number of Hours
and the Percentage of Time Devoted to the Subservices
Within Service Categories

Service Category	Subservice	Number of Hours	% of Yearly Time	% of Service Category Time
Assessment				
	Administration and scoring of formal and informal diagnostic tests	109 1/4	13.3	33.5
	Report writing	98	11.9	29.2
	[b]Consulting with other professionals[a] about assessment results	34	4.1	10.3

Table 2 (cont.)

The Yearly Total of the Number of Hours
and the Percentage of Time Devoted to the Subservices
Within Service Categories

Service Category	Subservice	Number of Hours	% of Yearly Time	% of Service Category Time
Diagnostic interviews with students		25	3.1	7.8
[b]Interviewing other professionals[a] to gather diagnostic information		22 1/4	2.7	6.8
[b]Teacher interviews to gather diagnostic information		11 3/4	1.4	3.5
[b]Parent interviews to gather diagnostic information		9	1.1	2.8
Observational techniques		10 1/2	1.2	3.0
Reviewing cumulative records		6	.7	2.4
Intervention				
Direct Intervention				
Counseling		65	7.9	32.0
Indirect Intervention				
[b]Parent consultation to recommend intervention strategies		49	5.9	24.0
[b]Teacher consultation to recommend intervention strategies		40 1/2	4.9	20.0
[b]Consultation with other professionals[a] about intervention strategies		22 1/2	2.7	11.0
[b]In-service meeting offered by the school psychologist		19 1/2	2.4	9.7
[b]Pupil staffings designed to determine appropriate placement and intervention strategies		6 1/2	.8	3.3

Table 2 (cont.)
The Yearly Total of the Number of Hours
and the Percentage of Time Devoted to the Subservices
Within Service Categories

Service Category	Subservice	Number of Hours	% of Yearly Time	% of Service Category Time
Evaluation				
	Research on the efficacy of school psychological services Follow-up conferences to determine the efficacy of intervention strategies	52 3/4	6.5	54.0
	[b]Parent conferences	18	2.2	18.1
	[b]Teacher conferences	17	2.1	17.3
	[b]Conferences with other professionals[a]	10 3/4	1.3	10.6
Administration				
	Travel to and from assigned schools	50 1/4	6.1	26.0
	Review of mail, correspondence, and copyreading psychologist reports	36	4.4	18.8
	Miscellaneous (primarily visiting in teacher lounge or visiting with staff psychologists during breaks)	31	3.8	16.2
	[b]Supervision of practicum student	25 1/4	3.1	13.2
	Preparation for testing and conferences	21	2.5	10.7
	Attendance at psychologist and faculty meetings	14	1.7	7.3
	Professional development – attending workshops or inservice programs offered by the school system or professional organizations	9	1.1	4.7
	Public relations – speaking to parents' groups, at career night, etc.	6 1/4	.7	3.0

[a]Refers to counselors, social workers, reading specialists, psychiatrists, physicians, etc.

[b]These subservices are considered consultation activities. When these activities were totaled together, they accounted for 34.7% of the writer's time.

Further inspection of Table 2 reveals data on the Evaluation and Administration service categories. Evaluation subservices included research on the efficacy of school psychological services and follow-up conferences designed to elicit feedback as to the effectiveness of recommended intervention strategies. Research on the efficacy of school psychological services involved comparison of two models of school psychological services, the traditional diagnostician service model and the consultant service model, to determine which was the more effective. During the first semester the writer operated within the diagnostician model; during the second semester the consultant model was adopted. The two models were evaluated by determining which provided more immediate feedback to teachers and which was most effective as indicated by teachers' responses on a follow-up questionnaire.

To follow up students to determine whether the recommended interventions were effective is crucial for accountability. The writer devoted 46% of his evaluation time to this subservice.

The Administrative service category required approximately one-quarter of the writer's time and included the following subservices. Travel consumed one-quarter of the administrative time, followed by review of mail, correspondence, copyreading reports, miscellaneous, supervisory duties, preparation for testing and conferences, attendance at meetings, professional development, and public relations, in order of percentage of time allotted to the subservice.

IMPLICATIONS FOR SCHOOL PSYCHOLOGY TRAINING PROGRAMS

When the amount of time devoted to various services is compared with the amount of attention that those services receive during the pre-service training, there appears to be a considerable discrepancy between the skills emphasized in the training programs and the skills actually required for successful on-the-job functioning. The data suggest that coursework related to traditional diagnostic testing needs to be deemphasized and that consultation skills need to receive increased attention. With consideration for the increased emphasis on accountability in education, the data suggest that formal preparation in self-evaluation skills should be mandatory during the preservice school psychologist training phase.

Traditional Diagnostic Testing Should be Deemphasized

Although the Assessment function required 40% of the writer's time, the administration and scoring of formal and informal diagnostic tests consumed only 13% of the total amount of time devoted to school psychological services. This percentage is corroborated by the time analysis data presented in the Martin, Duffey, and Fischman (1973) article, in which the Assessment function accounted for 33.5% of the interns' time; yet, test administration required only 37% of the

Assessment time, or 12% of the total amount of time devoted to school psychological services. This information indicates that less time is devoted to diagnostic testing than critics of school psychological services suspect.

Diagnostic testing accounted for 13% of the writer's time, yet disproportionate amounts of time in many programs are devoted to the training of school psychologists in diagnostic testing skills during the preservice training phase. A survey of school psychology training programs (Clair, et al., 1971) revealed that when coursework prerequisites to practicum experiences were ranked, assessment courses were ranked first and second out of 14 areas of coursework. Further data related to the type of desired training experiences to be obtained during the practicum and internship period indicated that the assessment experiences were highly desirable. Of the highly desirable experiences during the practicum period, assessment experiences were ranked first and third; during the internship period, assessment experiences were ranked second and third out of the 15 possible experiences.

Traditional diagnostic testing has been criticized on the grounds that it yields educationally irrelevant information (Dunn, 1968; Hammill, 1971; Neisworth, 1969; Valett, 1972). Personal experience has shown that frequently this is the case, which may account for the small amount of this writer's time that was consumed by traditional diagnostic testing. Because traditional diagnostic assessments frequently yield educationally irrelevant information, alternative methods of assessment need to be developed and utilized. School psychologists should be receiving training in other diversified areas of assessment, This training should include the development of skills in criterion-referenced measurement that relies on a knowledge of task analysis techniques. This would encompass the development and administration of informal tests based on task analysis and the designing of prescriptive intervention strategies. Skills in behavioral analysis and behavior management also should receive increased attention during the preservice phase.

Although alternative methods of assessment need to receive increased emphasis, the testing function needs to be included in training programs because it is used so much on the job, particularly to take care of special education demands. Although an important and necessary skill, the writer is concerned that the testing function may be receiving more emphasis than it legitimately should be accorded.

Consultation Skills Should Receive Increased Emphasis

When consultation activities are isolated from the Assessment, Intervention, Evaluation, and Administration Service categories in Table 2, the data reveal that 35% of the writer's time was allotted to consultation activities (see footnote, Table 2). The Martin, et al. (1973) time analysis revealed that 28.3% of the school psychologist intern's time was devoted to consultation functions while the interns were operating within a consultative model of school psychological services. This study showed that approximately one-third of the psychologist's services can be devoted to consultation activities if he can avoid operating within the traditional diagnostician framework and set forth specific guidelines to school personnel as to services that will be offered. Both the writer's analysis and the Martin, et al. analysis indicate that consultation activities consume a considerable share of the psychologist's time.

University trainers are aware of the importance of consultation skills. The Clair, et al. (1971) survey of school psychological training programs showed that consultation experience ranked high in desirability during the practicum and internship period, yet little formal coursework was provided by many training programs in the area of consultation.

Teachers prefer the consultation service. In the Martin, et al. (1973) study the consultation function was ranked higher than the diagnostician function when teachers were asked to rank preferred psychologist functions.

School psychologists are described as change agents within the schools. Since consultation is the primary vehicle for change when one is operating within a consultant role, school psychologists should have expertise in consultation skills. Psychologists, teachers, and university trainers all are aware of the importance of the consultation function. Since psychologists devote considerable time to the consultation function, school psychology training programs will need to provide opportunities within their programs for development of these skills.

The formal consultation skills coursework should cover content knowledge and provide process experiences. Counseling coursework might be required in order to provide the trainee with the knowledge of effective communication skills. Process experiences during the coursework phase could include simulated conferences, staffings, and in-service designed to provide a variety of consultation experiences with various professionals and nonprofessionals. Video-taped consultations could be presented and critiqued. Persons present during consultations could be followed up to determine that information was communicated to them. This information then would be compared to the information that was supposed to be communicated in order to ascertain whether the goals of the consultation had been met.

The skills learned in coursework necessarily would be applied during the practicum and internship periods. Coursework at this level would be confined to seminars or discussion groups in which students might discuss the consultation activities that they are engaged in, problems encountered during consultation, problem resolution, and determination of consultation effectiveness, among other relevant consultation topics.

Formal Training in Self-Evaluation Skills Should Be Provided

Educators have been bombarded with cries for accountability. Increased emphasis on accountability for teachers and administrators has resulted in increased accountability for special service personnel such as school psychologists. Psychologists have presumed that they are exempt from accounting for their services, yet the value of their services is being questioned. Psychologists are being called upon to justify their presence in the schools. Therefore it is essential that school psychologists learn the means whereby they can provide substantive proof with regard to the efficacy of their performance. Self-evaluation requires evaluation of one's professional effectiveness. The writer is particularly interested in accountability for school psychological services, so methods of accounting for services were developed while he was working in the Cedar Rapids schools. These methods were (1) keeping a daily log of services performed; (2) keeping a record of the amount of time that elapses from the time a student is referred until the person who made the referral gets meaningful feedback; (3) soliciting feedback from building staff with regard to services; (4) mailing brief follow-up questionnaires to teachers and parents in an effort to determine the efficacy of recommendations; (5) contacting the parents by phone after the initial conference in order to monitor progress; and (6) behavioral consultation, which involved the designing of a behavior management program with a classroom teacher.

The Evaluation service category accounted for 12% of the writer's time and included the above mentioned activities. Although the amount of time devoted to this service category was slightly less than the time devoted to diagnostic testing (13%), no formal preparation is given in self-evaluation skills during the preservice phase, whereas diagnostic testing skills receive considerable attention in coursework and practical experience.

If school psychologists are being called upon to provide evidence with regard to their effectiveness, school psychology training programs have an obligation to prepare school psychologists with self-evaluation skills. Since evaluation of school psychological services requires nearly as much time as diagnostic testing, the program emphasis should not be cursory. A formal course in self-evaluation and accountability techniques that outlines specific techniques should be provided. These techniques could be applied during the practicum or internship experiences, which would allow students to try them out first-hand and select the techniques that they can manage effectively, yet still would provide them with pertinent data as to the efficacy of their services.

References
_____

Catterall, C.D. A competency based school psychology internship. Journal of School Psychology, 1973, 11, 269-275.

Clair, T.N., Osterman, R.L., Kiraly, J., Jr., Klausmeir, R.D., & Graff, M.M. Practicum and internship experiences in school psychology: recent trends in graduate training. American Psychologist, 1971, 26, 566-574.

Dunn, L.M. Special education for the mildly retarded - is much of it justifiable? Exceptional Children, 1968, 35, 5-22.

Hammill, D.D. Evaluating children for instructional purposes. In D.D. Hammill and N.R. Bartel (Eds.), Educational perspectives in learning disabilities. New York: John Wiley, 1971.

Martin, R.P., Duffey, J., & Fischman, R. A time analysis and evaluation of an experimental internship program in school psychology. Journal of School Psychology, 1973, 11, 263-268.

Neisworth, J.T. The educational irrelevance of intelligence. In R.M. Smith (Ed.), Teacher diagnosis of educational difficulties. Columbus, O.: Charles E. Merrill, 1969.

Valett, R.E. Developmental task analysis and psychoeducational programming. Journal of School Psychology, 1972, 10, 127-133.